The Dayspring of Youth

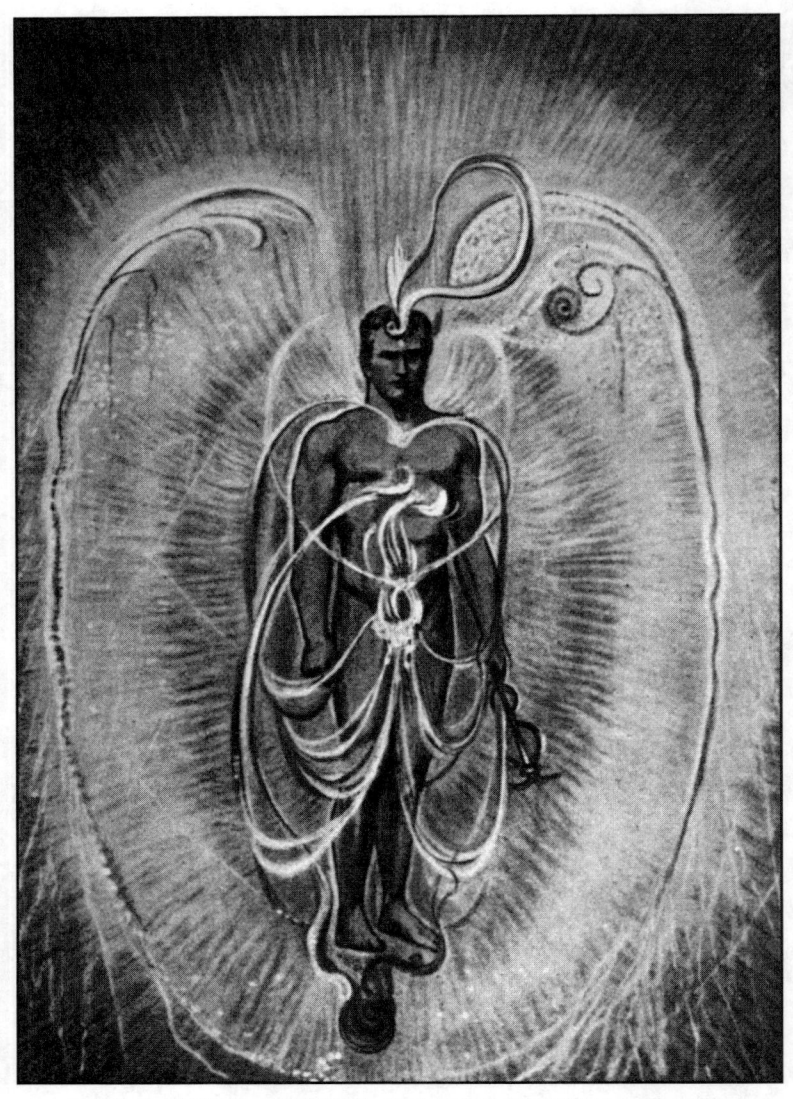

THE SILVER SHIELD OF THE MENTAL BODY

Frontispiece *See page 112*

The Dayspring of Youth

by M.

ILLUSTRATED

We Seek to Serve

GLORIAN

The Dayspring of Youth
A Glorian Book / 2012

Originally published in 1931.

Print ISBN 978-1-934206-68-3
Electronic ISBN 978-1-934206-61-4

Glorian Publishing is a non-profit organization. All proceeds further the distribution of these books. For more information, visit gnosticteachings.org

To
THOSE WHO HAVE SERVED AND
HAVE ATTAINED WE DEDICATE
THIS BOOK AS A MEMORIAL OF
BROTHERLY LOVE

PREFACE

THIS book has been written to meet the demands those who seek knowledge regarding the finer forces within Nature and man. The Great Initiate, under whose cloak America and the Western areas of Europe are being developed, has given me permission give forth these teachings.

This work is but a slight introduction to an unlimited science, and I hope it will help and meet the approval of those earnestly seeking deliverance from the illusions of this world.

It is published under the authority of the Brothers; and as certain people in the past have assumed authorship of some of my writings, all publications of the Brothers will be issued in future under their seal and copyrighted.

I also wish to render my great appreciation to W.L.R., and thanks to M.J., for having helped me this manuscript.

M.

CONTENTS

CHAPTER		PAGE
	Introduction	1
1	Atoms	3
2	The Nous Atom	13
3	Destructive Atoms	19
4	The Astral	29
5	Elemental Nature	39
6	The Eternal Lover	59
7	Nature	67
8	Health in Yoga	71
9	Advocate and Dweller on Threshold	83
10	Finer Forces	87
11	Breathing and Blood-stream	97
12	Animal Food	101
13	Reincarnation and Karma	103
14	Atmospheric Screen and Breathing	107
15	Mental Travelling	113
16	Masters	117
17	Submerged Worlds	127
18	The Silver Shield	145
19	The Elemental Advocate	153
20	Healing	163
21	Yoga Teachings	167
22	Summary of the Silver Shield	175
23	Determinative Energy	177
24	An Arcadian Contact	185
25	Mantras	191
26	Transformation Breathing	197
27	Cosmic Rays	199
28	Natural Magic	203
29	Egypt	209
30	Chinese Consciousness	219
31	The Element of Fire	223
32	The Solar Flame	233
33	Conclusion	247
	Index	255

LIST OF ILLUSTRATIONS

The Silver Shield of the Mental Body ii
The Astral Sheath 31
"Queen" Water Elemental 46
Black Magician 135

GLOSSARY

THE BROTHERS.—A Fraternity that has existed before man descended into matter, and who have worked and still work out in the world upon the Path of activity. They only appear as an active Brotherhood when the cosmic energy of a Dayspring of Youth brings them into manifestation to shield and bring its vibration and intelligence into the minds of those who seek their Innermost. When this cosmic energy is withdrawn they seemingly disappear from the world. The real name of the Order is only revealed at the initiation of a disciple. One of the tenets of Order is mental levitation or the process of travelling out of the body.

. . . . .

THE DAYSPRING OF YOUTH.—A cosmic hierarchal energy that appears at the beginning of a new age in man's development. It is now entering this world, and, through Yoga practice, the student attempts to tune himself into this directing consciousness and intelligence that is to revert man to an understanding of Nature's laws.

ATOMS.—Minute bodies of intelligence possessing the dual attributes of Nature and man.

ASPIRING ATOMS.—Those higher forms of energy and intelligence that, through Yoga practice, the student attracts to his physical and mental body.

NOUS ATOM.—The minute image of perfected man within the left ventricle of the heart.

SECONDARY SYSTEM.—These are centres or ganglia of the sympathetic system that extend each side of the spinal column and are contacted by the student when he aspires in his Yoga practice to enter his inner planes of consciousness and relate himself to the finer forces in Nature. They also review and re-experience him in his past lives and in those periods of inner development ahead of our objective time.

THE THIRD EYE OR PINEAL GLAND.—Through Yoga practice this seemingly atrophied organ within the head vibrates and attunes itself to man's nervous energy, and becomes the organ of the seer who visualises the activities of the finer states of consciousness in Nature and man.

DESTRUCTIVE ATOMS.—The opposing forces of Nature in man that seek to retard his development towards the Reality.

ATMOSPHERIC SCREEN.—A silken-webbed lining that holds the mental body in alignment to the physical body and is covered with a multitude of node points through which are received as well as transmitted thought-vibrations to and from the human brain.

NODE POINTS.—Small, truncated, cone-shaped projections.

THE SECRET ENEMY.—The principal atom of evil in man that directs the Destructive atoms.

INFORMER ATOMS.—Atoms that had worked for the Secret Enemy, but who have been liberated by the Aspiring atoms from bondage. They are a link between the Aspiring atoms and the atoms of the Secret Enemy and inform us about the nature of the evil plans that threaten us from the Secret Enemy and from outside influences.

THE ASTRAL BODY.—A sheath of radiant, fluidic atmosphere that envelops the physical form and is seen by the third eye. It registers our passions and desires and is a remnant of the past.

CAUSAL BODY SHEATH.—This is a lower atomic substance that registers racial consciousness and tendencies, and possesses the qualities of our individual parental stem.

DEATH ATOMS.—When the Solar and Lunar forces cease to operate in the body, and the Nous atom has left the arterial bloodstream, these Death atoms watch over the disintegration of man's lower vehicles and return the imprisoned atoms back to their natural elements.

THE ADVOCATE.—A powerful, collective atomic entity, otherwise known as the Higher Self, created from the best of man's aspirations during his descent and evolution through matter. It is the intermediary between man and his Innermost, and pleads for the remission of our past evil after we have reviewed this through Yoga practice.

THE ELEMENTAL ADVOCATE.—Similar to the Advocate, but created in our elemental past. It possesses the same attributes and works in union with the other Advocate. These two are known in zodiacal terminology as Castor and Pollux.

WHITE MAGICIAN.—They who seek to serve humanity impersonally and obey the directions of their Innermosts according to the degree of their occult development.

MANTRAS.—Sound invocations that the student uses to harmonise his body and its centres with the finer forces in Nature and man.

DETERMINATIVE ENERGY.—An energy that determines Nature's expression and that the student seeks to attain and obey.

THE SILVER SHIELD.—Through Yoga practice atoms called Transformation atoms of a higher voltage are attracted and formed into a mental shield that protects the student from opposing forces in Nature and man. It is the temple in which the Master atom of the mind will reside and is the condenser and transmitter of the powerful voltage of the Innermost.

MASTER ATOM.—An atomic energy within the seminal system that represents the student's individual record of intelligence gained through past experiences. When the Silver Shield is developed the Master atom ascends from the seminal system into the Silver Shield and becomes the intelligence that instructs the student about his mind-world and mental inheritance.

TRANSFORMATION ATOMS.—(See Silver Shield.)

INNERMOST.—That part of the Reality (GOD) within man that the Yogi seeks to attune himself to before attaining cosmic consciousness.

CENTRAL SYSTEM.—Represents the brain and spinal cord with its seven principal ganglia or atomic centres, and is the instrument that aids man to release—through Yoga practice—his Innermost from Its prison house of the body. (See Solar Force.)

SELF-DEVELOPED UNIVERSE.—That universe that man has built up through eternity under the guidance of the Innermost.

SOLAR FORCE.—It is of the nature of static electricity and remains latent in man till evoked and used through Yoga practice. This force can be governed by man and is the instrument the Innermost uses to build up Its solar or spiritual body.

SEMINAL SYSTEM.—The organs that create life as understood by man and by the student as the depository of the powerful forces attained to and made known to him in the elemental and objective states of his past. This brings about the birth of the Solar force.

INITIATE ATOMS.—Those atoms within the higher counterpart of the seminal system that relate the student to periods in advance of his time, and possess the attributes of a great Initiate's atmosphere.

SCHOLAR ATOMS.—Those atoms an atomic centre that relate themselves to the objective mind of the student and in his deeper states of Yoga inform him of his inner and objective attainments gained through countless lives.

PARENTAL STEM.—The individual expression of the Reality from which the Innermost sprang, and the directing force and individual expression of the student and his race.

"Before the false dawn came over this earth, those who survived the hurricane and the storm gave praise to the Innermost, and to them appeared the heralds of the dawn."
From *The Testament of Learning*

INTRODUCTION

THIS work is a record of instruction received during different states of Yoga practice; that sealed book opened by the aspiring student during his development into his own inner states of being. We have been permitted to reveal this in order that others, by similar practice, may develop and unfold their inner powers; for the body is a storehouse of past, present and—strange though it seems—future records.

At the beginning and end of each age there is a pouring forth of hierarchal cosmic streams of energy, and as they intermittently enter the earth's atmosphere and unite we find in this radiation that instruction best fitted for the time. Thus there is brought to birth a new period of discovery for the world.

This new force, called by Initiates "The Dayspring of Youth," has been in activity for some time, and they who respond to it and practise this Western Yoga can enter the new era and become its instrument.

This force, now working over Western Europe and America, possesses a new vitality and energy that will bring about a severance from past and inherited conditions. Minds that respond to it are clarified, and any opposition within the atmosphere of the mental body can no longer imprison them within its rebellious aura. For practice of this Yoga attracts an atomic energy of a finer nature and transmutes the consciousness.

The Great Initiates call this "The Churning of the Butter," the separation of the finer elements in man from the coarser. If the student responds to these finer forces he becomes aware of this manifestation within his physical body and mental atmosphere.

For over fifty years students have been side-tracked regarding the true methods of Yoga; for in nearly every book dealing with this subject they have been told to "Concentrate inwardly." This is false; as such concentration attracts atoms of personality and desire. Neither should the word "I" be used; for this again brings the personal element into play. It is impossible to pass inwardly by direct concentration unless one also aspires. Only through personal contact with a Master has a student been taught the true method.

Man is a prisoner within the atmosphere of this world, but his Higher self awaits the time when he will release himself from bondage and return to it. This union can be accomplished in one life if the student will but ASPIRE and bring into activity those dormant properties of matter within him of which he has been unaware.

Aspiration means that longing for the Reality's presence within one's own universe. Real aspiration should be impersonal; for personality attracts atomic intelligences of a personal nature besides parasitical and discarnate entities.

Within and about us are highly developed atoms, and in our breathing exercises we attract them into our bodies. They then supply our nervous systems with their energies, and as man is the result of his own type of atoms and atmosphere, he is judged by the quality of atoms he attracts, just as he is judged by the kind of people with whom he associates.

Man is a solar system in miniature, governed by his Innermost that dwells within Its sanctuary and seldom manifests beyond Its temple. If we are to gain Its recognition of our efforts to reach Its presence, we must aspire to this inner seat of government.

The objective body is not related to its Innermost until it can find a means of communication, and by attracting atoms possessing the nature of this Innermost we build a bridge between our inner and outer worlds. In this manner we regain our lost possessions in Nature: our true birthright.

THE DAYSPRING OF YOUTH

CHAPTER ONE

ATOMS

THE purpose of the science of union, or Yoga, as it is called in the East, is to acquaint man with his Innermost, and this work is but an introduction. The deeper knowledge is only given to the student when he is ready for it. They who teach Yoga to the unprepared suffer severe penalties.

The fragmentary teachings the Great Initiates have left us have frequently been appropriated and altered by certain religious bodies who were supposed to have kept them sacred from the time they were given forth. They changed them in order to strengthen their own personal beliefs, and these false transcriptions have plunged the world into darkness.

Occultism teaches us that the visible universe is but the lower counterpart of the higher one which, if perceived, would give us youth and happiness. All that we see about us is illusory and but a fragment of something greater; for our minds are imprisoned and held subject to our own illusion world. When we can pierce this we shall perceive in the depths of Nature a mind that directs and guides all things.

Many occult schools, especially American, teach us how to develop our inner powers by the improper use of what is known as conscious will power. These schools say that one's objective self can demand and receive things by impressing the subconscious self through will power. In the deeper states of Yoga the student directs things, but does not will them as this world understands the term, but uses the consciousness of the Reality within him. Thus in the higher schools the word "Will" is seldom used.

We do not wish to disturb anyone's faith; but we suggest that would man only learn to think inwardly and seek his own kingdom of Heaven, he would read therein the original books of the great world teachers that have not been altered; for our own books of wisdom are not distorted by the illusion world. As the prophet Mahomet has said: "To its own book shall every nation be summoned," meaning that in the future man will learn to distinguish the true from the false when he attains union with his Innermost.

This book also deals with the health of the body and self-analysis, and the student can begin these practices no matter how old he is.

The body is a composite form built up from many sources and periods of past and present experience. In our practices these are reviewed. The lower centres represent the lower periods and our animal nature, and are situated in the lower part of the spine. The centres above the navel represent the more developed states of evolution and consciousness. These lower centres must become our servants, not by conquest but by control. If we fail in this they will disturb and try to dominate us, thus making us not godlike men, but beasts.

Life will not be fully understood until we recognise the living forces within us and transplant atoms of a higher nature into the body. This will eventually help humanity to become the personification of justice.

Our atomic centres are similar to the starry clusters in the sky, and each atom is a minute intelligence revolving within its own atmosphere.

When we aspire we unite ourselves to atoms that have preceded us in evolution; for they evolve as we evolve: this body being their university, and they prepare the path for us to follow.

Different divisions of consciousness or beings intersect man's structure, and when the student enters his interior planes he will realise that this world is but an illusion, and that time and space are different when seen from these divisions. These planes will send their energy into his mind, and he will find himself part of a great universal scheme.

They who do not squander their time but work for the redemption of their lower natures will eventually enter their own domains and there find the peace of God "which passeth all understanding." They will be beyond affliction or pain and in complete harmony with their indwelling consciousness.

From these inner domains they will observe that Nature's atmosphere teems with intelligences, and they will be admitted into worlds of inspiring and radiant beauty. Creations that will ennoble them; for here the hidden glories of the planet are revealed. Here the elemental sovereigns await to admit them into their territories.

In this Yoga practice the increase of our wave-length responds to these elemental substances and helps us to develop, and there we receive the keynote of our characters. For these beings are nourished upon the finest forces and wisdom of their worlds, and they gladly serve and welcome those who enter their realms of understanding and excellence.

The problems that confuse us on earth become clear and simple when seen from the interior worlds; for there we become the very attributes of Truth, and from these planes any questions asked are instantly answered according to the experience we have gained in previous incarnations.

The atmosphere of the mental body is controlled by the atmosphere of this world, but by breathing in the energy manifesting in this new age through Yoga we can throw off this control. By aspiring when breathing we attract the atoms of this new energy into us and slowly conform to their wave-length. These atoms bring us a sensation of joy similar to a morning in Spring. The deeper the student goes the more does he assume an energy and directness unparalleled in his normal state. He will undergo a complete change and realise as never before the possibilities of his future welfare and how indolent he has hitherto been.

When we are correctly related to the atoms of the Universe we can command its powers. If the student has no love in his heart, however, he will be unable to attract those atoms that will help him to regain his lost inheritance. Mental effort alone will never unite him to his Central Universe.

Within us reside many atoms that impart their wisdom to our atmosphere in order to hasten their own development. Just as a chemist must know what he is placing in his medicines, so must the student acquire the power to analyse any atmosphere. This will teach him at what degree atoms respond, also their type of intelligence and outer appearance.

Every great master of this science has secretly taught his more advanced pupils how to converse with their own atomic intelligences that have evolved beyond them.

Man is the result of his own thoughts and thought environment. In the past he lived in periods of brightness and splendour and beyond illusion, and he can again contact atoms representing such periods. In this new age he may once more regain the properties of his lost inheritance: his divine birthright.

Once the student regains the power to review his past lives he can begin to remedy his faults and seek powers lost through selfishness and abuse. When these are regained he can then evoke in others a similar atomic attainment.

We often hear about the return of a World Saviour, yet are unaware that each man is potentially his own Saviour and possesses atoms that germinate in his mental atmosphere the qualities of supreme enlightenment. This Initiate atom dwells within every living thing as well as within man; but only appears when we have entered the deeper states of our inner worlds.

This intelligence is neither named Christ nor Buddha, but is called by a secret sound that possesses the principles of justice. Each centre in the body has its own note, and it responds when we sound it. He who sounds the proper vowels—the seven vowels of Nature—harmonises these centres to respond to a united vowel sound: the true name of his Innermost.

When the student meditates within his own university, vowels—that seemingly travel from a remote past—are taught him; for once he knew and understood the true names of things, and Nature, responding to his call, attuned him to her consciousness.

To-day we have lost our ancient inheritance, but within the living temple of the Innermost we can regain possession of this godlike science.

In the new age there will come a moment when the sincere student—who has attained his inner instruction—will accomplish all that has been written upon his illumined mind-body.

The Dayspring of Youth has touched the world in other periods. Where did Greece, whose splendour has never been eclipsed, derive her wonderful information? From whose school did her architects receive their wisdom-knowledge of architecture and the laws of balance, rhythm and proportion? Who taught Phidias, Praxiteles and Apelles their knowledge of form, colour and the spirit that permeated their work? Even to-day the illumined mind feels the vibration that the Praxiteles torso sends forth, and few living sculptors can impregnate marble with such pregnant vitality. Within such masterpieces were placed living atoms that still impress us with reverence and devotion. For they placed within their work their own atoms, and though centuries have passed the sensitive mind can still feel the artist's joy in his creation. Yet much of this rich and manifold creation of Greece arose within the range of two hundred and fifty years.

In the *Atlantean Testament of Learning*, a book preserved by the Brothers, we read the following concerning the origin of the Attic civilisation: "When the Great Initiate and his followers of the Sun came to the Mediterranean they halted for a time at the site upon which Athens was later built, and the Atlantean planted in the subsoil atoms that long afterwards stimulated the minds of those who came to dwell there. He then departed with his followers to the fertile valley of the Nile to build up the civilisation now called the Egyptian."

The developed student will find such records intensely interesting. In the Chapter House of the Brothers one can turn over the pages of the past written by the historians of the Order.

Few people analyse the atmosphere of this world, neither do they realise their place and part in its activity. They who do so are generally the prophets of a nation and draw upon and express its accumulated store of wisdom: it is this wisdom that unites a nation to its inheritance. Western Yoga will help us through many difficult processes and give us the wisdom that will enable us to fulfil our mission to this world, as well as attain to our individual and inner universe.

The secret of this form of Yoga lies in the breathing in of atoms of a developed nature; for their higher rate of vibration develops our atomic structures. This is done by inhaling into the nasal passages a certain type of atom called Aspiring atoms.

In certain past periods of this world we could unite ourselves to our inner centres, and to-day, through constant aspiration and purity of thought we hope to reach the summit of this attainment, and also gather the knowledge the developed atoms possess and bind ourselves to those who reflect our highest aspirations. Only by aspiring for purity can beauty be received; this will also bring us clarity of mind and an instant sense of rest, no matter how tired we may have been.

Through Yoga, the student will receive, besides enlightenment, growth to his spiritual nature and an interior understanding of the scientific world of today.

Though the Innermost may seldom interest Itself in outer things, we should always do so, and strive to conform to the laws of this world.

Old environments sap the atmospheres of young life. Such conditions are frequently found in old countries as well as in old cathedral and university towns, for we cannot awaken and train those who will not sever themselves from their old appetites and passions for the culture of a past age.

When the student begins to inhale this atomic energy of the new age it will give him some idea as to his future development; for the old atmosphere of this world has all the dust and filth of many ages, and therefore drags us back to the past. Thus a nation will decay if it fails to respond to its own manifestation of the Dayspring of Youth.

In the past we ascended the lower densities of matter into the higher, but as we did so we lost contact, being misled by our lower nature. Therefore we must not surrender to lower conditions; if we do so they will enslave us.

Men are different in their structures: some possess dense bodies as well as dense minds and do not respond to any inflow of energy, but drift along in a casual manner. These people are the slaves to other minds and impart such qualities to those below them.

In this practice of Yoga we no longer become the prey to other minds, nor revert to old standards of thinking when analysing the qualities of thought coming from the inner planes.

As energy can only be attracted by energy, think of the new energy in the atmosphere when aspiring; for these things can only be taken by force. When desirous for certain knowledge aspire and call upon the Innermost to connect you to that centre or division corresponding to that source of information.

In the deeper states of this practice we seek the essence of our past experiences after reviewing our past incarnations: whether good or evil.

When we have made the sum total of our experience into a wisdom intelligence we will then feel—if we are observant when practising—the attributes of courage and stimulation. This means that through aspiration we have inhaled those atoms possessing the consciousness belonging to the world of the Innermost.

We only become aware of our own atomic workers—who labour unceasingly upon the growths of our nervous system—when entering our interior planes. When we realise this we should give them love and encouragement.

If we wish to govern ourselves and analyse our conditions we must pass the barriers separating us from our own sovereignty and this illusion world; for we cannot expect the Innermost to promote the growths of our minds until we seek unity with It.

Each section of the body belongs to its individual atomic vibration, and we must analyse them in our practice as they collect within the nasal passage. We then call upon those atoms that instruct us and they will assist us by giving us the quality of balance.

As we inhale, a door seems to slowly open within us and we feel drawn into another sphere. In time this breathing will be controlled by the Innermost. When this occurs we shall then know for the first time the meaning of rhythmic breathing, and sense that other Being within us who takes charge and who gives us an alertness and perception never felt before. This is the borderland of our individual universe.

Within our nervous system lies a second set of nerves that respond to a greater wave-length. When we aspire we pass from the first into the second, and there collect atoms of a different nature. We also awaken currents of dynamic power that open to the secluded centres and prepare us for admission into our real world of being where atomic substances give us energy and intelligence.

In this study we must take each step with a feeling of security and courage. The illumination that comes to us comes through observation and study of our inner possessions. We are not blind like the mystic who, though radiating great love, has little to demonstrate; for the mystic and Yogi of this science are far apart. The mystic with fasting and praying weakens his body, seeking to make it subservient to its Higher Self, of whom he is ignorant, and only Its fragrance and peace remains in his heart; but the Yogi will develop and learn from his atomic intelligence his own great truth.

In the science of this Western Yoga there are preparatory, silent, active and scholastic periods. These four teach us how our inner and outer bodies operate. The presence of our Innermost has to be brought into manifestation on our objective world. Here we will add an important note about our Innermost: elsewhere we say that It is held prisoner; but this does not mean that It has no freedom of movement—on the contrary, It manifests through our central system, our secondary system, and objective body; but It cannot manifest beyond these until It is ultimately released through Yoga practice.

We do not consciously respond to the impressions of our Innermost—though religious teachers say we are in constant union with the Reality or God—until the Innermost, the instrument of the Reality, unites us to It.

In our present condition and atmosphere direct communication with our Innermost does not operate until we build into our system Its divisions of atomic structures. Yoga teaches us that only through the construction of such vehicles can we receive a response. We do not realise that when we reject these Aspiring atoms we likewise reject our own strength and serenity, or that in our practice we begin to fertilise our bodies another type of atom that evokes our hidden forces. Just as the gardener uses richer soil to nourish his plants.

A devout person often thinks he receives answers to his prayers from his deeper consciousness; for his heart is suddenly aflame and this convinces him that he has found God. Yet this is but the response of the atomic centre within his heart that has registered his appeal and aspiration. He believes this to be an illumination of God; whereas it is but the opening of a centre that has attracted Aspiring atoms that pour into his system and illuminate his consciousness, and pronounce their blessings upon one who has sought their atmosphere. To many this is called Divine Revelation. When centres in our secondary system are opened they also give us similar illuminations and periods of serenity and peace: not the peace of mind as we think, but determined energy personified by our own individuality: that composite body that calls to its Innermost.

Though we are always observed by the Reality and Its instrument, the Innermost, we are cast out of our own real kingdom until through aspiration we bring into our physical envelope those atoms that respond to the Innermost and the Reality. How can we know and receive the vibrations of the higher planes without an instrument upon which their vibrations can play and enter its consciousness? Man fails to endow himself with his own higher intelligences and is unaware of their reverence for his Innermost.

Thus the reader can now realise that this system of Western Yoga is to harmonise us to our finer states of being wherein dwells the presence of the Innermost.

There are many petals to a rose, but few breathe the perfume of its heart. Therefore seek the Innermost so that its fragrance may sweeten and heal the mind.

CHAPTER TWO
THE NOUS ATOM

IN the left ventricle of the heart rests the principal atom: that minute model the physical body must eventually conform to in its progress. This is a spinning body living within its own atmosphere and is called the Master Builder; for it has charge over all the constructive principles of our physical body. Like a general in command it has armies of atomic builders and engineers that carry out its directions. These are the Aspiring atoms who seek the Innermost as we do. This Master Builder has its staff of overseers who often sacrifice their own attainments for those beneath them in development.

Our first practice is to attract the notice of this Master Builder or Nous atom by the use of these Aspiring atoms that attune us to their intelligence.

The physical organism is like a foreign country to these willing atoms whose task is to attune it to its greater spiritual possibilities.

The Master Builder rests in the purest blood of the heart in absolute authority over the atoms that obey it. This bloodstream can exert pressure on these workers and thus stimulate them to greater activity. Increased pressure demands greater endurance from them as the body must be repaired regardless of the labourer's desires.

These myriad workers—whom we neither heed nor help—are often discouraged and seemingly helpless through our excesses in stimulants and labour. The student can encourage them every morning by this exercise: take a deep breath, stand upon the soles of the feet, pat the tip of the liver—the Robin Goodfellow of the Yogi—and send love and encouragement whilst doing so. The nerve centre at this spot is vitalised by our thought and love; for there lies the seat of the imagination, and a healthy imagination makes a healthy body.

These atoms respect an honest mind; for dishonesty in our dealings inflicts disorder in their atmosphere and they avoid us if possible. Thus only pure aspiration can contact us to their consciousness. They also bring the influences of the Innermost to our illusioned minds imprisoned in the mirages of this world.

Between man and Nature lies a vast void over which few have passed, and many Chinese artists have shown us these great conceptions dealing with the elemental realities that unite the mind to the consciousness of Nature.

It was the Nous atom or Master Builder that responded to the call of the Reality when asked to serve and incarnate into the lower stratas of the world before the coming of the sun to the mind.

The physical body only appears solid. When viewed from within it looks like a gaseous envelope, and is a protective screen for the Innermost, preventing the invasion of foreign, germlike substances. The penetration of our own thoughts can inflict great sufferings upon these atomic, faithful workers within us if these thoughts are intense with hatred, malice, or envy; for these qualities are far more destructive than we realise.

Our education teaches us to think outwardly. This prevents our minds from thinking inwardly. What we believe to be our own thoughts do not arise from our Innermost and are therefore not of our own individual Truth.

The Nous atom will never demand anything that is evil from us. On the contrary, it will suggest only those things that will be helpful for our inner development. Its work is to liberate us from our bondage in this illusion world. And as we are the architects of our own fate it is for us to decide.

As the student develops he contacts those periods when man was enveloped in an atmosphere full of divine wisdom, and he again recalls the plan he had determined to accomplish in this world ere incarnating—a plan forgotten as he descended into the dense matter of this world.

In those ancient days we knew we were composed of atoms possessing different qualities, and we are still encircled by a powerful protective shield into whose consciousness we must again enter.

When we receive illumination during our practice we help our atoms by giving them the same aspiration and aid that we receive. Only when immersed within our own interior planes do we realise the pain and misery we cause the workers of the Nous atom; for we re-experience their sufferings and we determine that in the future we will keep a healthy and normal mind in a clean and healthy body.

When the Master Builder or Nous atom leaves the body the body disintegrates. The Nous atom desires to establish laws that will cause the nations of the world to be as one.

Man to-day is only four-sevenths developed; but when the Nous atom and its workers respond to our practices we are taught to stimulate several divisions of the body seemingly atrophied through disuse.

The body is composed of two types of atoms: good and evil. Through them we re-experience the good and evil of our past lives.

Atoms resemble their owners, and those whose atoms are firm and solid have strong bodies; those with weak atoms have weak bodies.

When we enter our intermediate states we develop our hidden senses of perception and become aware of discarnate intelligences, and we must be careful not to confuse our intuitions with their communications. In order to know the differences between the true voice and the false we should feel a vibration that brings us a sense of victory and stillness: like the end of a great pronouncement.

Our inclinations to be alert and healthy will give us the steady reverence of the Aspiring atoms; therefore we should not eat impure foods, and be moderate in our stimulants.

Increased blood pressure accounts for abnormal appetites and desires and stimulates our lower natures to greater activities, and opposes our entry to our inner worlds. This pressure destroys the nerves that cause the cells of the brain to open and shut. As we breathe, these nerves open the cells to the energy passing through the body, and if they are shut through abnormal pressure from sudden exertion this increases the lower centres to a greater alertness and activity and shuts off the inner worlds from the student and prevents him from receiving their instructions.

We must therefore use a method whereby we can shut off the influences of our lower nature. In the heart there is a small valve that opens and shuts off interruptions from the lower seats of consciousness. Later we slowly realise that the Innermost uses a system of irrigation canals through which flow the beautiful substance that will fertilise our growth and understanding of our own possessions.

We not only breathe with our lungs but every brain cell is furnished with what we analyse as lung passages that collect atoms to impress us with their intelligence.

Aspiring atoms are often immersed in substances that destroy their communications with the Nous atom, and it is the indolent atoms that bring this to pass.

Our minds are collectors of decayed atmospheres of the past filled with the foulness that generates the taste for war and other great vices. In our practice these decayed conditions will give way to a Solar force that will burn them up. This fire will destroy those parasites that have inflicted their burdens upon us and cleanse us for our true minds to manifest.

Throughout history a World Saviour has appeared at the end or beginning of an age, and when we can read our own inner books of remembrance we shall then know what illumination each teacher brought to us and to the world; also that they could work miracles through the magical manipulations of vowel sounds, and that their work had been to attune man to the higher vibrations released by these atoms.

In every life we have had the same Nous atom, and in some lives obeyed its directions.

The world thinks that when a man becomes a Yogi and goes into retreat he wastes his life. It is true he may be known to but a few, yet the genuine Yogi has his place in the development of humanity, and his power increases as he withdraws from the atmosphere of the world that holds humanity prisoner. He possesses great power, and manipulates the thought-waves of mankind as the musician manipulates his keyboard.

As the student passes through the astral and mental planes in his journey inwards many of the subnormal beings that crowd these regions—some earthbound—often listen-in to his thoughts and strive to disturb and distort his mind.

The Aspiring atoms aid us in bringing to birth the latent energy within us: that sleeping force near our navel centre that liberates us from bondage. This force—similar to static electricity—is evoked, directed up the spinal tract, and opens our great hidden centres or schools; for in the central nervous system is the Sun intelligence of our miniature universe where man can gain oneness with the Reality.

We then come under the direction of a most powerful stream of intelligence that helps us to pass out of our bodies and gain information without resorting to normal methods. If we are observant we can scan the horizon of all endeavour and accustom ourselves to dwell inwardly regardless of the world's knowledge and partake of that inner nourishment we outwardly rejected.

In our central system we find certain atoms that represent the consciousness of the great leaders of humanity. These atoms form an atomic structure from whence one will now and again descend into the dense atmospheres of our bodies and contact us to those atomic intelligences that have followed their teachings. They will also flash before us the moving screen of our past experiences. And again, there will come over the student what he had previously suffered: feelings of having been conquered and of having conquered. He will aim, after having witnessed his good and evil deeds, to so live that there will no longer dwell within him those atoms that had "rebelled against their Lord."

No great administrator has ever used the standards of his age; instead he has created ideals and used his imagination in order to bring about progressive changes in his civilisation.

Nations have had periods of enlightenment when the moral worth of the individual was considered a national asset. The Greeks understood this ideal.

The organs of generation are of great importance in these teachings; for their creative power is not for sex alone, but also for the creation of ideal standards through the use of imagination.

The powerful energy that enters us has several strands, and each one vibrates a different division of the nervous system.

When seen inwardly these centres radiate different light-waves, like coals glowing in a dark night.

The energy of our central system keeps us awake; but when we sleep it also rests, and another form of energy takes its place. This is similar to an engineer overhauling the machinery after the workmen have left; for this energy repairs broken-down tissues and destroys all that is of an unhealthy nature. When we awake it ceases functioning and the previous atomic forces resume their tasks.

The governing intelligences of each atomic colony resist with all their power any outside influence that attempts to change their attitude towards one another.

It is necessary to be always alert for any message coming from the Nous atom; and there is an old hermetic saying, "Be alert for your Master's voice as he is alert for yours."

When we can respond to the Innermost we can remedy past ills, live deeper and nobler lives, and become initiated into the Lesser Mysteries.

CHAPTER THREE
DESTRUCTIVE ATOMS

AS we have said in the previous chapter there are two forces within man: good and evil. The Nous atom is sometimes called by the occultist the white or good principle of the heart. We will now speak of its opposite: the dark atom or Secret Enemy. In many ways its activities are similar to the Nous atom; for it has legions of atomic entities under its command; but they are destructive and not constructive. This Secret Enemy resides in the lower section of the spine, and its atoms oppose the student's attempts to unite himself to his Innermost. The Secret Enemy has so much power in the atmosphere of this world that they can limit our thoughts and imprison our minds. When we strive to hold the mind to one thing it will immediately attempt to disintegrate it. As a teacher once told me: "If you could hold a pristine thought for but three seconds you could become a master of the world."

These atoms evoke all that is evil within us, and in the history of the world it has its periods of power when it becomes greatly destructive. The last war was such a period.

As its powers predominate in this world it is easier for us to contact its schools in our Yoga practice; for from childhood we have been taught to think outwardly and not inwardly, and it is in the outer bodies that these atoms manifest more easily. Thus the kingdoms of Hell are easily entered, but the kingdoms of Heaven can only be entered by force.

Here we think a note upon faith should be of interest. Initiates say that its meaning has been misunderstood. Faith, as the world uses it, possesses no spiritual nature; though in the secondary system it means power and energy applied to action. All success in Yoga comes from this application; for the true quality of faith is a Solar force that illumines the mind and attracts to it atoms of power and energy.

More human wrecks have resulted from the misconception of this quality than man realises.

When Jesus used this word in the sentence "If ye had faith as a grain of mustard seed," He meant that one could work miracles if one possessed the atomic energy contained within a mustard seed. But in this world of illusion this is reversed, and the weak man sits still and believes that all will come to him if he has faith. It is not a force that should only be applied to religious belief. It is the power of the Innermost working through the densities of our bodies, and the more we respond to it the greater will be our powers.

Incidentally the student should know that when he enters his secondary system there is a reversal of things. For instance, here we say "The man runs," but in this inner division the sentence would read "Runs the man."

The Secret Enemy has never been allowed to enter the higher spheres of our being. In the beginning when the world was in a fiery state they refused the call of the Absolute, and "Rebelled against their Lord." Afterwards they followed the streams of the white atoms and incarnated. Their next opportunity of responding to the call will come at the creation of a new universe.

When the student re-experiences those past lives when he was dominated by evil, he also re-experiences the following lives when he repays such evil through much sufferings. And it may help those who suffer much poverty and pain to-day to know that they are paying the penalty of previous actions; for the Innermost within them is their judge.

When the student can balance his two types of atoms, the white and the black, their powers come under his control, and he can then enter his higher schools. In Eastern terminology this means, "He who has attained the middle of his Path." He is now under the jurisdiction of neither good nor evil.

As we enter the darker spheres of our nature we meet earthbound intelligences who would attach themselves to us were we to permit them. Later we have to face the composite body of our past evil—a thought-form of our own creation—and to whom we have given elements of a soul nature; for unknowingly we are all creators. This, called "The Dweller of the Threshold," will confront us, and is a living, dynamic force. Being elemental it can assume any shape of horror with which it wishes to impress us, and usually takes a feminine form. If we permit this evil to gain control over us for but a moment—for it is hypnotic—it will give the nervous system, especially to those uninitiated as to its true nature, a dangerous shock. But if at such a moment we aspire to the Reality for protection and understand, it will disintegrate like the ash of a cigarette. When this is destroyed it will remove the subconscious impressions of fear that children as well as men suffer from in their dreams.

In some Greek mysteries this "Dweller" is evoked and the neophyte is freed from it. There is also its opposite that we meet on the higher planes: the composite body of our past good and ideals. This is a godlike intelligence, terrible in its appearance of brightness and splendour. It is called the Advocate. We will speak about this in later chapters.

We also re-experience in our lower schools our evolution through the animal states, and we discover how they still strongly influence and control man.

As this world is closely related to the Secret Enemy it is far easier for the student to gain a knowledge of the evil side of Nature instead of the good; for operative magic deals more easily with the density of matter than with the finer forces of Nature.

The wisdom of the Secret Enemy is seemingly far greater than the wisdom of the Nous atom. As a great prophet once said, "The children of this world are in their generation wiser than the children of light."

Our atmosphere is moist, and when we attract an evil thought to it, this evil thought will surround us with atoms of a similar nature that will rotate about us like a swarm of bees. On the outer lining of the mental body are nodes of consciousness that attract certain types of good and evil thoughts. Such atoms differ in degrees of intelligence, and some can give us false conceptions of things as well as of people.

Students must adapt themselves to their environments and learn to govern their thoughts. By so doing they can increase their energy and feel a greater security and power from the atmosphere of the Nous atom. Remember that environments differ and evil places teem with destructive atoms.

The Innermost judges us by the atmosphere we attract. The Sun sends a great cleansing power into the atmosphere. You will notice this in Spring when new life and vitality is sensed everywhere; for the atoms of the Sun stimulate the central nervous system.

It is interesting to note that people infiltrated by atoms of the Secret Enemy cannot bear sunlight in the morning when the Sun is most vital. Those people who are dominated by their ancestors and live in rooms magnetised by their thoughts also generally prefer seclusion. But in the future people will no longer live in the begrimed and congested areas of cities where ancestral atoms of a decayed nature float; for the vibrations of the Dayspring of Youth will separate youth from such hereditary conditions.

People who build with old materials should remember that new wine should not be poured into old bottles. Our bodies must build with the new energy and be made healthy and conditions clarified.

Each person has an individual atmosphere and an individual intelligence. When we respond to the new energy and clothe ourselves with our own individuality we will have no affinity to other mental atmospheres. This separation will cause students difficulty at first in understanding people, for once on the Path we become different in thought as well as in ideas. We are again like little children entering another world surrounded by those pure atoms that came and remained with us in the first years of our birth, and, like children, we neither resist nor attract atoms of the Secret Enemy. In this way we are protected from evil. Incidentally it should be known that the opposition to good is the real cause of unhappiness.

The worst type of atom that confronts us to-day comes over from the remote Lemurian period. In this long past age, before this planet had reached a higher level of evolution, our bodies were of an animal nature divorced from its godlike mind and immersed in an atmosphere not unlike the atmosphere of to-day. We were constantly engaged in war, sacrificed our victims to our gods of destruction, and ate their flesh.

Our recreations consisted of opposing animals against one another and eating them afterwards. As blood is instantly transformed, in the heat of battle, into the evil qualities of the combatants, this helped the Secret Enemy to populate thickly the bodies with its destructive atoms and thus gain greater power over the physical bodies.

It was in this Lemurian period that we first broke bread. The more highly developed creatures harvested a grain similar to millet, and this disturbed the animal atoms within them, and created a desire to oppose those who followed war and ate the remains, and also to unite into a colony and brotherhood for the purpose of self-protection. Those who escaped from torture and death also joined them.

We were higher than the animals; for we could remember and repeat what we had heard from the elders of this colony—who could easily leave their bodies and had discovered how to receive instruction from another sphere—an overseer globe. At times there also came beings of a semidivine nature whose vibrations interpenetrated and stimulated our bodies.

These solar beings taught them an alphabet similar to that of the early Chinese. Also a lost art known only to Initiates that dealt with the vowel sounds of Nature. When these were sounded correctly they would evoke an audible response, and by the sound the true name of a thing would be known.

Our old Lemurian atoms are our most destructive enemies, as they still possess the inheritance of their ancient wisdom and the black magicians receive instruction from them. In the ritual of the Brothers we read: "Be masters of the black magicians by mastery over their masters of magic."[1]

Artists often succumb to the Secret Enemy and saturate their work with an evil beauty that contacts the beholder with a destructive atmosphere. What thought creates is penetrated by an atomic atmosphere, and beauty is often defiled by the thoughts cast upon it. In the lower spheres objects of

[1] See *The White Brother,* by Michael Juste.

great beauty can be seen; so lovely that we become almost entranced. Yet they would evoke all our evil natures if we permitted them to imprison our minds.

In this world the Secret Enemy transforms what has been created through great purity of mind into the opposite by the criticism of those darker minds controlled by the Secret Enemy. The criticism of Keats's poems is such an example; youthful genius is easily hurt, and sometimes destroyed, when the dark powers write through the pen of a critic.

Every man's past sleeps in the atmosphere of his constructive and destructive atoms, and according to his thoughts he awakens them and can inflict them upon others. He does not realise he can destroy the healthy radiations of others by the influence of his diseased atoms; for he is not always happy or normal when he evokes his past conditions. Sometimes healthy and positive bodies attract protective types of atoms in order to shield them when in the presence of unhealthy forces.

People controlled by the powers of the Secret Enemy discharge these foul qualities into the atmosphere, and sensitive people are not immune from this if they have not positive minds and the gift of sound bodies.

Depression and anger are the two doors through which the influences of the Secret Enemy enter, and when this occurs diseased germs invade the body. Anxiety and poor food will also destroy our Aspiring atoms. Our salvation therefore rests upon the possession of a happy and mentally balanced atmosphere; for our happiness is their happiness, and our miseries theirs also.

Instinct, that power we once possessed when evolving through the protean and animal elements, and which the animal calls upon for direction in moments of danger, still lies within us, and this will awaken again in the middle period of the new age. This power protects and warns us of evil minds, and they who use it will have nothing to fear from the Secret Enemy; since instinct comes from the Innermost and the opposition cannot work against it.

If we concentrate intensely upon the Secret Enemy we aid it and develop its powers within our atmosphere.

Within the lower spheres of our nature the Secret Enemy has its schools, and in our practices we are often confronted by one of its servants who promises to grant us any material wish if we be willing to associate with the powers and principalities of its master: though should we do so we must be prepared to give our souls into its possession. This is the student's great trial, for the white atoms do not promise us anything of an earthly nature save a wealth of wisdom and a sense of inner security.

Before the great war those minds responsive to its evil influences shadowed forth its ideal that "Might is Right," and sowed those seeds of destruction that unlocked the Secret Enemy within man. The workers of the Nous atom rebel at any prospect of war or destruction, physically or mentally, and will protect those who surrender themselves to their atmosphere.

Atoms of a demoniacal nature are appearing in the upper levels of Society, and no nation can secure peace and comfort when their leaders are under such domination.

Everyone has a caste mark written upon the forehead, and the initiated can distinguish the character of each man in this manner.

Man has several observation posts in his body, and he can see from them into the areas of the world wherein the darker forces are at work.

The lordship of a nation passes away when in the fields the scythes are made to serve the purposes of the few, and the harvest is distributed to profit but a small section of people. The harvest is abundant and can feed all the world, but the atoms of destruction corner the markets and many starve.

Humanity is like a feather on a stream—drifting without any real purpose in life beyond that of effacing those disagreeable things that would disturb its pleasure. When, in his practice, the student enters and peers into the present from a future time, he will see how much agony man could have prevented, and the unfertilised fields of the world.

To-day man must learn to think and become his own saviour, and not be led by a few minds selected by the Secret Enemy, whom we elect to offices of state in the hope that they will gratify our pleasures without any thought of future consequences.

The Secret Enemy works in every way to deny us any intelligence that would illuminate our minds, and would seek to stamp man into a machine cursed with similarity and a mind lacking all creative power. The machine-made man's mentality is only moulded to serve the machine, and the future progress of a race is restricted; for that which is not impregnated with the activity of thought belongs to a world of dead atoms. The machine may make a man useful to others and give him a clean method of living, but it impoverishes him in regard to his own importance as a unit of the great Reality.

A great dictator has said, "There is an empty throne in nearly every country in Europe." This is true if people will not think but be led by other minds who assume the powers of dictatorship.

The student should know that in the astral sheath surrounding the physical body—this is the coarser envelope of passion and desire—his lower thoughts attract intelligences of an evil nature to its fluidic and translucent substance, and there derange the mental body by impressing their thoughts into it, so weaken the character thus assailed. These spirits can foretell many interesting things and give us secret information in order to bind us to them; though there is little of real worth in such. Their astral fluids emit a very disagreeable odour; for they secrete and are nourished upon diseased forms of matter that we throw off.

In still lower regions we find forms similar to the lower astral forms but without their intelligence. These hover over the death-beds of people and exist upon decaying matter. They are of the vampire species, and the black magicians use this effete substance to direct into the atmosphere of their enemies.

When we discuss elemental nature we will speak of how its lower counterpart is permeated with these atoms of destruction; atoms that stimulate ferocity and hatred in animals.

In the future the energy of this new age will inflict upon us a series of mental disorders; for those minds that will not respond to its wisdom and power will recoil from it. The Secret Enemy will have no method of diverting its force, and those who have attracted this new energy will suffer from periods of illusion and depression. But the aspiring student will not be affected; he will be in tune with its vibration, and will render it homage and respect.

We are still under the spells the magicians of the past have cast over us.

The children of the Secret Enemy speak of their evil works as though they were great virtues.

Man easily degenerates when in the power of the Secret Enemy; it preys upon the burning furnace of his desires, and when he weakens he is lost and sometimes cannot regain contact with his Innermost for two or three lives wherein he works out the karma of his evil desires.

Our creative forces are made to be preserved and not dissipated; for stored energy is a wealth that can ennoble our characters. Beware the person who fouls his appetite with unhealthy passions and desires; he endangers his own health besides the health of those about him.

The Secret Enemy often gives those who indulge in dissipation greater opportunities to spread their foulness, they then being more easily directed to perform deeds of evil to which the normal and balanced mind would never succumb.

This dark power will, when possible, consume its victims by disease. If it cannot control you when you are poor, but recognises that you possess qualities that would respond to its direction, it will make you rich; for then you can scatter greater seeds of destruction and such evil will live generations after. Many who have attained to great power, fame and reputation have often been stimulated and work under its authority.

In order to collect their instruments the schools of the black magicians make sex worship one of their principal teachings.

The Advocate, previously mentioned, is an atom of great intelligence that always stands in the presence of the Reality, and if we are serious and faithful in our aspirations for union with our Innermost after we have entered our secondary system and re-experienced our past, it pleads that we should be forgiven our past misdeeds. When this happens a man is reborn.

This Advocate is a great shield of protection for the sincere student, but, if we desire, it will permit us to work for the Secret Enemy. If we do so we cannot come under its protection in this life. We alone must choose our Paths: the right or the left, the good or the evil.

CHAPTER FOUR
THE ASTRAL

JUST as there are people who talk with authority about life yet know but little, so are there people who talk about Yoga who have never practised it. When we review our past lives we find we have lived through but a fragment of a far greater experience. What the world calls life is but an objective experience. The efforts to trace the cause of things are the first steps given us to know the reason for our sufferings. If one asks a great Yogi "What is life?" he would reply "I know but a fragment." Or, as I have heard one say: "I am standing upon the shore of a vast and great Reality."

Our bodies differ in their radiations; for they absorb as well as radiate the waves of sound and colour that come within their range, and it is from these that one can see what is wrong with a person. When we find that these radiations are confused, then the vitality of the person is very low. In healthy people the astral, mental and several other currents are clear.

The astral body in the illustration shows a faint outline of grey with several interwoven strands near the axis of the spine that pass through the body to the navel centre where they unite in a closed sheath. It is from this that the seminal fluid is extracted when the medium wishes to materialise astral entities. The astral sheath is undeveloped and the sounding board that controls the sensitive when controlled by a discarnate entity. It takes several seconds for the semen to be collected in the sac-like sheath, and with this creative force we can project the astral body a short distance from the physical body; but it cannot record anything above its intelligence; for its radiation is not strong, and is foreign to our secondary and central system.

Every person is different in their range of passion and desire, and the seminal system responds to them. If we are animal in our passions we collect such atoms. Therefore we should aspire for purity and seek the greatest intelligence within our central system.

THE ASTRAL SHEATH

MAN has brought over the astral sheath from a remote past, and, like the foetus in its early stages, it represents man's past submerged worlds of consciousness. If the student immerses himself in its atomic structures it will revert him to his lower passions and desires. It is through Yoga practice that we free ourselves from its domination.

Its several strands are entwined into one cord attached near the navel. Gravity affects it, and its greatest densities are collected into a sac-like formation that extends below the feet, as in illustration. The atomic intelligence of this sac possesses a knowledge of good and evil forbidden to man and represents man's lower elemental and animal past. This has been symbolised in "Genesis," as the tree of knowledge that grew the forbidden fruit of good and evil, and it is this that the black magician contacts. But such intercourse will retard the student's entrance into the atmosphere for several incarnations. The Egyptian magicians used this knowledge to perform their greatest miracles. It is one of the teachings of the Brothers that this sac should be sloughed off and thus give the adept power to levitate and prevent him from ever being earthbound or revert to past periods.

We have shown only the main strands; from these numerous others branch out. The astral body is a pattern body or matrix upon which man's physical framework is constructed; it is most akin to the physical body and registers its emotions and desires. It has several node points that intersect into the mental planes, and this produces annoying astral conditions; for the developed mental atoms have contact with the lower astral atoms, and thus the mind receives messages from astral intelligences. Each principal nerve ganglia of the coarser nervous system has an atomic link with the fibres of the astral sheath, and when the student removes the astral framework from any part of his body that part will not register any pain. This is easily demonstrated in hypnotic control and an Initiate can use this method if tortured.

The illustration shows only the skeleton of the astral body and not the complicated, weblike appearance as seen by the clairvoyant.

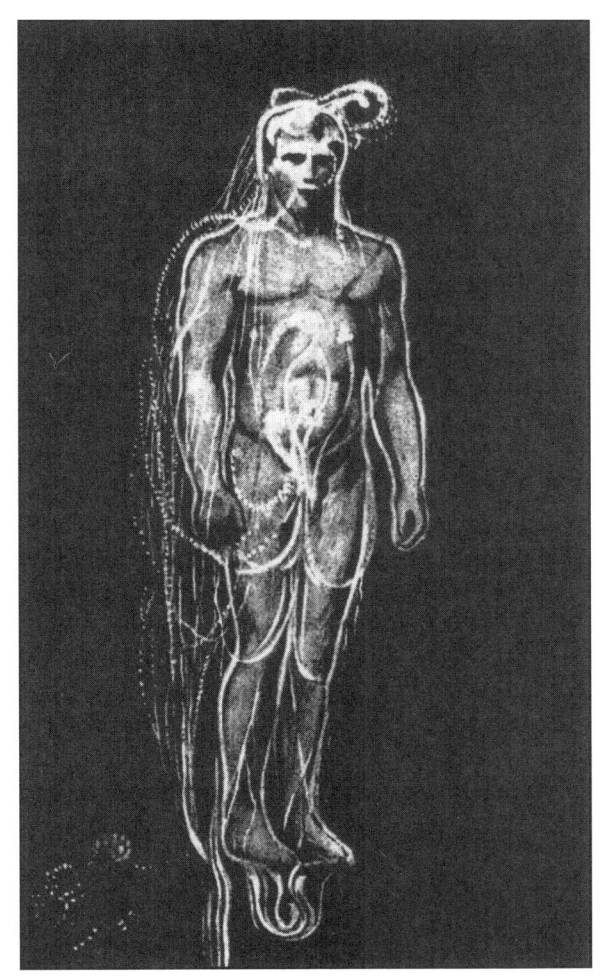

THE ASTRAL SHEATH

As the student develops in his practice he will notice several changes in his astral body. It begins to assume a new development and appear more lustrous. This is caused by atoms in the seminal system being transferred to it, and this grows more pronounced as we develop our power to emerge into our secondary and central system.

The astral body registers all that is foreign to our Innermost, and belongs to the submerged states of our existence: worlds of an ancient day when we were of the substance of the animal and antediluvian period.

As we do not go into the lower levels of Society to meet great minds, neither do we enter the astral planes for wisdom; for they possess very little of true worth.

The astral body consists of numerous fibres held together by a composite body of matter similar to the translucent membrane of a fish's eye. This membrane has the power to extend its area of activity several inches beyond the surface of the physical body during our waking state.

The subconscious world of sex-animalism is very strong in many people; though they would shudder at such a thought, yet they unconsciously revert to their animal ancestry. Psychoanalysts will discover this; for they often analyse astral conditions, and place them in regions of their patient's subconscious mind wherein astral conditions are unlocked and disturbed. For these reasons it would be better for these psychoanalysts to study Yoga, as they can then consciously enter these submerged states of man's animal worlds of disease and destruction.

The greatest use we can find in the most developed atoms in the astral sheath is that they possess great influence over minds closely related to their atmosphere. Though this astral intelligence might be of an animal nature, if it is cleansed through the purity and aspiration of the Silver Shield—to which we will devote a chapter later—it will become radiant and a sounding board for the thoughts of animals that will also receive our thoughts. Thus in time we can converse with animals as did Appolonius of Tyana.

There is some confusion regarding this astral sheath. In occult literature we read about astral travels. This is a wrong term, since we cannot travel more than about twenty feet from the physical body as we are attached to it by the silver cord.

When we travel into the astral plane we climb in our mental body to a high altitude and from this height project ourselves into these planes; though the student will not waste much time in such worlds.

There are three belts of illusion around the world, and as the student passes through these he attracts hosts of entities, and if he halts and listens to their demands for aid and instruction he might become beclouded by their ignorance. When entering the secondary system he casts a light behind, and like a candle in the darkness he attracts a multitude of rebellious atoms.

Spirits are seldom interesting though we often test them, when we realise that they possess but little intelligence beyond this world. Though they presume to hold great secrets they cannot enter into the secondary system. Therefore the student should avoid those who claim to be great beings. As we scatter them with our power we see that they radiate but little of that light they claim to possess. Too close a relationship with them will result in the degradation and sapping of our vitality.

We should keep aloof from those lower orders whose morals and views of life are of the nature of the animal kingdom, and to consort with gangsters and rum-runners is not the goal of a refined soul. Developed souls do not linger on the lower levels infested by these spirits. Hell is full of those who still long to keep their place and position in a Society that has at last divorced them. Such unfortunates are seldom willing to work on the lower levels to assist those beneath them. Though sacrifice of self can place them on a higher plane and in time evolve them into higher spheres. Evil natures bring sorrows to those who have their interests at heart. This is how the good are frequently persecuted by the Secret Enemy.

In our practices we often descend into a lower sphere in order to liberate someone imprisoned there. The atoms of the Innermost observe those truly repentant of their evil deeds, and have watchmen who report upon those who are to be redeemed from their periods of illusion; just as the student is observed and given that initial effort that will enable him to gain a higher note.

There is a consciousness called the Overseer planet that retards our progress in order that we may gain sufficient power to overcome obstacles placed in our path. This planet is a secret of initiation and casts a pink light over the Initiated and gives them a new consciousness of a militant nature. This is the symbol of one who has conquered atoms of the Secret Enemy within his astral and lower mental envelope.

Mars—that is the instrument of this overseer planet—impresses a warlike quality upon those who are intermittently governed by its attributes of justice.

Within the astral sheath are migratory atoms possessing our passions and desires. We do not realise that we attract myriads of these into this sheath. When we can visualise this atmosphere we shall see a moving and livid mass of small clusters revolving around their own centres. These atoms absorb the life and nourishment we radiate. Such atoms are particularly fond of the diseased centres caused by our unnatural passions and desires and states belonging to our past and submerged nature. We have often created images of a subnormal kind, and these are perceived and impressed upon us by our Secret Enemy. This causes our astral envelope to be invaded by hordes of lower atoms.

We speak of entities living within a definite range of astral fluid and not of those entities that infest the atmosphere of the lower mind-body; for these belong to a more intelligent class.

The astral nodes of communication are comparatively few, whereas the mental body has many, and we are often aware of some astral entity who seeks information about the plane above that it cannot enter. These are like certain beasts that neither toil nor enrich the world, but are parasites of the life force of others. Those contacting them become likewise—devitalising and indolent, with no incentive to work.

To overcome and sever one from such conditions one should cultivate a sense of prosperity and activity. This comes to those who have collected the Aspiring atoms. Vitality throws them off just as laziness attracts, and sunlight also severs them from such conditions. If a student becomes infected with these lower conditions flowers of sulphur shaken into the stockings will eradicate them. Several kinds of obsessions can also be remedied by this process; for these conditions refuse to inhabit the astral fluid when the odour of sulphur permeates its sheath. People who have died from accidents and whose skins have been lacerated make it easy for these entities to impersonate them; gathering the astral and mental moisture oozing from such wounds and creating apparitions at seances.

The attachments of such entities to a sensitive can be broken by the application of vinegar to the rectum. This increases the voltage of the seminal fluid and produces greater resisting powers to foreign entities.

In the atmosphere that divides us from our secondary system are innumerable places where certain atomic species suspend themselves like weaver-birds' nests. These colonies distort our minds. Imagine myriads of these drifting unresistingly in space. They hover unseen about one's atmosphere, and are more easily received upon the surface of our mental sheath in wet weather, and there remain, infesting it like ants swarming about a mound.

People who receive them become anxious and distressed, particularly in a storm, for these colonies are deflated in the rain and, becoming denser, increase the depression of the people who receive them.

The only way to check them is by radiating health by means of physical culture and any other healthy activity.

The student should not aspire when the air is heavy and depressing; such conditions will impair his mental envelope; as aspiration breathing makes one a magnet for other atoms as well. These atoms are the parasites and drones of the atomic species: lazy, useless, devitalising. Sensitive people who attract such conditions need more nourishment. They should form regular and normal habits in order to eradicate refuse from their system.

We are constantly surrounded by the cast-off shells of those whom we loved and who have reached their own true spheres of attainment. To visit them is easy to the advanced student, who reaches them by going inwardly and not reacting to the objecting atmosphere that is full of these shells.

There are times when a person living within a loftier sphere may appear to us. This is not often, and occurs when one of the greater Beings pilots or guides a person through the Purgatory states of illusion into our objective atmosphere, and then only when it is deemed necessary for the loved one on Earth.

Survival after death is easily learned during the first steps in Yoga. Afterwards the student will not think of survival at all as it is usually conceived; for he learns about space-time and it does not distress him.

We do not apply right methods in burial. Immediately after death place the body in a dark room without draughts, then place a warm water-bottle to the feet and raise them to a slightly vertical position. This improves the circulation of the sheaths so that they can be easily loosened and withdrawn from the body. For we often bury people when their astral sheaths are still in the atmosphere of the body, and this causes great distress to the atoms that compose them, and afterwards react upon the higher mentality of the person who has left the shell.

The processes of disintegration are carried on for a considerable time, and the body should not be buried before three days unless in a warm climate. But above all it is better to cremate the body, as this gives the person peace of mind and his sufferings are lessened. When the astral shell still clings to the corpse it is then that its apparition appears to the sensitive mind.

Thoughtless people think little about the care of the dead; they imagine that no further care is needed. But if a person has died suddenly and his body has become chilled it causes him acute agony, and a low nature will avenge itself upon those responsible for its sufferings. Incidentally when assisting drowning people while out of the body I have not witnessed this agony; for there is an affinity between the astral sheath and water, both being of a protean nature.

Death has not its sting for the occultist as for the normal man: for whenever he enters his interior systems he goes through a form of death, but religions have so impressed their followers about the terrors of after death that many devout Christians fight against that which should sometimes be welcomed.

It is well that the femoral artery should be severed after the doctor has definitely decided that death has ensued, there having been cases of coma or trance state.

As the Earth breathes in and out as we do, graveyards are a menace to civilisation; in time cremation will take its place, and people will have an altar in their house for the ashes of those who have showered their love upon them when alive, but not the ashes of those who gave no love: the youth of the future will not worship their ancestors indiscriminately, but will only send the pressure of their love to those deserving it, and evolve them to higher levels of consciousness. In these ashes will lie the atmospheric links between their ancestors and themselves. Incidentally the pressure of a child's prayer is one of the most protective forces known to the occultist, and in occult history Egypt was once saved from calamity through the prayer of a child. This will show wherein the Chinese have a greater wisdom regarding these things.

The Initiates say that the living should be respected, and when death awakens them into their own states of the Reality they will be given their incense and perfume. This means that when a person who has loved others and has been loved passes over, his love is perfume and incense to our mind, and as we inhale this we contact those who are far beyond us in the inner states of being.

Death is but an awakening into another state of consciousness, and the Greeks treated this beautifully, as can be seen in their sculptures. It should be awaited with joy and not with misgiving, seeing that we return to those spheres that are of the nature of our being.

CHAPTER FIVE
ELEMENTAL NATURE

IN the great sealed book of Nature I have read these words: "In everything there rests an absolute Presence," and in other books of the Initiates we read similar thoughts. In everything rests the presence of the Absolute, or as the more developed Brothers have written: "The name of a body of matter if spelled or spoken correctly will evoke an answer; for in all substance there lies an intelligence that replies to the note in a spoken word, and this intelligence is not of the nature of its matter but of the objective minds that bind it to Nature."

As the student progresses he becomes familiar with and aware of the elemental intelligences of Nature. He learns that Nature is divided into two divisions: that the world is the lower counterpart of something that exists in the finer atmosphere of Nature, and that it has much information for him. As the records of the Brothers read: "And what others have not observed they take up and make known to their followers."

In these finer atmospheres the student contacts the mentalities of fire, water, and earth, and if he is pure enough he can enter their kingdoms and principalities; as we all know, our bodies are composed of such elements.

Sooner or later man will return to his natural surroundings and regain that ancient wisdom to which he had attained ere plunging into the dense matter of this world.

When the student contacts these great elemental forces he will enter a storehouse of wisdom and information far beyond our own, and if he can gain the confidence and interest of these forces his own sensitivity will be enlarged and quickened.

Within us there is an atmospheric sheath that is the archive of our racial consciousness; its centre is situated in the knees, and man is more subject to his racial consciousness than he realises, and this explains why his knees tremble when anything endangers his body or the directing power of his race.

We should remember that we are obnoxious to those pure beings of Nature's higher altitudes.

The mind must be vigorous and alert in order to gain entrance into Nature's higher counterpart. Through Yoga it is possible to reach these realms if we possess courage; but without preparation it is doubtful if we would succeed. The method that brings us in touch with our secondary nature also contacts us with these elemental spheres.

When in these higher realms we are above all those things that disturb our minds, and we do not demand anything from Nature that would retard our inner growth.

We analyse things from a different angle when in these realms: that is, we study the causes of things instead of the effects, and a process of levitation: the power to pass from a dense state of mind-matter into a finer state. In a certain book a student relates such experiences.[1]

Though active inwardly these vibrations do not register objectively.

There comes a time when the student is taken out of his body in full consciousness by his teacher, and he learns to journey to other spheres. This is part of his education, when, like Paul of Tarsus, he will say: "I met such a man, whether in the body or out of the body I could not tell." [2 Corinthians 12:2-3]

Remember Nature is our great mother and it is she who nourishes her children when they return to her. She is very stern but loving, and her joy when attaining her consciousness is deep: for she desires that her sons should regain their lost sovereignty, as man was born to command the elementals.

As we pass through each division of Nature we are taught the laws and customs of each sphere. From these we learn what is known as Nature's magic. The elementals working with us can manipulate mind-stuff and produce illusions that to the beholders would seem miracles. These helpers are our subjects and can give us the secret formulas of their magic. To distort the vision is one.

Though the student may be instructed in such knowledge there is a law regarding the production of such phenomena,

---

1: The White Brother, by Michael Juste.

which is only shown to the initiated who will not use these powers illegitimately. It is regarded as a sacred science given alone to those who possess Nature's intelligence.

These elemental beings are called angels in sacred literature, and are important in man's future evolution, as they were once in his past. There is magnitude in their expression and they give man a sense of majesty and power when he is immersed in their atmosphere.

They teach us how to develop our minds so that we can magnify a thing till it can embrace the whole world. Meaning that a single line of verse can be enlarged and fixed into many minds by their magical power of focusing so that it can be constantly repeated. The great poets—who have been elemental—have given this power to thousands of minor poets. Something that is charged with beauty and is the forerunner of a virtuous thought.

The great poet is the dominator of the world's atmosphere, and this kingly substance has given him power to unlock his own elemental doorway.

Though the student may enter Nature's kingdoms she will not always unveil her face to him, after consulting his past records. Yet sinners as well as saints have entered them; it depends upon the material of their clothing whether they will reach the Innermost, whilst the more ignorant will grope for instruction in her lower spheres wherein they can obtain knowledge that will give them power over the lower elemental forces.

The ancient prophets all taught their pupils to go to Nature and learn of her systems of government, then pass such laws down to humanity. For if we are to govern wisely we must be given that wisdom Nature holds for us.

We must be impersonal; for personality cannot enter these kingdoms. Individuality possesses nothing that is outside one's rightful domain, but if we are personal Nature recoils from our demands as this quality is dreaded by her subjects. Real individuality is the light of our intelligence shining through us.

We are kin to Nature if we are producers of real wealth, but such wealth cannot be purchased in the world's marketplaces; the greatest wealth being that which was engendered in us at the beginning of our creation—it is the great hub upon which we place our whole being, our central seats of government that will restore to us those possessions Nature has in her keeping.

Few students realise that if they wish to contact their own inner systems of government it is necessary for them to ally themselves to Nature, and if they first prefer to accumulate a fortune and succeed in business then afterwards study the secrets of Nature it will be more difficult for them. Possessions beyond the amount that will give us a clean, healthy life in clean surroundings often accumulate passions and desires that will govern the brain and shut us out from our sovereignty in Nature's higher counterpart.

The law of Proserpine is needed so that man will first acquaint himself with his own inner possessions ere entering the world of Mammon.

Nature will seek us if we will but open the way to her understanding; but as man destroys her work she withdraws her interest in him. The destruction of animals regardless of their proper use also destroys our approach to these higher elementals.

The different properties of matter that are under their jurisdiction are worked over and evolved as we are evolved.

Those who are cruel to animals and dominate them are often open to a concerted attack from the higher elemental spheres, and substances are discharged upon them that will hamper the normal functioning of their minds.

By loving an animal we protect its intelligence, but if we are cruel to it after we have gained its affection we have to pay the penalty; for it has its protection—a bodyguard similar to its master—and the evil we send it is quickly returned to us.

When elemental beings appear to us they are clothed in garments that represent their place and position in their own sphere. It is imperative that the student should know this, for the black magicians of the lower elemental planes can appear before him "clothed like the sun," though, if properly challenged, their hideous characteristics are quickly unmasked. Everything has its own keynote and colour, and when responding cannot hide them. "By a man's light is he known."

In these higher spheres the Beings have neither the sadness nor the so-called virtues of this world in their atmosphere. They are a creation apart and look upon us as objects of compassion. When they enter our world it is like coming amid decayed conditions where the odours are disagreeable and the atmosphere unpleasant.

Many of the world's great teachers were fathered by the Lords of the elemental worlds. Appolonius of Tyana, Merlin—a professed Christian born in the fifth century—and others. They possess the mingled bodies of elemental and human nature—such men are natural magicians. We have also magicians of a lower nature fathered by evil elementals who aim at personal power and who evoke abnormal appetites in men's minds.

There are also people in whom the elemental forces are most prominent and such are of an unmoral nature. We should not judge them too harshly; they are dominated by the lower conditions of these realms. But the higher types are Nature's sensitives and their bodies recoil at the approach of an unclean atmosphere. This can be noticed among children before their sensitivity is dulled by their surroundings. For this reason teachers of the young should be examined for their mental atmosphere and bodily cleanliness, as such can retain the love of their pupils all their lives. As is well known, it is in the child's first seven years that its future character can be determined.

Races receive their stimulation in the arts and sciences from these elemental worlds. Once in conversation with a sylph, who instructed me in the attainment of a certain kind of purity, he suddenly paused and said: "Do you not realise that the Christ consciousness works through our spheres as well as through yours? And sends its teachers to us as well as to you." Yet this Being, that the uninitiated would mistake for the ideal representation of Jesus in a shining amber robe, was but a sylph, who, according to ecclesiastical history, was one denied the kingdom of God.

These elemental people have a great regard for those seeking to enter their world and express themselves very frankly when we are accepted. They can give us information that cannot be heard by the listeners-in of the lower spheres or the magician of the Secret Enemy.

Also they allow us to see the workings of the internal organs of the physical body, and show us how one mind-body functions against the wishes of another mind-body. They can cause the evil that a man sends forth to return to him.

The properties of matter vary as the seasons change, just as the substances that surround our physical bodies do. And this change of season should warn us that our mental vestures will also undergo another change.

We do not realise what beauty and form can attain to until we enter these kingdoms: for the elementals can manipulate mind-stuff till its loveliness leaves us breathless. As an instance: a queen elemental can arrange precious stones as a garment; not only beautiful in design and arrangement, but with the hidden luminosity within the stones revealed.

After an illumination, when the student contacts the higher forces of Nature, he is sent to study these kingdoms; beginning with the mineral.

THE GNOME ELEMENTALS

In the mineral kingdoms are intelligences that learn to communicate with human beings. They live, as they express it, in the interspaces of rock. Their higher orders are like quicksilver in their activity, but they can appear in bodies similar to ours, and by their power over mind-stuff can clothe themselves in the fashions of the people to whom they appear. As they live for many centuries they generally adopt the costumes of an old-fashioned style. People in whom the mineral properties predominate are easily impressed by their vibrations and they inspire the giants of the engineering world in their inventions.

Such men are industrious, they will drive others' to work for them and profit by their labours. They seldom respond to the finer things of life, though they often possess bold, buoyant spirits and great capability for exactness in detail and construction. Such men, if married to women of sylphlike natures, dominate and cause them great anxiety and suffering. They cannot realise that above their machines there is another country filled with beauty and activity. They are also fond of manufacturing destructive weapons. Nature's great stumbling-blocks, they seek to dominate her, and will be unheaved and remorselessly destroyed when she again levels all opposition to her manifestations that periodically sweep over the world. These men are the reincarnation of the Atlantean engineers, and the new architecture in America is similar to that which once rose on that sunken continent; but in Atlantis they dug deeply into the earth for security from their enemies' engines of warfare. Thus American architecture has not been created solely through economic conditions.

Students are extremely interested in the constructive work of the gnomes; for their material substances differ from ours as ours differ from those of the East, and they can manipulate substances to harmonise them. They call this distilling the perfume of minerals, and tell us that each mineral has its distinct odour. Gnomes recognise our individual atmosphere as a dog does, and this they use instead of sight. The gnomes resemble the dog in many ways; like it they are most egotistical, and are easily affected by ridicule or laughter. The more ignorant gnomes are great pretenders, and I have seen a gnome wearing ancient spectacles, goose-quill pen, ink horn attached to his girdle and a doctor's hood. He brought me an ancient tome nearly as big as himself.

We learn to love these little fellows with their grey beards and august mien. They can give us valuable information, and their lives are an example for any clean man to follow.

By listening to our conversation they remember the topics of the day, and also take charge of troops of children in their sleep—usually the children of the poor—to unite their minds with theirs. Thus, small children often pass a happy time with

"QUEEN" WATER ELEMENTAL

them before they awake. Children dream of these gnomes and tell us about them. We could relate many quaint tales about these people, and in a later work hope to do so.

The higher gnomes are always aware of the atoms of the Advocate and will often ask the student for his Advocate's blessings, and for the student's true wisdom.

They have strong religious tendencies, and, as they can see and hear better in semi-twilight, know much about the Scriptures by listening to old people reading their Bibles in the evening.

Sometimes their attraction to a student is the result of some early life when he had evoked them by white magic, and they can remind him of secret things he had hidden away in the past.

A king elemental directs them. They have great constructive ability, but do not permit their architectural works to last, disintegrating them when they wish to create new forms. This they constantly do.

In the Masonic guilds they have a knowledge of ceremonial Masonry that would be of great interest to the Masonic Lodges of today. The early Jews, owing to their constant association with metals and precious stones, were also in close harmony with these interesting elementals.

When we enter our past consciousness we find that we also possess such a gnome nature within our own submerged atoms, and that we can contact these little beings of our past.

WATER ELEMENTALS

We will now deal with the protean or water states of consciousness.

Our bodies are mainly fluidic, and the protean forces of Nature are closely allied to them; and, as students know, we are entering the Aquarian age that can be symbolised by water.

As we go inward we contact these higher water elementals and enter a cloud of singular density—the atmosphere in which they live—it is not water, but a peculiar etheric vapour. They can play upon our sensitivity as a musician plays upon an instrument, more especially when the moon reaches fullness, and can intensify our impressions of a thing or mood.

As their wisdom deals with the wisdom of the moon this study will need great preparation by the student, for the greatest wisdom that has reached the earth came from a remote moon period—incidentally, the Sphinx is the symbol of the wisdom of that time—and in an inner sphere we can visit the Temple of the Sphinx and meet the great elemental intelligence that guards its teachings. Many monuments left by ancient civilisations are the graven images of elemental forces.

We have so many protean elements in our nature that when we enter such realms we almost lose consciousness of our own individuality by plunging into the memories of eons ago when on our pilgrimage into the density of matter.

When a water elemental first appears before a student it is like a starry cluster that slowly takes form as it manipulates mind-stuff till it takes on the guise it wishes to represent. [See page 46.]

Nature will respond to us when we love her, and the elemental kings bring to us a remembrance of that time when Nature was worshipped and they were appealed to by the Arcadian peoples who called them the "Sons of the Morning." To these water gods the first fruits of the earth were offered in token of their power to fertilise the land and send it welcome showers. The student can enter such past days when he lived according to Nature and possessed her intelligence he has now lost. This was a time when semi-divine beings taught him the craft of tillage, the shaping of tools, and how to dig and delve in Nature's storehouse.

The soil in those days was different from the soil of the present; for man has distorted Nature by destroying her loveliness and peace.

The water elementals have never, to my knowledge, been reproduced or analysed in a painting save by some Chinese adept artists and some primitive Japanese Buddhist priests.

Sometimes they will appear as women wearing wonderful enrichments and hair that has the sheen of an otter's back with an electrical quality. They are apt to devitalise the student at first, as they have to absorb from the surrounding atmosphere those properties that endow them with density. When one studies their powers of adorning themselves one will realise how limited in range is the art of today. Their materials and designs are foreign to us. For example: a fluidic material, that when stationary looks like pumiced coral or greyish-pink sandstone, is used and seems to be the natural flux for all their range in colour and decoration. Unlike the gnomes they keep subdued harmonies in their designs and would seem to have a wonderful control over colour notation.

They radiate the light of pure minds and will reveal to the student his own similar qualities till he will suddenly realise with a shock the density of his own mind and body.

Those who attract the lower water beings, and the student is impressed by his teaching not to do so, as curiosity often leads the student astray, are frequently enslaved by a jelly-like elemental that can travel and partly materialise, being seen by sensitive people. It appears during the sleeping states of its dissipated victims. This parasite collects in brothels and places where vice abounds. It is called an octopus elemental and is created from the diseased thoughts and passions of different races united in a composite unit. It can also impress its weight upon its victims.

The higher elementals have little reverence for our laws and customs; for we have not yet allied ourselves to the teachings of our Initiates.

Their methods of communication are like a machine gun in their rapidity: a swift moving screen of sentences wherein certain words are particularly impressed upon the memory, so that after hearing a dozen sentences we find that the accented words form themselves into a sentence meaning something different, and is the key to the meaning of the conversation.

The complexions of these beings are generally blonde and a phosphorescent odour emanates from them. Their kings usually signal their appearance by the symbol of the trident.

Although many occult organisations use symbols few of them understand their right use. Few people have been given the wisdom of using elemental substances in symbol forms.

Symbols handed down to us have their higher counterpart and when properly used will pass us through inner schools of instruction. This knowledge has never been given to the uninitiated. Each division in Nature has its key symbol and the keepers of these measure the aspirations and worth of those seeking entrance to their realms.

By close allegiance to these beings man is often privileged to give them part of the substance of his Innermost and thus confer upon them an immortality akin to man.[1]

THE AIR ELEMENTALS

In Nature's higher counterpart of air her beings play an important role in the evolution of man. In their worlds we find the ancient inheritance of our minds; for we should constantly remember that Nature is the storehouse of our past records, and it is quite possible for the man with literary or artistic tendencies to again find those works of worth he had long ago created. The student will then realise why we reverence these higher intelligences, and will never again take an interest in the phenomena of spiritualism wherein swarm earth-bound spirits.

The higher sylphs and sylphides are great scholars and possess remarkable memories. As they prolong their lives to a considerable period they can draw upon a tremendous range of experience and information, remember what has been written by the world's scholars, and present different systems of philosophy in a naive manner. They view these studies from an entirely different angle to ours; we approach subjects with the desire to know what the philosopher has to impart; but they will tell us what they did not impart.

They will tell us about the processes that take place at the moment of death; a section of them volunteering to shield us during our passage through the hallucination realms known as Purgatory.

When a sylph stands beside us he radiates a sun-like quality that stimulates us to greater thought. Their method of instruction is often through vision, creating pageants of

1: See *The Comte de Gabalis*, with commentaries.

pastoral life of an Arcadian nature. It is as though one had a touch of cosmic consciousness when one becomes part of a past that becomes real. They also give us the knowledge of Nature's rituals when we worshipped the gods and the stars; we can also learn about the lost books of antiquity.

They consider that a thing is of value only when it possesses the impregnation of the sun's atoms, just as the water beings judge the worth of a thing by the moon or Neptunian qualities in it. For they say: "Where real worth is hidden there the sun's rays shine." It is interesting to note that they will say of certain religious vestments and images that the possessors had drawn into their atmosphere the rays of the sun. They also speak about the intolerance and cruelty of humanity.

They impress upon the student the importance of gaining what is called the "Knower consciousness," that is: to know a thing without thought. An instantaneous method. For example: if you were to ask an advanced Yogi where you would be at ten o'clock the following morning, he would immediately reply, as you would later discover, correctly. All of us possess this principle of sudden direction, but sporadically. This can explain the meaning of the old saying: "He who hesitates is lost."

Animal life uses this method, for when danger threatens it knows what to do without any thought operation, neither does it in its natural state suffer from anxiety, as man, after the danger has passed. The sylphs say that when danger threatens, meet it; but do not think of it until it happens.

They have recorded the sayings of many prophets and possess the secrets of many hidden organisations that still flourish.

The skins of beautiful sylphides glow as though illumined by a hidden sun, and show the ripeness and abundance of health. They have whimsical natures and think that the vanities of our women are somewhat backward. The type of sylph or sylphide the student contacts is the reflection of his own. They are past-masters in reading and analysing one's thoughts, nothing escapes their observation, and they can remind us of all our thoughts during the day; including those we would like least known.

To an occult artist they have a wonderful power of presenting any costume he wishes to see; though this is tantalising, for they flash by in all their splendour and leave in the mind but the memory of an alluring smile.

The lower divisions of these air elementals is a world about which we care very little; for we enter the fields of necromancy, witchcraft, and magic. These lower sylphs and sylphides can supply sensitives by their impersonations of historical characters, and inflict a medium with illness and disease. They can destroy the fluidic elasticity of the astral envelope by what occultists call broken vowel sounds, and send into it qualities of a mineral nature. This is like shell shock, though of a different kind, and brings about mental disturbances and sometimes insanity. Incidentally, we think it would interest the student to know something about the place and position the true medium should occupy in Society.

In the remote past such people were treated with care and reverence; for sometimes the elemental gods spoke through them and they were called semi-divine on that account. In the future we will hold our sensitive in respect, and care for their moral and social welfare, and give them opportunities to develop their higher powers without endangering their gifts in their struggle for a livelihood.

The law in the East is that no one should take money for such gifts. This is known as the Great Law.

The sensitive is one who has developed an astral and lower mental body that can respond to a higher vibration. It is here that the sylphs take their place by the side of those sensitives who are pure in heart in order to shield their precious armour from those minds controlled by the Secret Enemy, and we pity that mind that demands of a sensitive those things that are beyond their natural range of receptivity. Trance subjects are often dominated by the hypnotic minds of others and, similar to the third degree of the police, are forced to enquire into the private affairs of other people. But as the hypnotic mind seeks to break the laws of Nature so will it eventually meet those guardians of Nature who will demand justice. For the sylphs of the higher planes often speak of their own Innermosts who direct them and group them together in order that they may work destruction upon their enemies.

The world is honeycombed with people who prey upon the credulity of the public, and often through poverty a sensitive, worthy of great attainments, is brutalised by the ignorant. Because of this mediums should be examined for their moral, physical, and spiritual worth, and again placed as oracles within their temples.

Today, many people overshadowed by their Secret Enemy, ask the sensitive to do things that they themselves would reject. This, being against the inner law, injures their astral membranes as well as the body that could be used to enrich the mind with knowledge far beyond human perception.

The sylphs dislike those who boast of their own powers and possessions.

They can magnetise an object to which devout minds have prayed, and entering into the atmosphere of such an image can give it at times a radiance and movement to the eyes—the lids opening and closing—and sensitive minds seeing this say that a miracle has occurred. The reason they do this is that the adoration sent to these images possesses elements similar to their own. Teraphim, or speaking images, of which there are more than is realised, are of a like nature.

THE FIRE ELEMENTALS

When we enter the kingdoms of fire we enter a vast territory that has more to do with the inner development of man than he realises. From fire we gain the directing force that moulds and leads towards a loftier standard of spiritual enlightenment. This force can intermittently lead and control the welfare of a nation; it deals more with masses than with individuals. The sincere student should not fear if brought in touch with it; for it brings harmony to the world. It should be known that we do not speak of the physical side of fire but of its higher counterpart, and these Beings will cause the student to pass the ordeal of being faced with self; his higher nature facing his lower nature. He will then know his degree of attainment, and it will suggest to him the greater possibilities in his life and the original plan of his evolution through matter; but he will also be conscious of a void he cannot pass in his mental travels save through far greater aspirations towards his Innermost. If the student were to ask what lies beyond the spheres of flame, the fire Beings would reply: "It is not for us to answer."

We sense their dominant power and a consciousness far beyond human beings. Nothing escapes them, nothing moves them, and among the higher ones there is a Jove-like serenity and austerity that is particularly felt when they take on the form of an adept Pharaoh or Greek god.

These powers who have been worshipped as gods have spoken through the mouths of the prophets for the betterment of the nations, and in Greece the great fire elemental known as Apollo guided through his pythoness at Delphi their spiritual welfare and that of the surrounding nations.[1] Sometimes they can impress a sensitive to lead a nation out of its moments of peril. Joan of Arc is an example.

The Delphic oracles have moulded many minds with their illuminative qualities, and Initiates speak with great reverence of those whom they call the "Stillborn Children of the Flame." This means those who appear in this world but are not of it.

When the student can evoke the element of fire within his body he creates a shield of protection from his lower nature; for as the lower elements of the body resist this flame they are consumed by its energy. The awakening of this force is the instrument of the godlike man, and with this we will deal in a later chapter. The reason for its importance is that within such realms Nature preserves our highest records.

When the student can work from this fire consciousness he is given a greater conception of the Reality's manifestation in humanity.

Having accustomed himself to the vibratory range of fire he will then possess and understand the characteristics of an oracle. These sovereigns of fire can then unite in a future

1: See *The Comte de Gabalis*.

period wherein are those laws that are to be given to man in his approach to his own Innermost.

The student should always bear in mind that when he wishes to enter these kingdoms he must be clean in body and mind, otherwise he will be like a savage attempting to enter the portals of a university.

Just as the world is divided into continents and countries so is there a map showing the divisions and the king or queen elementals that reign over them. Similarly in our world each nation has its special protector who guides it and strives to keep it true to its intended unfoldment.

One of the turning-points in the student's life is when his prayers and aspirations are answered by the appearance of one of these great Beings. Advanced occultists call them by name such as: "The Green-faced Man who instructs one in the wisdom of the moon," or "the Beautiful Greek" or "the Great Atlantean."

Students find it pleasant to compare notes with their brothers regarding similar experiences, and though each has his own individuality to develop, there is a likeness in their initiations.

Where fires break out the lower fire elementals are attracted with great rapidity. As a fireman once told me: "It is uncanny the way a fire will suddenly spread just when you think you have controlled it." People impregnated with this element are often stimulated by the Secret Enemy to destroy by this means. Pyromaniacs should not be imprisoned but should be treated as mental cases where a different atmosphere might slowly heal such tendencies.

Far from expecting heat the student will experience just the opposite when entering such realms. And we are told that the reason why the sun radiates heat is because its density rebels against its higher counterpart known to the occultist as the Sun behind the sun.

History records many stories about the appearance of these elemental Masters to the great men of the past.

Here we include a message from a fire elemental to a student: "Before you were born I was acquainted with you in the inner spheres and we agreed to meet when you would return and harmonise yourself to my intelligence. After this long period I have come over to you in order to instruct you in the work that had interested both of us. The fire that you perceived to-day with your sixth sense was the signal we will always give you when we are here; for I have a following that will help and support you. We once spoke about your work at a time when you were born in Egypt; and I witnessed your insurrection in a certain province. You gained great power in your efforts to undermine the authority of the ruler under whose sceptre you had command. You failed in this conspiracy and were decapitated. But you were able to win the interests of the great elementals of the Fire mists. Much of your knowledge was locked; but we can unlock this and serve you faithfully."

·   ·   ·   ·   ·

In the Temple of the Sphinx there is a lawchamber wherein are hung festoons of Nature's essences that vibrate to her rhythm and gives to the mind the power to analyse their elements; and overhanging this chamber is a dome-shaped vessel that can be called Nature's sounding board. Thoughts are things possessing sound, colour, and form, and are formed by this instrument into visible speech—for it registers the silent chords of music that shape our thoughts—and the student is permitted to watch his thoughts materialise. This knowledge will teach the student how to place in his thoughts that activity that will stimulate other minds to think and to enable him to project his thoughts into any part of the world. As Nature also possesses this power, he is taught how to protect himself against the lower side of elemental creation and the astral world. This is also the method used by the Yogis when they wish to telephone to any part of the earth.

The College of the elemental Sphinx is the half-way house to Nature's understanding, and here we are introduced to her laws.

Our minds are not disturbed in this chamber and we aspire to the great Reality Whose presence is ever within it, and place ourselves in its manifold time. Here we realise that the urge we have felt throughout life has been Nature's signalling to us from her Innermost to gain her attributes. None can escape this strong urge: Nature's call to return to her.

The elemental sovereigns give their atmospheres to the students, and this clarifies and transmutes the debris in their auras into another substance. It awakens their sleeping sentinels who open their doors to the inflow of cosmic energy, and he is lifted into their source from whence springs the immortal hour of remembrance.

The kingly purpose of Nature is to destroy all illusion in our atmospheres and instil into us her expression, and an instructor awaits us all in the elemental paradises.

CHAPTER SIX

THE ETERNAL LOVER

THEY who possess much elemental nature are often given visions, and as they easily enter the elemental realms we have been privileged to record such inspiration by a pupil.

This will give the student some ideas about these realms from whence inspiration is derived. It is given in her own language.

.   .   .   .   .

Natural beauty and music are the links that hold her to this plane. She is highly religious; but of a pagan nature, and this world seems to her one of toil and suffering. When taken into these higher spheres she begins to grow younger and childlike and is happy and at peace with all things. Past records show her to have possessed an imperative nature, and to have been a courtesan as well as a nun; but the elemental source of her being constantly beckons to her. Having suffered greatly in past incarnations, she lost touch with her elemental guardian, who possesses great enlightenment and power.

I can trace her incarnations from her elemental spheres—her source of enlightenment—to this dark world. Though bearing her karma with rebellion, she is not divorced from those elementals who come and guide her thoughts. Certain beings of a hierarchal nature have also appeared to her and their beauty and serenity are wonderful to behold.

Her life has been a constant giving without, as she thinks, much return. As a child she felt that this world was an illusion. She easily senses any dishonesty or hypocrisy in people who possess such and has the elemental power of the sylph of placing a finger upon the weak spot of a person's character.

THE ETERNAL LOVER

I heard a voice that called to me saying, "Come, my beloved, and follow me. I am he who lives in the land of Perpetual Fragrance, whose walls are of crystal."

And the sound of the voice caused the Tree of Love to put forth her branches within me. The Tree of Love whose flowers are light with music and whose leaves are inscribed with gold.

I sought my Beloved for many days, but I found him not, neither did the echo of his voice come to me upon the wind, and I journeyed far into the Valley of Despair.

Now while I walked in this valley, from the mountain on the farthest side there came a horseman, whose spear and shield shone, and he lifted me and carried me through the illusion of the world where there was an altar garlanded with the blossoms of sensation, and the corners of it were carved very curiously with the heads of rams.

Behind it stood One crowned and above his head was the nimbus of the moon. He stretched out his hands and anointed me and held towards me an ewer out of which he drew necklaces of pearl and sapphire and emerald, and as I tossed them up to the laughter of the sun I heard again the voice of my Beloved bidding me sit beside the Stream of Lost Remembrance.

Now the waters of this stream ran clear, yet when I put my hand in it I drew out precious stones, and each stone had its own particular fragrance; and from the thickets and hedges there came fauns and elves, playfellows of a bygone age, and they decked me with the jewels, singing songs that were like the gentle spray of fountains, and they showed me the path my Beloved had taken.

Like a bird that was freed, happiness soared up within me, my mind became calm and like a net that floats upon a moonlit sea I drifted into sleep.

In the distance of a dream I saw my Beloved standing beside the watch-tower of my soul, and he cried to me saying: "Prepare the way, for I come to you with a new body and a new mind; with a casket of precious ointment and a chalice from the moon.

"The pastures of your brain will be made fertile and about your feet will be spread the net of expression to enable you to hold the imagination of other minds.

"No father has begotten me, no mother has suckled me. A symbol of time, and an advocate of justice I stand serene in the resting-place of silence.

"I am the crystal wall built about the garden of Nature, on the ramparts of which are the storehouses of understanding.

"Out of my land comes song and laughter and the rhythm of the dance. My messengers run before thought with the rush and fluttering of wings.

"Sowing and reaping I have followed you through the fields of yesterday. In Arcady I permeated your mind with the Dayspring of Youth, for I am the eternal lover before whom all others fade. Each holds for you but a facet of me and so cannot satisfy your hunger or assuage your thirst.

"Babylon was known to me. Through the rites of Istar you have worshipped me. Asshur heard the sound of my voice, but I remained hidden from them. Egypt unveiled my face, Greece cast her treasures at my feet and listened to my songs.

"Through the eyes of many lovers I have looked on you, drawing aside my veils by the magic of colour and perfume and sound.

"The going down of the sun and the rising thereof have been but links in the chain that forged you to me; for I am He who comforted you in the pangs of birth and folded about you the sheltering wings of death. Your eternal star."

.   .   .   .   .

In answer to my Beloved a messenger came forth to the watch-tower of my soul, and he touched my forehead so that my mind was caught up into a higher Heaven.

Circular like a great courtyard, it was divided into twelve divisions in which each sign of the Zodiac had its place, and from each sign wound spiral staircases that led to a balcony of crystal where the people of the sun walked with the daughters of the moon.

In the centre of the courtyard rose a fountain, greater than the one that encircled its walls, and the sound of it seemed the source of all music, and over it high up till it merged with the innermost Heaven curved a rainbow that paled and quickened as the waters rose and fell.

Then he who guided me bade me look into the dusky cities of the world, and I saw that the only light that came to the earth was the reflection from the crystal wall, and where the spray of the fountains chanced to fall it illumined the minds of poets, it coloured the brushes of painters, and made dreams stir in the hearts of men.

And as I looked the spirit of the fountain spoke to me saying: "Whom do you seek?" and I, thinking it was the voice of him whom I sought, held out my arms crying: "My Beloved, my Beloved, upon whose forehead shines the eternal star."

Swiftly the jagged icicle of torment entered my heart, for the voice answered: "Already he has journeyed far from here. Seek him in the world through the door of service." The fountain shimmered to silence. The rainbow stood still.

I passed through the gateway into the outer courtyard that I saw dimly through my tears. Leaning against a pillar, for all strength seemed to have left me, I waited; and out of the shadows moved a form, and I called to it, for I thought I recognised one whom I loved, but as it came towards me up the steps of the loggia, I saw it was no mortal, but the goddess Venus with one of her handmaidens, and I ran to her delirious with delight. Under my hand I felt the roundness of her breast and my whole body was filled with the wonder of her beauty, but when I touched her she turned and looked at me with wounded eyes, and uttering a cry of pain fled from me. Stooping, I picked up a spray of blossoms she had dropped in her flight; it seemed but lately picked from the Tree of Youth, for the bees of happiness followed after it, humming the song of Spring.

· · · · ·

I returned to the world fettered with poverty, and Fate led me into strange paths. I who had looked upon service as my right now was called upon to serve.

I heard the roar of the jungle called Commerce where the mind of the machine rules supreme. I saw men whose souls had dwindled till they had become like shrivelled leaves. I heard the hollow laughter of the rich, as with indifferent feet they trod the wine press of wealth, demanding more and yet more and seldom seeking to give; seeking happiness and pleasure and finding the Cask of emptiness.

I moved among many so bowed with the stress and struggle of existence that they had almost forgotten that there existed such a thing as beauty. To them I gave a blossom from the branch that I carried, and where I plucked a flower another budded in its place; and those who looked at or held these fragile petals felt hope revive within them, and loveliness entering in made of their minds gardens of escape from this world.

Yet I was lonely and sad. I caught no glimpse of him whom I sought; he seemed distant as the rose that grows in some far land, perfuming only my dreams.

One day as I walked along a street a figure beckoned me, and I followed her through narrow passages and devious ways till we seemed deep under the earth; and in an alcove of the wall behind grated bars I saw something which vibrated. Looking closer I recognised the Stone of Remembrance that like a shuttle travels back and forth through the space of time. Putting my hands through the bars I held it and it gave me the power to see into the past and to understand the reason of suffering.

. . . . .

That night in a vision I again saw the Beloved, and in one hand he held a casket and in the other a chalice.

I took the casket and opened it only to find in it seven other caskets, and he said to me: "Open the third casket." And when I had unlocked it I saw within it an image of myself embalmed in fine linen, and he said again: "Open the second casket," and I did so, finding another body similar to the first, but on the brow was a diadem of seven pearls.

He bade me unlock the fifth casket. With fear I did so, and in it lay a decomposed body, and knowing that it came from the evil of my thoughts I shrank from it in loathing; but the Beloved poured over it the contents of the chalice that he held transforming the malice of it into the wisdom of experience.

Then a voice came from the seventh casket, and at my touch it sprang open, and in it was a sprig of amber and mother of pearl cunningly joined together and entwined; and I lifted it out and planted it in the earth, watering it with my tears. New life flowed up the amber stem, yet its smell was rancid, but the entwining twig of mother of pearl gave of itself and nourished it, and as it did so the amber faded to primrose and finally into the likeness of the pearl.

The voice of the Beloved cried: "Prepare the way, for I am he who returns to you." And stooping over me he sealed my lips. Yet there was singing in my heart.

Then, looking at the caskets, he turned and said to me in anger: "Open the first." I did so. In it was my soul enkindled, and it gave to me its message. Then did the Beloved with gentleness unseal my lips.

Opening the fourth casket he showed to me that it contained nothing, yet as I wondered there rose from it a cloud of perfume, fragrance of happiness I had given to others.

And in the sixth casket was a ball of crystal, and looking in the crystal I saw stretched out of Heaven the great arm of a God, and down this arm came chariots and horsemen, all the pageant of bygone days; and entering my mind they revealed to me the lost beauty of each century.

Unscathed by death, unmarred by time, Love stood before me; and he passed his hands over the caskets enveloping them in a rosy flame, and with my Beloved and him I passed into the glory of the sunrise.

But the time for fulfilment was not yet come. I was left alone in the land of solitude where stillness hovered with the outstretched wings of some menacing bird; and from under the earth came a muffled sound like the repeated note of a tolling bell.

I wandered through the desolate coldness of the valleys seeking some way of escape, but the mountains bound me in on every side.

In my hopelessness I prayed, and as I did so I saw far away in the distance many men pulling at a rope that seemed immeasurable; stretching into the very beginning of time.

Guided by a light I found my way, and when I came to the place, I saw that the men were careworn and fatigued, yet buoyant with an inward strength, and on each of their foreheads shone a lambent flame. Then I knew that they were the Chain of Initiates who bear the burden of the world and I asked their blessings. And one of them bade me place my hand over his as it clasped the rope; like an electric current there vibrated through me the cruelty of man and the sorrow and suffering of humanity. It crashed through my senses like lightning, till a merciful darkness overtook me.

When consciousness returned I found myself on a pinnacle of a mountain and before me stretched a path leading to the open country. I lay there looking up into the sky, and as I looked the clouds opened and out of Heaven came two hands bearing a chalice, pouring a crystalline substance over me. I stood upright and before me rose a tree.

The Tree of Love, whose flowers are filled with music and whose leaves shine with gold, and about it thronged the sylphs of the air, the fauns and dryads of the woods, and the little people of the fields.

Around my neck they placed an amaranthine garland, and the children of the moonbeams clothed me in shimmering garments and placed a crown of stars about my head.

Through the groves of Arcady they led me to an altar, answering the voice of my Beloved with their singing, and as the morning mist is caught up and interpenetrated by the sun I was made one with beauty, Conquistador of Love.

CHAPTER SEVEN
NATURE

Humanity tugs at the skirts of Mother Nature till, wearying, she rummages in her bag of tricks and says: "Here is something new to play with." Thus she gives to us some new invention like wireless, areoplanes, television, and so forth, in order that her children should be amused and happy in a dim and discordant world.

WHEN we have learned to bridge the void and enter our Secondary system we unconsciously acquire the habit of always being in communication with an atomic intelligence, and this contacts us to any period in time we wish to enter. We also find that this thread of atomic current will communicate with us from its end, and we are often called up to listen-in to some direction to be given us, and we are sometimes startled to learn that what occurs in our environment is known and inwardly registered by the watchmen of these centres.

When we realise what powers have been placed within us by Nature we appreciate them and do not use them heedlessly; though at first we do not know the minuteness of its detail. One of Nature's laws is that no one should use them to the disadvantage of another person, no matter how ignorant or learned he may be. The student is apt to experiment before he knows the laws that govern its expression. Being human, he desires to display his powers; but when he burns his fingers he learns not to display them until he becomes part of them. Those who have attained this consciousness will not direct it to those who do not aspire; for a simple phenomenon is often far greater in its after effects than is at first recognised.

Nature's laws are subservient to the sum total of one's own wisdom and no further, although through magical rites and ceremonies we can evoke a still greater power; but this is not permissible. This was the cause of the destruction of Atlantis.

It is possible to have a mind that can increase or diminish its wavelength. This is what the advanced Yogi does; he unites himself to the atmospheric sheaths surrounding his body, and seeks to attune his mind to move in harmony with each sheath. In his highest sheath he can recognise his own individuality working in unison with his atomic intelligence;

but in his lowest depths he will not find this harmony, for there the atoms of his past—that he has discarded as he has developed—are related to his lower sheaths, and amid their darkness and squalor he cannot register their vibrations and attune himself to them.

We will often be asked, "What does this aspiration mean?" The answer is simply this: "To be one with the Innermost and obey it."

The proper use of symbols begins when we enter our secondary system. We cannot reach unknown countries in different planes of consciousness unless we use them. These are the doors leading into those regions charted by the Innermost. Each division is represented by a symbol, and in our secondary system we are often given one upon which to meditate. Symbols are also used as short cuts when we wish to contact an elemental sphere quickly.

To-day and in the past the hierarchal streams—each composed of three forces—were represented by such signs. Each great civilisation possessed three symbols: each represented one strand of these forces, and these, if correctly used, will again immerse the student into their civilisation now withdrawn. This is one of the arts lost and forgotten to-day. The ancient Initiate artists sometimes drew these three into one composite design.

These symbols, left behind by the wise men of the past, will constantly repeat themselves in our minds when we concentrate upon them. This repetition gives them life through atoms similar to their nature being attracted. Man little realises the vast storehouse of creative intelligences locked within his atmosphere and never used.

By concentrating upon this symbol we become creators; for we clothe it as an apparition clothes itself about a semi-developed entity. Only we do not clothe an entity but an elemental consciousness that we ennoble with a soul-like atmosphere. Thus we create messengers and send them into those spheres their creations represent. The symbol will be received, the thoughts cast into its creation analysed, and returned to us as the signal from that sphere to which it had been sent. In this manner we contact the intelligence of past spheres.

Our created symbols are also the lower counterparts of higher ones, and those left on earth also have higher counterparts, and if we receive them we know that our symbols have reached their source.

As an example: if the Solomon's seal is visualised and created into an elemental messenger and is passed by the guardian of its sphere, it will signal to us its acceptance. We are then given the higher key symbol to unlock the door of a temple whence we shall receive guidance and instruction. This kind of study is needed for the Masons.

This is but one aspect of symbol study. The cross also has its higher counterpart, and when properly used can give the student surprising results. Its Initiates call this higher counterpart, "A mind glorified by its Creator." Those to whom it is given are swept into its truth and consciousness, and discover that the parables reveal a great mystery far beyond the understanding of the public.

The sayings of Jesus have to be read in this manner. The cross does not alone represent a cross upon which a man was hung, but also a thing upon which glory descended. The cross is the symbol of one crucified and reborn into the Innermost, and not a thing of torture and pain. Crucifixion means one who has mastered his lower nature, and has been made clean in the consciousness of the Innermost.

The Aspiring atoms gather round the symbols we create, and transform them into an image representing our thoughts and aspirations. As they go inward they leave behind a trail of atoms that connects us to the source of the symbol, whether it be of a higher or lower nature.

In the past this science was known to all Initiates, and many occult societies left behind the symbols of their orders, like the marks of Masons left in different countries and easily read by those who can understand them.

There are also evil symbols that can evoke disaster and destruction, and many well-known symbols are used for commercial purposes. If their true meanings were known they would be immediately discarded. Religious associations have also borrowed symbols that, if concentrated upon, would place the consciousness in the lower spheres of evil. This ignorance in the use of symbols is to be avoided. Symbols are dynamic things, and should not be fooled with.

The anchor, so commonly used by seamen, symbolised a period far beyond our own in evolution. The Chinese Initiates also have a profound knowledge of this art and science, and some day we shall appreciate this. If the West would approach them understandingly they might reveal many lost occult arts that would help us.

They have a method of blessing one by the proper use of a symbol. They fashion them and send them to students on the anniversaries of their initiations into their sacred sciences. If a Western student was fortunate enough to receive one he would sense an atmosphere of well-being and fortune, and the fragrance of it would last some time.

It is difficult to describe the working of a symbol, for few have attained to that quality of sense perception needed for such work. The atmosphere of this world rebels against any outside and inner knowledge given us. It also objects to our forming symbols and sending them inwardly.

In our Silver Shield we often find symbols being used by our Master atom who creates them for our benefit and shows us their use within our secondary system.

We consider that the symbol of this new hierarchal outpouring of the Dayspring of Youth will be one of the discoveries of this age. Those who will enter their secondary system will be given its use to develop the powers and attain the wealth and greatness of this new energy.

This is a secret symbol, and must be guarded by those to whom it is revealed, and no one may give it forth without the consent of its directing intelligence.

Nature's laws will become civil laws when understood, and when we look back from those periods that are to be man's future and see what is happening in the present, we sense the pressure of opposition and evil, as though a great cloud has swept man out of the real world of common sense and justice. May this new symbol revert man to his own place and plan in Nature's consciousness.

CHAPTER EIGHT
HEALTH IN YOGA

WE will now deal with the first steps in health in Yoga practice, and how to bring into the physical body the qualities of the finer atmospheres and their atoms.

Few students realise how difficult are Yoga practices, for though they seem simple at first few have the vitality and patience to continue till they attain results. If the youth of today expended in Yoga practice half the energy used to become successful athletes, they would become master minds.

It is to our regret that the seekers we frequently meet lack that physical stamina possessed by the average college athlete. For the body must be fit and alert to respond to any call, as it is a store-house of strength that will later be necessary for his development.

The first law is bodily poise, to learn to sit and stand erect; for as the spinal column is similar to a magician's wand, each vertebra must be held in its proper place, and no bone should press upon the nerve channels to hinder their nourishment. One should learn to stand upon the balls of the feet, having only a pressure of a pound and a half on each heel. It will be a little hard at first to acquire this habit, but later you will feel a sense of well-being. Any qualified osteopath will correct any vertebrae out of alignment, and before the student begins these practices he should have a working knowledge of anatomy.

The student should know that from the first moment he takes these steps he will come under the observation of the Elder Brothers, and though he may feel he is alone he will never be permitted to go too far either in good or evil; for balance is needed and the student will later realise that weakness is sometimes worse than wickedness. It is people who do things in life that count. White and black magicians enjoy opposing one another; for they respect the other's vital qualities, and are stimulated by such. Cranks, who should be avoided, do not possess these strong qualities. When we speak of cranks, we mean those unstable idealists who carry rational theories to irrational lengths.

A ninety-two-year old Yogi, who was as vital as a youth, once visited this country and was questioned regarding certain statements he made by a well-known lecturer on occult subjects. The Yogi quietly told him to sit down, but the lecturer, full of energy and argument, continued. The Yogi placed a finger on the man's body and the lecturer promptly collapsed. He was a long time recovering from the shock; when he did so the Yogi, smiling sweetly, said, "Real strength comes from gentleness." To this day he cannot explain what happened to him.

We know that "as above so below," and the strength in the physical body has its counterpart in the mind-body, and just as the Japanese received secret teachings from the Hatchet men of China—the militant Hatha Yoga adepts, now called Ju-Jitsu, the art of overcoming one's enemy by softness—so is there a Ju-Jitsu on the mental plane. The Elder Brothers use this secret knowledge to protect students in moments of emergency; for the Secret Enemy will attack mentally as well as physically.

Students are often watched and protected if they possess qualities that, when developed, will produce great genius in the arts and sciences. In the early days of the Klondyke two students were sent two years before the rush to live over the Klondyke Pass with medical supplies in order to protect the body of a young miner, among others, whose possibilities for the future were carefully watched. We ourselves have been sent into strange countries and places for similar purposes. We are never commanded to do this or even told what we are to do; only later does the reason for such action dawn upon us.

The moment you begin these studies you will become a magnet and attract people, some of whom will talk about their souls. Such are usually selfish and weak, and form a floating population of worthless materials who do not flow with the tide of humanity's endeavour, but drift along, entering those movements that will give them the incense and perfume of self-praise as well as borrowed bread and butter.

These are not genuine seekers, but vagabonds who prey upon the sympathy of the serious student. But the sincere student is welcomed with open arms, no matter what his race, caste, colour, or position in life. Sometimes the seeker who seems most backward and may not be able to harmonise himself with others or possess social qualifications, will suddenly receive an illumination that will place him in the position to lead the rest. These people—who invariably have fine bodies in their youth—sometimes become the headstones of the corner.

It is well for the student to have some trade, profession, or art by which he can support himself no matter in what country he happens to be.

Our bodies take on the nature of our environment, and the air we breathe affects its fitness. We breathe with vigour when fit, and easily throw out our destructive properties from our lungs; for weak breathing will ultimately produce disease. Later we will unconsciously breathe in harmony with the rhythmic impulse of Nature.

The body should be exercised daily in order to have a flexibility of spine and feel the healthy glow of life. But do not go to extremes in these things. Do not shock the system by too hot or by too cold water, though it is advisable to accustom the body in time to cold water, and rub it with vigour. Accustom the body to sun baths, but wrap a damp towel round the head; for the base of the skull should be kept cool, as the sun's rays are destructive as well as curative, and there is a reservoir of vital energy at the base that supplies the nerves with vital fluid.

The student should not rely upon the back of the chair to support his spine, neither should he lounge nor sit crosslegged in his practices as in the East, for the Western body is not adapted for this posture.

When exercising do not cast the shadows of worry or anxiety over the atoms within you; for the body being of a gaseous nature is easily penetrated by them and reacts upon those workers who look after it.

Civilisation's great gift to humanity is constipation; we have become unnatural in our habits, causing pressure at the base of the rectum and many children are born with the lower intestine not held in its proper alignment.

The moment the physical body disposes of its waste a signal is sent to the different centres of the body to do likewise, and each nerve centre also responds. This occurs in the mental atmosphere as well. Remember that regular habits of this kind clarify the mind, and one should always keep this tract open and clean.

We should use common sense in our diet, and not favour one kind of food more than another. For this the student need only read some book upon dietetics; yet should not waste too much time about thinking what passes through his mouth, for the food crank generally makes himself most objectionable to his friends. We do not enter the kingdom of Heaven through the food that enters the mouth, as some occult fraternities would have us believe.

When united to the Nous atom, the student will be told the kind of food best suited for the atomic workers within. This can be noticed in women who have certain cravings for food not in their normal diet before the birth of their children. This is because the incarnating ego is conscious of certain deficiencies needed for its physical structure. A child can often communicate with a Yogi before its birth and tell him what it needs for its physical nourishment, as well as the things it will need when incarnating. Yogis in the East will sometimes tell their brothers before death where they will incarnate, and they watch for his appearance. They will sometimes travel for long distances to see that the child is properly protected and give it early instruction.

If it is possible, one should live upon sun-enriched foods; though we should remember that in a war of commercial ferocity, where tiger-man fights tiger-man and it is a case of the survival of the fittest, the vegetarian stands little chance of survival if he has to build up his business from the beginning. What you feed your atoms upon you become. Rule your food and do not let it rule you.

Generally speaking, there are three types of man: physical, mental, and spiritual, and the gestures of each type are different, and the physical is most easy to read, especially when dominated by his Secret Enemy. They can also be distinguished by the hand-shake and posture. The face is also divided into three types.

Observation is the student's second step in his training; for many important things that pass before us are unobserved, and when out of the body the student must try to remember what he has seen, and this is difficult; for if he will try to visualise the entrance to his front door he will be surprised to know how little he has observed. Those who have read Kipling's book *Kim* will gain some idea as to how a student is trained after meeting his teacher.

In our trips out of the body the visions of the interior planes are more difficult to see than those of the physical; for the finer essences of Nature are more subtle. Our methods of reading—especially newspapers—in time impairs our powers to think about what we have read, and to remember it with precision.

This power to see with one's third eye is not what is usually called a spiritual gift, and this can be developed in the same way that an athlete can develop his muscles. There are many centres seemingly atrophied from disuse within our bodies; these can be awakened to a normal condition by this Yoga practice.

We again remind the student that he must use common sense in these things, particularly in his food and sleep. A three months' course in a gymnasium will prepare him for his plunge into his Yoga practice.

The physical type must keep his liver healthy, and if he does not feel well applications of hot and cold water by means of a pad of cloth should be alternately placed at the tip of the liver. The whole operation should not take longer than five minutes.

If the mental type needs a mental rest he should do the same to the upper third of his lungs.

If the spiritual type feels the need of vitality he should bathe his generative organs alternately in hot and cold bowls of water.

The spiritual type are most often obsessed by thoughts of sex, and those belonging to celibate religions have to control this; for the controlling of the sex nature builds up a reservoir of strength, and it is this strength that opens the door to the Innermost.

The occultist who has passed inward quickly recognises those religious teachers who possess such attributes, and often protects and aids them with his own protective force; for such men are frequently attacked by members of their own denomination.

The Eastern mind quickly recognises such qualities in a man and calls him a saint, but the Western mind has not yet arrived at this stage, though in future when the West has developed such men will also be given support and respect as in the East.

Although we have said that man can be classed into three main types—physical, mental, and spiritual—they can all attain to the same source.

Before beginning your breathing exercises take a drink of water; for we should remember that the body will take as much water as we will give it. It is often thirsting for it, as otherwise it cannot clear itself of its impurities. We should drink fresh water between meals and keep a pitcher where we can see it.

We should also cleanse the nostrils by inhaling water. This will assist the actions of the atoms that we attract, and also strengthen the tissues and membranes. The water we take acts as a filter, and the positive atoms find it easier to communicate when the stomach is clean and full of water.

In your breathing you will quickly notice that you inhale in one side of the nostril at a time, and you will learn to change the current of your breathing from one side to the other as you wish.

There are many different types of atoms to attract and place in their proper position on the membranes—that plate the occultist calls the magnetic field—we attract one kind at a time, and the type we build with mostly are the Aspiring atoms. The passages in the nostril are known as the Sun and

Moon passages; and the Aspiring atoms enter the right passage. Later, when we try to attract the atoms of the Lunar force we breathe through the left nostril.

When you find that you are breathing through the left passage in your practice, take up anything, a small roll of cloth or a book or paper, and place it under the left armpit. This brings pressure upon a certain nerve in the arm, and before long you should begin breathing through the right nostril and bring in the Aspiring atoms of the Solar force. If this does not bring results pressure on the bobtail nerve on the muscle of the calf of the left leg should succeed.

This alternate process should be done in order to carry out opposite results. Some time will be required before we can change the breath.

In the East you will see Initiate priests carrying umbrellas under the left armpits; they will not reveal the reason, but this breathing through the right nostril whilst walking will conserve our energy. The student should remember this when taking a long walking trip.

The student should also try to sleep on his left side with his head on his hand. This attitude will cause the breath to flow through the right nostril and produce the same result as when walking, and the life currents will restore the tired body more quickly. Middle-aged students will also notice that their digestive organs will function more easily.

The reason why Western bodies cannot adopt Eastern Yoga methods successfully is because we live in a Northern atmosphere, and the currents change as they approach the Equator.

In the first exercise sit erect with chin in and chest out, hands clasped with the thumbs crossing each other: the reason being that no obsessing force of a psychic nature can enter. Do this whenever practising. Aspire inwardly with the utmost purity of thought, and as you inhale think of the word "Aspire." Do this six times with the mind centred upon the roots of the nose; for behind it lies the magnetic field that collects the Aspiring atoms.

In this exercise do not strain, but breathe naturally with an alert mind; for in your practice you must never allow your mind to become sleepy.

Repeat the same exercise, holding the breath for an instant whilst concentrating upon the magnetic field, then send the atoms collected there down to the Nous atom in the heart.

By this method we call upon the Nous atom to respond and the first time it does so the student may feel a slight pain in the heart. This exercise should be repeated daily at regular times, and in about two weeks he should feel a sensation of heat on the magnetic field. This is a process of building a bridge of communication between the inner and outer worlds by means of atomic substances.

When Aspiring send all your love to the Nous atom and its workers, and listen for a response. When this occurs these atoms rejoice, for, as Initiates say, "There is joy in Heaven." For now we begin to journey inwardly and place our feet upon the Path of realisation.

The response will not be in words or sounds, but a thought-emotion that we learn to translate into words. So with practice we shall in time bring through clear and definite instruction. As we have said elsewhere, our true information comes from within and not from without.

This exercise is all that is needed to deal with the Aspiring atom. The Nous atom collects them into its atmosphere, and distributes them through the bloodstream: a foreign invasion of atoms of a higher vibration than the vibration the body normally responds to, and these attune us to that higher wave-length of intelligence we call the Dayspring of Youth.

Whatever you do in your daily work put your aspiration into it until it becomes a habit. This will bring out your constructive powers.

When the workers within your body receive aid and instruction from the more advanced type of atom, they are immediately stimulated to a greater activity and take on themselves the characteristics of those more developed atoms who inspire them to seek closer union with their Innermost.

Hence the physical body is no longer indolent, but receives a new life and vitality; for the atoms that respond go through a transformation period.

The Aspiring atoms predominate in the human system and also in the seminal system, and assist in the building up of the procreative elements. If we can converse with these Aspiring atoms we can then send our thoughts into the groups and sections they are developing. And as we increase their energy by Aspiration breathing we bring into their sections our more advanced type of Aspiring atom, and this gives them happiness: for they gain a period of upliftment and, as this also increases their energy, our body benefits. This is reflected back into our minds, and for the first time we feel that they respect us.

This increase of energy causes the indolent atoms within our secondary system and physical body to respond also.

When we vibrate to the intelligence within the Silver Shield it sends to the Aspiring atoms an added appreciation of their efforts, and from that moment we feel an individual responsibility for their welfare.

After the first steps we begin to aspire for another kind of atom called the Transformation atoms, that bring about what we call "Rebirth," for we are transmuted into another kind of substance. Though ere this happens we have to pass through our inner schools of instruction to which our Aspiring atoms have introduced us, and our progress depends upon our quickness in reviewing our past lives. This is a process similar to the embryo in the womb that draws upon its material from its past development.

The student will naturally want to know what is meant by school of instruction. We have six big centres in the body: atomic substances similar to star clusters called in the East the "Petals of the Lotus." In time these centres will open to us and reveal intelligences that will re-experience us through our past lives. For the student cannot attain any great achievement without a knowledge of these inner universities and the forces within the Sun and the moon.

These schools record to him his evolution from his lower states to his highest attainments, and he will know two natures within him: one that unites him to good, and the other to evil.

In Eastern literature the schools are described in this manner: the lowest centres have but four petals, whilst the highest has a thousand, and is called "The Thousand Petalled Lotus."

The student must not be afraid of contacting the evil as well as the good; for each centre is a store-house of wisdom, and he will study the evil he has done and the suffering he has had to undergo, and he will know what to avoid. He should also know that he can govern the influences of the planets when he can open these centres.

When we have acclimatised ourselves to the energy of the Transformation atoms we get a sense of being lifted out of darkness, as we are no longer resisting the intermittent streams of energy that flow into us, and we bring to birth the latent energies within the central nervous system and its branches about the spinal cord.

We have met very few who have been aware of this interior world without also being students of Yoga. And though we have met saint-like men, we have seldom found them the possessors of this science of spiritual unfoldment. We hope that this new knowledge will harmonise and bridge the void between science and religion.

In the West we find few fitted for this study, for it calls forth great fortitude, perseverance, and well-being towards others. The pupils we usually select are well grounded in the literature of the past, and are acquainted with teachings the more advanced students possess. Such men are found in every walk of life, imparting wisdom and instruction to the ignorant as well as to the scientific mind, and demonstrating the things about which they speak. It is useless to waste one's time with a seeker who does not possess the courage and balance needed for the Brother's work. It is also imperative that the moral character should be above suspicion; for the student has to demand the use of the Solar force in his work, and if he is immoral or sexually weak he will soon befoul himself with the lower substances of the world's atmosphere.

The reader would assume from the above qualifications that we ask for Godlike men in order to make them Godlike. This is not so. No matter what the student's past might have been, when he begins his Yoga practices and sincerely aspires to his Innermost, he begins with a new garment, and, if he succeeds, he will later discover within his inner universe a powerful atom known as the Advocate, who stands in the presence of the Reality and pleads our cause. If we are worthy much of our past evil karma will be forgiven us, and we shall be free from further incarnations to balance our past evil. Meeting this Advocate or Daemon is a great moment in the student's life.

The higher atoms possess three qualities: virtue, wisdom, truth. When Yoga unites virtue and wisdom it brings to birth our torch of Truth. In other words, the balancing of the Solar and Lunar forces awakens that current known and sometimes called "The Flaming Sword of Justice," and like the Aspiring atoms also bridges that void that separates us from our Innermost. In the East it is called "The Serpent Fire." In scientific terms it can be analysed as static electricity, and once evoked passes up the central nervous system, increasing in velocity as it pierces each centre. We will write about this later.

Previously we said that the greatest wisdom we can record came from the moon; but beyond that is a wisdom that comes from the Sun behind the sun. It has power over the sun, moon, and stars, and this wisdom will show the student that he has celestial as well as terrestrial bodies.

In time the student will reduce the nature within him into its first element; for from this sacred fire spring all things. This essence of Nature—the fixed principle in all things—builds within him his divine inheritance and his lost treasure. When he has accomplished has purpose he will be filled with vigour and strength.

The way of the spirit is called the way of the Innermost, and each of us will come to a moment when we are to lose all or accept all. We seek union with this inner power; for there is a power stored within us for the use of future generations; this invisible ray is a sword, striking when least expected. Like "A thief in the night," it will enter our atmosphere and create disease and disorder to all who reject its presence. For that reason we should prepare ourselves for its instruction.

In Yoga the Nous atom directs us to those atomic intelligences that are to instruct us. After we have learned the process of communication between the inner and outer worlds we are then permitted to regain our knowledge by entering into any period of the past. Only later will it dawn on us that the Nous atom knows best what is necessary for our development, as it works under the direction of a great atomic intelligence called the Architect, who places before it the plan it has to follow. We should remember that the Nous atom is the Master Mason of the body.

The Nous atom is responsible for the work it has to do, and chooses its own kind of workmen, for whom he is also responsible as well as for the edifice.

The student will now understand why this intelligence rejoices when we bring to it superior atomic workmen of an aspiring nature.

Students who have regained their past knowledge often burn their fingers by researching into the lower recesses of their nature in order to gain powers and become magicians. When this occurs they soon humbly return to that source that will give them instruction best needed for their present development.

As the student passes deeper into the finer planes of his being this vibratory bridge will also link him to similar depths within his lower nature. This is a struggle for purity of thought, and his aspiring breathing, that in time becomes rhythmic, supports him at moments of peril. The physical body is the occultist's support and foundation, and places him in a stronger position than the angels or demons: for he has the earth to spring from and their feet have no resistance for they dwell amid floating substances.

CHAPTER NINE
ADVOCATE AND DWELLER ON THRESHOLD

WE will now speak of two great forces of intelligence that represent man's higher and lower nature. They are called the Advocate and the Dweller on the Threshold, and now appear before the student as definite personalities.

If we are familiar with Greek literature we know about the Daemon of Socrates, and how he was often found in an attitude of listening-in to its guidance. We all possess a similar Daemon or Advocate, and he constantly stimulates us to purify our aspirations and breathing; the higher elementals give similar advice, and it is the Advocate who passes us, if worthy, into higher phases of development. This, as we have elsewhere said, is a great moment in the student's life, and the Advocate appears as one clothed in shining raiment. He is terrible to behold, and often the light is so great that one cannot open one's eyes.

The Dweller on the Threshold, our Dark Angel of Destruction, can also appear, and possesses radiance and beauty, but it is evil and its presence is more easily sensed.

As the student goes deeper he will be aware of these presences always overshadowing him, and they impress him with their advice. Slowly he will realise that there is a dual intelligence within him.

Before we go further an explanation of the above beings is necessary. We have built up through myriad lives two composite thought-forms of an opposite nature. The higher has collected atoms of our loftiest aspirations and actions; the lower has collected, and is the composite thought-form of our evil passions and desires.

These we have endowed with forces of a soul-like nature and with a tremendous range of knowledge, yet ere we can feel the presence of our Innermost and not be impressed by these personal elements of the past we must disintegrate them and return their atoms to their rightful place in Nature; for it is the Innermost who is the true expression of the Reality within us, and possesses greater wisdom than our personal creation. The student will naturally ask why we should disintegrate the Advocate. Here is the reason. By unconscious magic we have drawn atoms from their rightful spheres, and have imprisoned them in the body of our thought-creations, and this, being contrary to the law of Nature, must be freed and returned to their own elements, just as we wish for freedom to enter our own worlds of being.

Yet this disintegration does not occur until we have reached a certain period in our development. The student can now realise how we are impressed by our own creations of Heaven and Hell.

The Advocate assists us to separate the true substance from the false; that is, the coarse debris of our bodies is passed down into the sheath of the Secret Enemy, and this foreign substance nullifies its force and power to unite itself again to our lower mental, astral, and physical body. We slowly begin to bring into our bodies by this process the consuming atoms of the flame that will imprison and take away the Secret Enemy's powers.

The student should remember that all of this occurs within his own self-created universe.

Concentration as the world knows it is different in the inner worlds. When we project our minds into the substance of a thing—for thought is penetrative—we prevent its approach to our minds, and we are also exposed to a similar pressure.

True concentration is to know a thing by becoming it, and true thought is an activity far beyond the comprehension of our objective mind-body. When we unite ourselves to the intelligence within a thing it repeats itself as long as we concentrate upon it. In concentration we also try to get the response of the Solar atomic intelligence within a substance.

When we think of a friend and send our love to him with a concentrated vision, we unite our atmosphere to his, and it will respond as we press our thoughts upon the silken web of his mind-body. This pressure brings a response from his inner self, though his objective mind is unaware. His inner self will reply if we adopt the real method of concentration; for as it registers thought it brings to birth a composite mass of atoms of the same nature that it returns to us. This is like a crystal formation; the seed crystal collects and builds about it similar crystals. This means that what we send to others is returned in abundance, and this is for good or for evil.

This process, that is objective, also takes place interiorly, and we receive our information in this manner. This is far different from those who teach meditation and concentration without knowledge of these laws and methods, and this gives their pupils little of real worth. When the Yogi concentrates he seeks knowledge and receives it.

Another important thing: we shall constantly evoke our personality if we are without the knowledge of these correct practices, and wilt always be thinking of it.

We have seemingly wandered from the subject of Yoga practice, but we have done so in order to impress upon the student the importance of purity in thought and aspiration and cleanliness of body and life.

There are many schools of Yoga and seven paths; but there are many byways that unite man to hidden things in Nature, and three broad paths that will unite man to God. These the student must find for himself.

CHAPTER TEN
FINER FORCES

THERE are several unregistered colours in the spectrum of the Innermost whose rates of vibration are far beyond our range of receptivity. There is likewise a range of vibration that we do not receive from our Nous atom. When we receive this through the interspaces that separate one atom from another our real higher development begins. This energy, called the Solar force, is our real building material that the lower atoms refused to build with.

This material is to be the "Headstone of the Corner," and when this occurs we arrive at our real constructive period; for the true material has been placed in the Mason's hand, and he must fashion his own stone. This force can destroy all opposition to the Architect's plan, and when directed will work and develop our latent sources of inspiration attuned to its activity. This intelligence is a secret instructor who gives us its constructive material. It conserves its energy in the finer substance of the central nervous system, and releases in this substance that great energy that has brought to birth the World's Saviours.

When this sleeping energy is awakened it is similar to particles of ether charged with an intense vibration that causes our bodies to respond to it.

When this energy rises up the central nervous system and attunes the many centres to its own note it leaves the top of the head, known as "The Door of Jesus, or Buddha, or Brahma," according to the Lesser Mysteries of these religions, but this is not the same kind of opening in the skull that a child has at birth. It is one of the most sensitive spots in the adept's body, and is sometimes known to take two years and a half to open. When this happens the Innermost is no longer imprisoned in the body.

From now on the student has periods of intense bliss and relationship with his Innermost. Yet this is not the Reality; he who attains the Reality enters into union with God.

After the student's union with his Innermost he has the choice of two ways: to return to the world and become its instrument, or become at one with the Reality. Usually he seeks such union: the greatest attainment man can achieve, but others prefer the other way: those who remembered that they incarnated with a determined plan to remain behind until the last member of their Order had gained freedom from incarnation.

To be practical is a synonym of being thorough in any work we wish to accomplish, and the student will now begin to recover some of his lost possessions. In this Yoga we must return again and again to those experiences of our remote days when we were animals and afterwards men of an animal nature, until we reach those epochs wherein lie the lost records of our past. We often do this in our sleep, though remember little on awakening. We can go back to the morning of our creation and forward till we see the Great Initiates, who direct the world in their present bodies.

· · · ·

The student now enters a new atmosphere wherein he is taught by atoms called the Transformation atoms. Before this he worked under the guidance of the Nous atom, but now these new atoms take him into his wisdom schools where he is instructed, and each experience for which he incarnated is summed up.

Before this the student had no inward guidance for his material welfare—though he might have had communications with discarnate intelligences—but now he will begin to sense this. He will no longer rely upon his personal domination over conditions, but upon groups of Aspiring atoms sent into his aura. For now the trowel has been placed in his hands and he can labour constructively and prosper.

The Aspiring atoms that have successfully carried out their apprenticeship under the Nous atom are now taken over by the Transformation atoms, who send them inwardly to that which they have been seeking, and there for a time they rest from their labours. Later they will work under the Architect.

The illumination of the Transformation atoms is like light entering the atmosphere of the Nous atom, and everything seems to be enclosed in a vapour of yellow light slightly tinged with green. One feels the consciousness of a higher intelligence, as though some great Lord of Mercury had touched one with his wand. This power can contact us with other planets in this Solar system.

This power, which adepts call the Justice Ray, carries us farther into the lower strata of our nature, whose vibrations we have hitherto not registered, as well as into the inner worlds.

From this we are instructed about the human mind: its anatomy and activity. This is the wisdom school's teachings. Just as there are temples on the physical plane so are they on the mental plane, and from these we receive mental attributes and knowledge. There are also hospitals where diseased minds are treated, and many books by Initiates wherein are written the wisdom of this plane.

Here the student will learn about the great intelligence—the master creator of the mental world—who places within his universe a wisdom atom that reveals to him the sum of his past mental experiences. For we often reincarnate three or four times in order to gain a certain type of experience, and the Transformation and Master atoms bring him the wisdom he has gained.

Evolution on the lower planes is slower than on the inner planes, and when we look back from these we can see that we have evolved beyond the present into what the normal man would call the future.

When our inner powers are developed and we can view things from the inner worlds, we shall be able so to live as to absorb nourishment without heeding the desires of the material body—for such desires are not of the inner world. But as we have developed our bodies to respond to the lusts of our surroundings we have become a part of an illusion world that does not exist within our true being.

Just as great Initiates have come to earth to individualise the members of a soul-group, so have they visited the mental world to individualise the mind, and in the Atlantean Testament of Learning we read: "Before man was, an angel said: "This world has passed away, and another will be born in remembrance of the sign of the Thrice-Born Hermes, the Messenger of Light, and the chosen one of the mind-world.

"'This sign shall be known to all men that the Thrice-Born Hermes staff of righteousness shall be given to those who await his coming.

"'The Transformation atoms rejoiced and said: "We await-his coming: this Thrice-Born Mercury, the mind of the Source that is glorious in itself."

"'Then those who followed after—the atoms of the Secret Enemy—came upon this planet and swallowed it up in their clouds of darkness.

"'They buried Hermes the Thrice-Born, and said: "He is not the messenger sent for us, but a Master who brought his light to another world and not to this one. And they buried this prophet, but afterwards found in his place of burial a staff inscribed with these words: 'The mind has advanced into the dwelling place of the soul. Take this staff and follow me into my world.' And the minds of those who did so were instantly brought into its presence." ' "

The above is but a feeble translation from an archaic work.

Two thousand years ago there came another great Initiate to enkindle the sleeping embers in the heart, just as Thrice-Born Hermes came to ancient Atlantis to bring to the mind the Master atom.

The true source of individual expression comes from the mind's central luminary: this is the sovereign intelligence that moves and directs all mental bodies within its orbit.

In order to attract these Transformation atoms we must practise a new kind of breathing: the inner planes call it natural breathing. This form of breathing can be seen after a child is born and before the objective atmosphere begins to control it. We now breathe in harmony to the rhythmic pulse of the universe, to which the Innermost responds: for the Innermost now takes charge and controls our normal breathing; but this can only occur when the student has entered his own Central universe.

As we breathe these Transformation atoms, they build upon the silken lining of the mental body a shield that registers thoughts from our own inner spheres that give us instruction. The atoms of this shield are under the guidance of the Master atom. We are also given our hidden knowledge and encounter the Lords of the Mind who give us information and strive to bring us closer to our Innermost.

Here the God Hermes stands radiant and serene; the messenger of those spheres upon whose temple walls are portrayed his attributes and works, and from here we can also descend into the lower ranges of intelligence as well as into the higher.

Besides the building up of this Transformation or Silver Shield we also breathe atoms that do not register the lower type of objective thought. This dams up any leakage of our mental spheres and helps to increase our reservoir of mental energy. This is one of the Yogi's great qualities; for he can close the doorways of his mind from foreign invasion and shut out the five senses. He can then receive direction from his inner worlds without interference. As he has built up his physical energy so does he build up his mental energy.

The great sealed records of the universe will open when we enter the inner planes and there read about the possessions mankind has stored up. The inner planes will also reveal the natural causes of things, and bring us in contact with those invisible Beings who scourge this world in order to bring into the atmosphere Beings of their own caste whom we call prophets, and to us peace and tranquillity. These Beings also forgive those who have been destructive, and give them a certain atomic substance that will help them to aspire.

The scourge has to be applied to us till we renounce our warlike habits and seek our Innermost. Our animal atoms must be given aid and instruction in order that they be not cast out of this world's atmosphere when earthquakes and plagues descend upon it. Nations that possess such animal tendencies will sooner or later be destroyed as were ancient nations that plundered others, and the Secret Enemy will again have them enslaved by their dictators and military caste. The direction of the masses by a single individual will sooner or later be demolished.

We have only to look back in history to confirm this, and in the inner planes we can read the records of such despotic minds. In the records in the Temple of the Sphinx we can see why they were permitted to destroy that which they had created. We scan these records and note that in their early days these despots ruled under the guidance of celestial Beings, but were later directed by their own personality, and were thus severed from the direction of the Master atom of the mind-body. Here we can also read about those unborn despots who are to come, and as we enter a period far beyond the present, we find these great soldiers gathered into a mass of atomic substance—for in the inner planes souls do not appear in their human form—and slowly incarnating.

The Great Initiates have to prepare the ground for those who are to govern wisely and build up a nation's usefulness and prosperity. These despots often follow these Initiate leaders, so that they can converse with them in their moments of depression; for then the Secret Enemy has power to drag them down.

Men who bring real worth to a country are always overshadowed by what the Initiates call the Great Illuminate Crown of Victory.

During the transformation period the student will find much to interest him in those who, similar to himself, have achieved this consciousness. And when he looks from the inner planes he will see the creative work of the despots that will later become destructive. We shudder when we gaze into the past camps of the Secret Enemy's Initiates; for there we see the evil geniuses who foster destruction and create war. Yet these are the instruments by which the Great Initiates scourge the world.

At this period the student's Dæmon will begin to teach him about his future progress, and attune him to its vibration, and to the Master atom within his Silver Shield. This will bring him joy, for he will now know his own powers. This comes suddenly, and is known as "The illumination to the Mind," for we are then in direct communication with the Great Initiate who guides the destiny of the Western areas of the world.

Our atoms are not directed by the Initiates' energy, but by the Solar energy within us, and this Silver Shield vibrates to the consciousness of certain Initiates who place certain powers within it that protect us from outer destructive forces; for such students who can progress to this state have treasures for those who follow in their footsteps. The Great Illuminate Crown of Victory is that consciousness that we are to reach when we have evolved beyond the instruction of the Master Atom. It is a directing force of the mind about which we know little, as it is beyond our comprehension. Yet we know that it guides and governs our Innermost, and is a universal body of substance, and that the Great Initiates are of its nature, who, though seldom heard of, can suddenly appear in a material body when needed; for they can clothe themselves when they wish. They sometimes speak through the Silver Shield to the student if necessary.

The Advocate also has his place within this Shield, and his great work is to release from imprisonment his own atomic intelligence. When this occurs he will disintegrate as he will be no longer needed; for he has contacted us to our Innermost. This is a process similar to the Innermost returning to its Reality or Nirvana after His work has been accomplished.

As we increase our sensitivity and develop our Silver Shield, we begin to receive instruction within our normal consciousness, and this process of listening-in or bringing things through should not be confused with clairaudience: a process of listening-in to the voices of discarnate spirits.

The physical relationship with our secondary system, that we now tap, is done by positive aspiration. The more positive we are the more clearly do we hear that which is not normal to the human ear. This is a process of hearing from the inner schools without having to go inward as we did when reviewing our past experiences by the aid of our Aspiring atoms or using any of our sense perceptions.

During this process we have a strong impression of the dominant power of the Innermost: similar to an oversoul directing things, and the deeper we go the stronger becomes Its pressure.

Here we will speak about the positivity needed for a clear receptivity from the inner states.

A positive body is a healthy body, and reflects a healthy mind. This does not mean egotism, nor people who seek to impress others with their personality; for the great men whom I have been privileged to meet and associate with have been invariably sensitive, shy, and simple, and did not exhibit their wonderful powers or attainments unless necessary to do so. It is this positivity, the real determinative energy within us, that enables us to contact our secondary system. A positive body radiates atoms of health; a negative body attracts atoms of the Secret Enemy. If we are positive our secondary system will instruct us and apply its forces with a positive energy that will disintegrate the atoms of the destructive class and nullify their power. These destructive atoms can only exert pressure upon us when they take the shape of battering rams that press upon the sensitive membranes of our mental and causal bodies.

Negative peoples seldom render great service to their fellow men, and talk a great deal, and unthinking talk is responsible for much of the worry and anxiety in this world; for it distorts the imagination. Constant conversation often hinders the currents that flow into our system, and this hampers one's development. Hence the student should not indulge too much in trivial conversation. When he does speak he should endeavour to ennoble the thoughts of others. Some teachers place their pupils under a vow of silence; for by saying little they protect themselves from onslaughts upon their atmospheric sheaths.

The Nous atom and its builder atoms make this inner contact also possible, and we are inspired in a manner difficult to express in words; for they form bridges between the centres of our secondary system and this objective world. This aspiration for the higher intelligences ultimately connects us with our central system.

These wavelengths differ in different people and the type of intelligence we inwardly possess determine the nature and character of our expression. A poet or author will often read his works from an inner plane when his body sleeps; but only dimly remembers them when awaking; for it should be known that any creative work produced here has already been created on an inner plane, and this study will enable him to bring into his objective consciousness the work he has already produced. There are many authors and poets who have this gift, and they will often say: "This thing wrote itself after I got into my stride."

There are also a class of sensitives who possess the power of listening-in to the elementary spirits of the astral world, and to elemental bodies that possess intelligence and information. These sensitives often write books that, though sometimes instructive and beautiful in sentiment, lade the consciousness of the inner states and resemble the voices of children. A soul usually childlike in spirit is often entranced by a discarnate intelligence who uses it as a mouthpiece in order to speak to the sensitive, and books are often produced in this manner, though showing a low grade of intelligence similar to those spheres beneath us in development. There is little instruction of worth from these spheres, and the higher states of intelligence are far above the reach of the usual sensitive.

Those sensitives who seek the Innermost are frequently given instruction through another process, though not in the form of books, that brings to birth in the sensitive a determination to seek a higher plane of enlightenment that will lead him from Spiritualism to Theosophy and onwards.

Whilst we are building up our Silver Shield we are given for the first time by the Innermost a power over certain sections of our secondary system. Living in the objective world we understand some of its operations, and we must now do likewise with our secondary system. Initiates call this "The wise beginning." As we are given power over our Aspiring atoms we must also care for and help them, and as we bring through the higher instruction we give these atoms periods of rest and they receive the same instruction and illumination that we receive; for they aspire as we do.

When we have learned to govern our secondary system we are then eligible to pass into our central system. Man little realises the powers he possesses when he can harmonise his secondary system with his objective body.

The objective body protects the secondary system and the secondary system protects the central system, just as in the cranium our most delicate organs are protected by coarser fibres.

When the student has arrived at the state of physical communication with the inner planes he can then read the books and revelations of those Initiates who have come from their home to pass their lives in the service of humanity, and secure for us that freedom that will eventually take us into the presence of our Innermost.

When such Initiates appear they are often mistaken for the Being known as Jesus; but on the inner planes the student sees them in their own natural forms that are similar to elongated prisms shining with a crystalline radiance. They appear more frequently than the world realises to the humble and the pure in mind.

CHAPTER ELEVEN
BREATHING AND BLOOD-STREAM

WE do not realise that we inhale distinct kinds of air and that the physical body is a highly sensitive magnet to the alternate day and night currents of the earth. We attract atoms with distinct characteristics; similar natures attract similar atoms, and we know not that when thinking we attract atoms that sheathe us in their vibration. We also inhale a dust of decomposing matter, whose organisms would greatly disturb us if seen under a microscope, that inflicts our worker atoms with their diseases as well as sins.

The kind of food we eat also attracts similar conditions that can impoverish and make our blood-stream impure, and thus prevent us from responding to the higher vibration that the current of the life force pours into us. The pure blood of a Yogi enables him to attract pure atoms that give him an energy that impure blood would reject.

This is why a healthy body as well as a healthy mental and physical environment are important. Decayed substances that infest the blood must be eradicated ere the inner seats of government can be opened.

Many people do not care what they eat and drink or how ill-ventilated are the rooms in which they live. They should immediately alter such habits when they take up this practice.

When we analyse the atmosphere in this world after we return from a mental flight we find that it possesses a most disagreeable and fetid quality; particularly over congested areas, and I have often wondered how those Beings of splendour and light must feel when they visit the student and sense this unhealthy smoke and atmosphere.

Sometimes when a student is mentally travelling with a teacher to a place in order to prevent something occurring there, he is asked to analyse the odour; for by distinguishing the odour he can tell what kind of disease infests the spot.

The air we breathe on clear frosty nights is full of atoms that charge the atmosphere with vitality and power, and a long walk in the snow clears the system of germs foreign to the body. Winter sports teach us the value of this; for these atoms quickly gather and absorb the moisture wherein atoms of a lower nature are collected and give them strength and vitality.

It is necessary to prepare our minds for purity of thought and action when aspiring. Sit still, breathe normally, for this kind of thought, and so attract atoms with such qualities. When thinking we breathe in atoms of the nature of our thought, and our blood is an exact replica of these. In the future scientists will measure and weigh our thoughts, also discover the nature and energy that direct our blood-stream.

A normal blood-stream represents the activity of a normal mind; though often it is inflicted with disease and worry. We can discern within a person's atmosphere the exact nature of the energy in his blood-stream and can systematise it when registering the radiations of his mental aura.

Scientists have discovered many different properties in the blood, but have not yet measured the atomic substances that enable the blood-stream to operate under the guidance of the Nous atom. This atom's atmosphere will in time be located by them. As yet we cannot measure it by mechanical means, nor observe the Nous atom spinning in its centre.

The blood determines our growth and inner relationship. When we analyse this by its radiation we find that no two people are similar and that the particles of matter in the aura give us the keynote of the student's real worth.

When a student is inwardly related he carries an atmosphere that even the insensitive mind recognises for its cleanliness, and we can clairvoyantly tell a person's position in Nature by the brilliance of his aura. This clairvoyance is considered abnormal by the world; but this can be easily developed by one whose mind is clean and seeks purity of thought and action.

One with this gift can give it to another who is in harmony with him. When he energises his third eye the vibration from it enters the left ventricle of his heart and here, the Nous atom perceiving these waves, seeks to discover what has called it to the objective mind. As it analyses the seeker's thoughts and aspirations it sends its atoms to the Pineal gland to develop it. Thus this atom is the real instrument that can awaken an atrophied centre.

We again feel it necessary to remind the student about his physical development as this is one of the secrets of Yoga, also that he should become united to his Master atom and increase his power of breathing into his system those more highly developed atoms, which then become Overseers to the atoms that build up the physical body.

As anatomists know, the purest blood is sent directly to the seminal tract; but they do not know that it is directed by the Nous atom. Yet the best blood is impure compared with the blood of a Yogi; though normal blood is slowly changing into a higher vibration.

We have often heard the term "Blue-blooded aristocracy." To the occultist this means that too much inbreeding and dissipation has brought impurities into the ancestral blood and weakened its constitution.

When the Solar force is evoked our blood has the qualities of sunlight and vigour and in time will resemble a clear stream of life-bringing energy.

When we enter our secondary system our arterial bloodstream pressure increases; that is: as we breathe our Aspiring atoms they force the blood into areas hitherto unaffected, and these respond by building up their structures. The normal man cannot do this as the Yogi does, who intensifies the pressure when practising, and unites the Solar and Lunar currents into one energy. This gives the mind thoughtful impressions of a deep nature and destroys sluggish currents. The blood cells become vital in order to supply these newly opened territories of the body. This develops the physical body into another state of consciousness, in that it is impelled to assume a more direct positive energy and promote the growth of its lesser dominant nature. This change in the blood takes place the moment we have brought a sufficient number of Aspiring atoms into the body.

This change is not physical but of an atomic and gaseous nature that adheres to the walls of the arteries and energises the blood. The Transformation atom directs this energy into weak nerve cells and brings life to them. This is how the blood-stream assists us; it opens our principal centres and eradicates impurities.

Atomic pressure within the blood-stream does not mean an increased pressure within the arteries, but an increase of energy among the atoms, and this greater energy eradicates the destructive forces within the body.

CHAPTER TWELVE
ANIMAL FOOD

THE elemental world in our nature will not register our minds if we are impure in thought and action. From this world of beauty we learn that service is the path to its source. We do not perceive these higher forms easily until we, like them, seek our Innermost.

These Beings often cast their spells about us, and we are taught by their wisdom religion that if man would only follow Nature's wisdom there would be less pain and sorrow in our world; for they subsist upon their energy alone and thus their bodies are free from disease and torment, whilst we unceasingly torment our Worker atoms by needless worry and privation and do not respond to their cry for proper nourishment, but defile our bodies with unnatural appetites and desires.

Animals when killed for food should not be shocked by the fear of death if possible. The animal instinctively knows when it is to be destroyed, and its sufferings and torture permeate the flesh that we eat. This hampers the growth of the Builder atoms within our blood; and much time is lost in their constructive work whilst defeating these animal atoms that destroy their creation.

In some of the older races certain veins are cut and the impure blood drained out. The arterial blood is pure but the venous blood is impure.

Animal food will survive as long as man is animal in his lusts. When man will aspire he will give animal life its fullest development. If we impose our strength upon those animals that have been created for us to love and who toil unceasingly for us, this will weigh upon our karma in the future.

In the present state of humanity, animal life is necessary to hasten the development of certain structures in the physical body, and animal atoms predominate in those with strong animal natures, but through Yoga the body is weaned from such forms of atomic life and the student will naturally acquire the taste for non-animal food. We should also be ruled by the impressions sent to us from the Nous atom.

The student should remember not to show disapproval of any food given to him by those whose food he eats. This we have mentioned elsewhere. Though obviously, if the food should be of a poisonous nature to his system, he should say so tactfully to his host.

What do the higher elementals say about the destruction of animal life? They reply: "These lower creatures are made to serve the purpose of their creation, and not be heedlessly sacrificed." Though, in the past, animals were given to the gods for sacrifice we explain the reason for this elsewhere.

Cereals are the right foods, and fruit and vegetables will some day be our universal diet. In the future scientists will assist humanity to nourish the body.

They will discover a singular germinating substance that will supply all that is needed for the body; also several similar liquids.

It is from these elemental worlds that we begin to perceive the cause of things, and are told not to worry about their effects upon the earth; for the elementals consider the cause of things to be of greater importance than the effect.

There are hordes of migratory atoms that infest our atmospheric sheath and seek to build therein colonies that will disturb it. This is the cause of much of man's woes; for they impress the node points of our atmospheric sheath with their demands and desires. It is to render himself immune from these parasitic conditions that the Yogi will often fast for some days. This starves and dislodges them. He will fast until he clears his atmosphere. By fasting we do not mean abstention from water; in fact he should drink quantities for cleansing and purifying.

Fasting should never be attempted when conditions are unfavourable, and it is best done under the observation of a teacher.

Meat eaters find it difficult to fast; for the meat gives these migratory atoms a more secure hold, therefore meat eaters suffer much from fasting, but vegetarians suffer little.

Fasting brings great enjoyment to the Worker atoms in the blood; for they are no longer crowded with animal structures that oppose them.

CHAPTER THIRTEEN
REINCARNATION AND KARMA

ERE we are born we collect all the materials that disintegrated at the death of our last incarnation. Thus man attracts his old body and its atomic structures, and inherits his previous diseases and character, besides the physical conditions of his ancestors.

Often through misadventure the Innermost is unable to attract all those elements necessary to complete its physical body, and this produces malformation and pains in the bones that cannot be traced. Sometimes a skeleton has had certain substances poured over it that bind the atomic energy within it, producing after rebirth an atomic deficiency.

We are told that the greatest atomic force known to the occultist, and which scientists will some day unlock, can only be imprisoned in pumice.

By karma we mean the law of cause and effect. If we injure others we must pay the penalty in this life or in another. In Theosophic literature we read about physical, mental, and spiritual karma. But in our secondary system we begin to analyse and find that things are different from that which we have been led to believe, and are astonished to learn that we have often borne in past lives burdens far in excess of our creation of evil. We then are told by an Instructor atom to observe the following life. We do so and discover that we were singularly free from anxiety and pain; for the evils of our youth had been previously balanced. The cause of our anxiety and pain is our karma that hangs over us; but this sense of freedom again returns to us when we take up our Yoga practice, for we determine to be as free as possible from evil in order to attain to our Innermost.

We reserve a karmic reservoir as we would a supply of energy. We should always remember that we ourselves choose and analyse the body into which we are to incarnate. We search for bodies that we think wilt give us that environment and experience we most need.

Often in our zeal to return quickly to our Innermost, we will plunge deeply into the densities of matter in order to gain a greater round of experience in one life.

The greater the soul, the more deeply does he plunge; and though he may suffer exceedingly and all light will seem to have left him, he attains a nearness to his Innermost that few who incarnate into the laps of luxury and indolence gain, for they receive but little of that greater experience of the world that would help them in their growth.

We often meet men seemingly free in everything they do: free to travel, free from worry and affliction, free to associate with those whom they choose. These people accumulate a great experience that deals with hidden things not known to the usual mind and have stored up this reservoir of good karma for this life.

There are also people who do not incarnate for a long period, and store up a great amount of energy; adding to and storing up a great reservoir of power that they will draw upon when incarnating. This is a determinative energy: Napoleon is an example of such a type.

As the student slowly works into his higher schools he will meet and be taught by Elder atoms, and he will frequently ask for a certain type of instruction. But if he has not reached their canons of perfection this will not be revealed.

We do not realise that we are all fugitives from Justice, and that we must shoulder the burdens that we have caused others to bear before we are permitted to gain such knowledge. These Elder atoms impress upon us that we must pass justice upon ourselves for any past wrong doing and administrate our own laws. Though our Advocate pleads that we should be forgiven we find we must repay certain karmic debts before we are allowed to travel farther into our own universe.

Afterwards we realise that our Innermost was just, and we manfully attempt to remedy the distress we have caused others in this and in previous lives. Debts to one's fellows will always find one out, and as we re-experience our past we soon learn what our past debts to humanity are and humanity's just debts to us. When these are balanced we are grateful to our Innermost; for at last we know where we stand.

Justice is the aim of all creatures, and when we receive justice we seek to awaken this sense in others.

A child's environment is often inflicted by the thought-atmosphere of its parents who, overshadowed by their conscience, unknowingly place such atoms within the child's atmosphere.

The student often prays for forgiveness and wonders why he did certain things. When he enters his secondary system and reviews his past he is sometimes surprised at what happens. He sees people who have physically and mentally tortured him in other lives, and the people he has not treated justly in this life, and for which he suffers acutely. He then discovers that those people who had once tormented him are those whom he now repays. The moment he realises this his remorse vanishes and he discovers later that the reason for this is that his debt has been repaid either way. He also understands the principle that as we judge so shall we be judged. This is why the Elder atoms constantly impress him to be careful in his speech.

Students should remember that they have often been illumined in past lives by their Yoga practice and are credited with their past endeavour.

CHAPTER FOURTEEN
ATMOSPHERIC SCREEN AND BREATHING

WE have already spoken about the inhaling of certain atoms. In the atmosphere are numerous kinds of atoms that distract and injure the mind. If we can live in the country away from congested areas we breathe fresh air and healthy atoms, and open a number of nodes of consciousness that were closed when we lived in the city. These nodes sense the country conditions and relate us to its rural nature; but the opening of such nodes depends upon the receptivity of the person to Nature.

Our mental screens are impregnated with atoms of past civilisations, and though we think of them as dead and buried, yet within these screens these atoms will still contact us to those civilisations that are now far in advance of our own. And the student can contact their golden ages of culture and intelligence; civilisations that will take this world many centuries to achieve. For example, although Egypt is considered but a remnant of an ardent glory, in the inner planes we can still enter her periods of illumination and wisdom, and discover what the world can gain from such a consciousness.

The student should always remember that space-time is non-existent on the inner planes. That everything IS. Thus he will learn that within him are atoms representing higher developments than his. But when he enters his secondary system he will find it difficult at first to discriminate between his own Instructor atoms and those of a foreign nature attracted to his mental screen. These atoms also attract intelligences of other civilisations. These foreign atoms and entities are injurious to our screen; for they do not represent the student's past experience and wisdom.

If we attract the past it is apt to becloud and retard our own growth; for we must develop from within and not from without, no matter how highly evolved is the period.

In the student's later progress he will easily rid himself from any outside interference by radiating his own Solar force.

A torn mental screen brings disease and often insanity; for in this wound hordes of atoms and entities find a place to build their structures, and in some desperate cases we have found several colonies adhering to the envelope. In this manner they can speak into the mind of the subject and the normal personality is often replaced by others. These severe cases can be healed by proper care and judgment by the doctor; but he must be able to locate the cause and not judge it objectively. The coming century will produce a new school that will deal with such cases successfully, and a mind harassed by such conditions will greatly benefit if the patient can live in a very high altitude; for such atoms and entities cannot rise owing to their density and weight.

In the East those instructed in certain systems in Yoga are taken into retreat far above sea-level; for a clear atmosphere enables the student to enter his secondary system more easily.

Incense properly used could drive away lower conditions from the screen and cause a number of node points to become active; for the odour will attract different atoms that will clarify the atmosphere.

The mental screen is often bent from its normal shape if the tissues of the body are destroyed and will appear like an elongated balloon, and when the body is unable to radiate into the mental screen a hollow depression is seen. This tells the developed student what organ is diseased. A sudden fall or shock can sometimes injure a membrane of this screen, and some period will elapse ere it will return to its normal shape.

We have frequently met people whose auras were out of shape, so we knew that all was not well with their physical bodies.

A normal and healthy body has a normal and healthy screen. If we have foul minds we are not physically healthy. Aspiration and inward seeking will engender our atoms with a healthy appetite, for they are fed upon the higher nature of one's seminal fluid: this is the energy we have brought over from past lives and provides us with a greater energy similar to seminal fluid. We should remember that if we procreate children we bequeath to them the strength of our past, and this inheritance gives them stamina and courage. The two qualities with which weakness is bequeathed are weak in their powers of observation and endurance.

Mental distortions are caused, as we have said previously, by the silken linings of the membrane being inflicted by the diseased germs of the Secret Enemy. In this silken web project unprotected node points, and germinating fluids, collecting about them, produce erosion. This hampers their receptivity when registering thoughts and distorts them in the physical brain. When we are healthy the node points are strong.

In some cases these nodes have been shattered by shell shock, which also produces distorted imagination and great mental sufferings. This is one of the great penalties of war, and few realise how such cases suffer.

From year to year the thought-waves about us are increasing, and this pressure upon humanity brings an ever-increasing agitation to sensitive minds. It is by aspiration that we protect ourselves from this thought bombardment. Hence it is imperative to erect a protective shield about these node points. This bombardment is caused by man's uncontrolled thought agitation that will later return and inflict him with certain forms of mental disorders. The rapid voltage of the Dayspring of Youth will add to this state of mind. War has also loosened conditions that seek to destroy the healthy mind.

When we wish to close down the node points to the illusion-thought of this world and open them to a higher note, we use this method: we aspire, and multitudes of dormant node points will suddenly open as we go inward to receive information. Our normal node points will then close down, thus shut out the thoughts of the physical world. This is the method that helps us to receive instruction from our interior centres.

When we can shut out the objective plane and the organs that receive its impressions we shall be able to exist for certain periods within our self-developed universe; for there we find we possess an interior set of sensory organs that relate us to the activities of our inner systems.

A higher voltage within our atmospheric sheath is caused when we enter our secondary system, and this removes the accumulation and mental debris we have collected.

When the student has combined Nature's consciousness with his own and energised the latent node points of his mental sheath, he then commences his deeper education.

As he proceeds inwardly he brings into activity more and more node points of his atmospheric sheath. When he has attained this illumination, he possesses a consciousness that the physical brain responds to and registers the inner waves of thought as well as the teachings from distant stars.

The cell life in us also rejoices when we begin to water their parched soil; for we had not considered their efforts of labour or supplying us with a habitation for the Innermost, who is our guide as well as our saviour.

.   .   .   .   .

When breathing excessively, through exhaustion, we collect atoms of a most disagreeable nature. We should bear this in mind while exercising; for such atoms are of the Secret Enemy, and elderly people often asphyxiate themselves with this energy when breathing them into an exhausted body; for these, travelling to the generative organs, inflict them with diseased atoms that can at times cause instantaneous death. The protective screen grid of Nature has broken down, and we thus breathe a distinct type of Death atom that will irrigate the system with their corrupting substances, and cause diseases suddenly to spring up.

When we breathe normally we do not exhale all the air from our lungs, and this remaining carbon-dioxide gas ultimately produces death.

Year in and year out we have been infiltrating our bodies with this carbon-dioxide gas. We leave about a hundred cubic inches of this deadly gas in our lungs; for when we inhale we use three times the muscular energy than when we exhale. Only when we can develop our breathing muscles to a high degree as the Yogi does can we keep our lungs pure. By careful exercise we learn to breathe outwardly. When this becomes a habit our body will be greatly refreshed and our mind-atmosphere cleared of its debris.

In order to destroy the attraction our lungs and nasal passages have for these atoms we learn to inhale atom of a more advanced nature; for in their higher vibratory current they destroy this poisonous gas that is the cause of old age.

We learn to breathe from the lower regions of the abdomen, so that the muscles and walls of our lungs become elastic and powerful. It must become second nature with us; for we must exhale these impurities with force insects do. This will then teach the student what wonderful activity goes on in his body. He will sense the activity of the divisions and analyse them.

When he has perfected his body into a finer instrument the Nous atom will take this breathing over. We have written about this elsewhere.

Later in his practice the student will learn to retain his breath, its higher counterpart—magnetic oxygen, the real vital breath—and pass this through his stomach into his abdomen. The atoms there will also receive a higher vibration, and assist him to awaken his Solar force and a trance state of bliss.

THE MENTAL BODY

THE mental body is a collective energy that determines man's place and position in Nature.

This illustration shows the mental body of the advanced student who has built up his Silver Shield of Transformation atoms through Yoga practice. The atmosphere of the mental body from which emanates our hidden energy is a radiant vapour that can be easily seen—if one has developed this—by the advanced student.

The mental body possesses the energy of the Nous atom as well as the powerful currents of the seminal system. The principal currents that arise and pass out of the body as well as enter it can be seen in the illustration.

The current above the head is the magician's crest and sounding board. When the Solar and Lunar currents unite at the apex of the spine this swirling wave or current becomes more pronounced, for it registers the deeper activities of the Solar and Lunar universe within us. By its use as a feeler we tap any node point upon the silken lining of the mental body, and this conveys to us the impressions of any intelligence that seek to attune its activities to our atmosphere. As we have brought this sounding board—similar to our third eye—over from a remote, elemental past in Nature's consciousness, it registers Nature's activities within us and passes them into our Silver Shield, which then collects and distributes them into us.

Our Elemental Advocate as well as the higher elemental beings have several of these streamers upon their heads, and these can be seen in the ancient sculptures that show the great elemental being who brought the Aztec civilisation to a high state of development ere the people rebelled against Nature's instruction and were governed by a decadent priesthood.

The sac at the feet in the illustration is the higher counterpart of that shown in the picture of the astral body.

The reader can also note how the powers within the seminal system's energy is drawn upon by the thinker and that the sounding board of the Yogi represents the awakening consciousness inherent within man and within his Solar and Lunar atoms.

[See frontispiece.]

CHAPTER FIFTEEN
MENTAL TRAVELLING

WHEN the student is united to his secondary system he contacts another condition that will enable him to pass out of his physical body. An experienced teacher does not at first take his pupil into the astral or lower realms, but into the higher, and the student learns about the different degrees of densities that compose these atmospheres. Such experiences are very interesting and exhausting at first, for it will take some time before he can rise by the power of his own will to any place he is directed.

His teacher will first take him to the top of a high mountain. This is difficult on account of the seeming weight of his body. When this is accomplished he is given a load to carry to the same height. This is still more difficult, and at times he is assisted by his teacher, who encourages him and takes the load from him when he is exhausted. The process of levitation gives him, later on, the power to enter the clearer atmospheres of the inner worlds and learn about them.

When he develops this power he becomes a worker of a higher type of service. He is taught by his teacher how disaster may be prevented by his power to impress minds that are determined to lull or injure the innocent, and, if he is sufficiently developed, he is shown the evil of the world. This will cause him great depression, for the things he witnesses are terrible and could not be written down.

At this time the Secret Enemy will try to impress upon him the uselessness of combating its powers, and will suggest that he should leave this world wherein there is so little good.

The student will now realise that those who strive to lead noble and clean lives are not without their invisible helpers. Kind hearts, no matter what their degrees of intelligence, are more carefully watched than they realise. No prayer is unheard, though they may not receive a reply from their Advocate at the time.

The student is taught to prepare people for death when out of the body. Sometimes in a storm at sea the teacher takes him round to the stern of a sinking ship so that he can read and memorise its name and port. Then before the vessel goes down they appear before the crew and passengers. Sometimes the drowning people take them for higher beings. The teacher and student tell these people to breathe in the water as naturally as they breathe in air, and that they should not be afraid.

The student never forgets such trips and the care and attention he receives from his teacher. He is also greatly impressed by the noble manner in which those who had lived fine lives meet their deaths. At such times the student has the power to sense their characters instantly and deal with them according to their intelligence.

Sometimes he is taken by his teacher into the councils of the great—such as the Warlords of the Secret Enemy—and he can sense their conversation as though it were audible.

Only one country in Europe had advanced sufficiently to call upon the services of their great occultists during the Great War, and in the future no secret will be hidden in the hearts of any opposing force.

Passing through a rainstorm whilst in the astral is like passing through a fine mist.

· · · · ·

The magician is submerged within everyone's nature; for long ago we worked with Nature's materials and could produce her phenomena. When we recover our lost consciousness the magician within us will arise. The invisible forces of Nature are very quick in their movements, and we have to learn to follow the waves of their thought with an alertness not easy to gain. We receive an extended range of hearing. That is: these finer vibrations react upon our coarser nervous system.

The student cries to the Reality: "Why is my body so coarse? Why have I not these finer perceptions? Why can I not see? Why can I not receive knowledge?" Here are the reasons.

When we leave our bodies on mental flights we often pause and look at them, and we suddenly realise how coarse a vehicle the body is. We are surprised to find that we view it with indifference and often disdain; for its density seems to absorb one and conceal the light that we see when out of its sheath. We also find that it tries to shut out our memories of journeys we long to bring back. Artists have often felt this loss of remembrance and keen regret for failing to record some moment of beauty.

We meet exalted Beings who impress us with their clarity of atmosphere. Their thoughts are as brilliant as clear streams of water flowing over a fall in early morning, and standing in wonder at this majesty of beauty we become regardless of our own body awaiting our return.

It is sometimes difficult for a teacher to get his pupil to travel to his own plane; for when he arrives at an inner sphere he finds it so interesting that it is difficult for the teacher to levitate him further. The pupil is like a small boy at a circus who will persist in lingering at the cages. Women pupils are more susceptible to this gazing in the shop windows of Nature and afterwards regret having done so; for their disregard of time has kept them from attending some council.

The laws of man vary with races. Nature's laws are also often contrary to our own. This can sometimes shock the student and give him much suffering; but until he can understand the cause of a thing he will be unable to pronounce judgment. Therefore if he cannot arrive at a cause he should remain silent. This law is strongly impressed upon us by Nature.

CHAPTER SIXTEEN
MASTERS[1]

"A faint far horn was blown—I listened—and the hollow North grew thunderous and sweet with sound!
"From vaulted caves of ice, where the lone sea boomed, wild echoes of voices sprang.
"Voices, everywhere voices; snarls of vengeance, shouts of defiance, wails of anguish;
"Women white-bodied and splendid, veiled with shining hair, lay faint on dead lover's breasts.
"Symphonies infinite, wide as despair, sad, deep as regret, arose from the pit; all waking moved and sang and fought again.
"In the golden rose-shot mists of lover's land, and wandering in horror strange as sweet, I cried:
"'O dreams of Darkness, who hath conjured you to match me with a soul unmated,
"'I, who fain would be alone, and yes, unloved, to follow out my life's desire in paths of wisdom found?'
"And in the dim light they turned and lifted their hands while the sea snarled on, and in a sound which whelmed me like an ocean's roar, they cried: "The Master.""

Wagner

TO-DAY there are living in their physical bodies a number of men and women similar to the "Saviours of the World," and in their atmospheres are atoms that resist the impressions of this earth. If we could contact their cloaks or Shekinahs we could hasten the development of some of our atomic structures. Also working silently and unknown are groups of people united to their own inner energy. These attract many who wish to join their administration.

Such people are in the Western part of Europe as well as in the East, and they work in their own areas. In their atmosphere much that is latent within us can be brought to birth. In the West some have given up their whole existence to the call and need of humanity to help it relate itself to its lost inner possessions.

We little realise what goes on in the world. We take things for granted and only at times of great distress do we call out to the Reality. Our thoughts revert to the past; to the days when great Initiates and prophets lived, not realising that they are still living in our midst, though seldom recognised.

Much occult literature has been written on this subject; but we think it as part of an imaginary world to have exalted

[1] We wish to thank the Editor of *The Occult Review* for kindly giving us permission to reprint portions of an article entitled "Masters or Teachers."

views and idealise such great people. Thirty-six such men are now living among us who have attained a high degree of consciousness; though they vary in their receptivity to their Innermost and Reality. And should these men reveal themselves to the world they would be crucified by the very forces they seek to help.

The personal appearance of these Masters vary greatly. We have been told how they are supposed to look, and idealised pictures are sold by some societies for students to meditate upon. But idealists often make serious mistakes; and if the truth were told people would be greatly surprised.

Out of his body a Master appears as he desires; but in his physical body he is similar to the inhabitants of his country. I well remember my surprise when I first met my teacher: the merry laugh he gave me and the pleasure he took over his cake and ice-cream. My ideal of a Master fell from the skies; yet when one learns and begins to understand the great work he has done to bring about industrial relationship between capital and labour in the United States, one realises how great a man he is. He remarked to me: "To-day you must work from the top downwards; from the cause of things if you wish to help humanity, not from the bottom upwards as the Master Jesus did." Also: "Keep your feet on the ground, live in the world, sense its activities and become its instrument. Then you can help humanity and give it enlightenment."

This is why the physical body must be made strong; for it is the stepping-stone to the greater Reality. Get knowledge. Go where wisdom is found. Do not meditate on the way. The East is the East, and to build with material different from your own is to destroy that which you have laid down as your foundation. The Masters unite in saying: "Where your soul is planted bring to birth other souls as well. The seed is planted in the Earth; destroy it not with the seeds of other earths." We have often noticed that teachers coming from the East to the West seemingly lose their clear atmosphere and become subject to their new environment.

I have never been told to address any of these great Initiates by the title Master: "We are nothing, the WORK is everything," was the answer of a Master when I asked how I should address him. He added further as he looked at me and held out his hand: "Call me friend." With this reply a great stream of energy swept over me and I felt that my real work had become implanted into my mind.

It makes no difference where one is born to gain the attention of a Master. Though unknown at first to the student, desire and prayer bring about a physical change, and the body and mind are severed from conditions that formerly possessed them. The light that shines above the brow of the aspiring student is recognised by the teacher, who calls its rays to his own mental atmosphere. It is by this symbol that the teacher recognises the student's intelligence; for by a "Man's light is he known." This attraction comes from an intense desire to be of assistance to others and from a willingness to give up everything in order to gain a knowledge of the Reality. It is this aspiration and longing that brings the assistance of a teacher.

If we are really in the presence of a teacher he does not demand anything from us; yet his presence is sensed as something that gives us a new conception and impresses our atmosphere with a newer and more developed consciousness.

The world is divided into sections and each teacher has his own division wherein he is best suited to work; and the cry of the seeker is not passed over by the teacher in his section.

The teachers vary according to the density of the mental atmospheres in which they work; for they have to adjust their bodies according to their locality, and they adopt a vibratory balance and train themselves and their sensory systems to accord with their environment. If you looked into the face of the Atlantean or the great soul working in Russia, who looks like a Finn, you would realise what wonderful work they were doing, and what great strain their physical bodies must bear.

The great teachers will develop us if we are really in earnest; but we are often blinded by our own individuality, and desire to carry out its expression rather than react to the force of the sun in our mental atmosphere.

No teacher should be accepted who cannot demonstrate his ability to transfer his activities to his pupils. Many who teach cannot do this; and often surrender themselves to the mental atmospheres of others, so that they can be given the instruction needed, being unable themselves to contact their own spheres of intelligence.

The pupil expects when meeting a teacher that all obnoxious conditions will be swept away, and that he will be given powers and knowledge of wonderful things, be placed immediately upon the Path towards adeptship, be taught how to produce phenomena and be *en rapport* with the gods and Mahatmas. He does not realise that he must first shape and chisel his own stone; that he must construct his own foundations and build upwards with his own hands; and that he is not permitted to talk freely about those things he cannot demonstrate.

Though these great teachers know that the supply is limited, they do not take pupils willingly; for their atmosphere is not pleasing to them, and they have learned from experience that the student is apt to become conceited when immersed in their atmosphere. Being placed in condition that stimulate his mind, and having contact with a higher intelligence within his own mental atmosphere, the student begins to feel elevated to a knowledge not revealed to his fellows.

The teacher's individuality expresses itself in the student's atmosphere, and the teacher is responsible for the student's activities in those spheres wherein Nature balances the mind-body's atmosphere. Later on all intercourse is severed, and the student must rely upon his own efforts. This is a dark period for him. He is not mentally individualised and must progress along his own Path.

After the teacher has contacted the student's mind with its higher counterpart's activities he is sometimes sent to another teacher—for each one is a specialist—till the student is slowly absorbed into the centre of his own self-created universe and into the tri-unity of Nature.

The student cries OUT into the material world for a Master to accept him; but he will receive no answer; for the mind generates discord and the vowel sounds will not reach him. But if the student asks INWARDLY he will receive a reply; for the teacher can answer his pupil from any distance.

It will probably surprise the reader to know that many Masters live by the sweat of the brow. In Egypt there are two: one who intermittently carries on a humble vocation, and another, whose age we do not know; for his atmosphere expresses eternity and his name has been mentioned in ancient religious books. In America a great Initiate has at times worked in the fields as a labourer; but where his feet have trodden a more vital life springs up. To witness how he holds great forces in check and governs destructive minds would take a great author to describe.

We have records in our history of the death of sixty-two such men. That is: they met their deaths according to the methods of their day; but all were similar to crucifixion.

Does history know who it was drew the armed hosts of Mediaeval Europe to perish in the sands of Syria and Palestine in order that the wheat might again spring up in Europe and its youth be protected?

The history of these sacred men remains to be written. During these Crusades Initiates were among the Muslims as well as among the Christians. Women have taken a high place among the Initiates. Many teachers have left small occult schools, varying in different degrees of worth, behind them. A school may be latent for centuries until the world is again ready for its new manifestation.

It is through such people that the principles of the religions have been preserved from great antiquity, and the time will come when each race will return to its own racial stem of religious instruction, and Nature will return man to his own parental stem: his source of determined expression, and he will be tolerant to those who differ from him in religion.

Men who do things and do not borrow their ideas from the past and have consciously or unconsciously inwardly related themselves to a future period of development, are master minds. These increase the wealth of the world and are usually interested in the future welfare of their nation. They possess the greater wisdom of their inner planes, and when we meet them out of the body we find them working far in advance of their time.

The Yogi dominates himself before he dominates the thought-world of other minds. A positive attitude is needed for the student, as we have stated elsewhere; for a positive mind promotes the growth of other minds and does not sap their vitality. Yet the Yogi does not seek to dominate any mind about him; but as he lives his own truth his influence impresses thousands. Just as a great book can attract the minds of its readers to the author's atmosphere.

There is always an atomic link between a creator and his public; his creative atoms permeate his manuscripts and the atmospheres of his readers. Thus is the reader unconsciously carried into the remotest places of Heaven and Hell through atomic influences.

We have the power of projecting our atoms into any substance that interests us, and a student can easily read the records of a family by projecting his mind into the surroundings of the fireplace; for generally when people's minds are at leisure they concentrate and unconsciously magnetise this spot.

A teacher who has attained to Nature's consciousness and his inner systems can link up those same qualities in a student; for an accepted pupil always has the right to challenge his teacher to demonstrate the things he teaches.

Students with artistic, poetical, or literary tendencies can be linked by their teachers to their sources of inspiration; for they are largely elemental in their atoms.

There have been many instances of a great teacher radiating a light through his pupils that has had a far-reaching effect upon the world. Socrates is an example. When the Delphic Oracle was asked: "Who was the greatest soul that Greece has produced?" the reply was: "Socrates." For Socrates contacted many of his pupils to their inner spheres of creative activity.

Some years ago there retired to Philadelphia a great surgeon, and the master minds in industry and commerce when in great trouble would call and spend the night at his house.

They were told to say nothing about their worries, but in the morning when this Master accompanied them to the station they would suddenly exclaim: "I have it!" And a light dawned on their minds showing them how to solve their problems. One of such instances occurred to myself, for I came away with a link in my consciousness from which I have never been severed.

There is a strange attraction that will draw a student into the atmosphere of those more developed than himself and through apparent chance meet such people.

Certain students are trained to step out of their bodies and allow their teachers, who may be physically in some distant country, to step in and do things that are beyond the student's strength. This is called an Avesa. The pupil is fully conscious of this operation, for the radiation given his physical body is like the birth of a new consciousness; as though he were suddenly ushered into splendour and brightness from out a dark age of conflicting emotions in the astral world. He feels a peace never felt before.

Sometimes an Initiate's body is used by the Reality for deeds of healing and many heavy burdens are removed by this atomic energy liberated at the descent of the Innermost's power. Jesus said when a woman touched the hem of His robe: "Who touched My clothes?" For he felt that the energy of the Christ consciousness had withdrawn Itself from Him.

When we stand in the presence of our Innermost and demand our freedom it will come suddenly to us; a freedom the world knows nothing about; a freedom from bondage no matter where and how we may be placed in this world. For having released ourselves from our lower objective nature we know what freedom means for the first time. In *The White Brother*, elsewhere mentioned, we have said that the soul desires three things: freedom, love, creation. This freedom comes when our Master atom enters our Silver Shield, and this ascent of a higher intelligence severs us from many weights that have dragged us down to our animal nature and our body feels a lightness never sensed before. This sudden illumination awaits us when our Silver Shield is sufficiently strong to provide a temple for its presiding genius who is the wisdom intelligence of our mental plane. This great Being is a lawgiver, and in the secondary system guides and administers the law within its territories. He represents a half-way station between our objective selves and our Innermost.

In ancient occult literature they speak of seven steps or seven rungs of a ladder. When we reach our secondary system we arrive at our second rung. When the Master atom ascends its throne we are on the third rung; and when we enter Nature's consciousness we arrive at our fourth rung; for the Master atom does not release itself from the seminal fluid until we have become conscious of the determinative energy in Nature.

As man is only four-sevenths developed into the image that the Nous atom represents, many occultists will tell you that they have arrived at their fourth step, whereas they are really but standing on their first or second. Only to those related to their higher centres will be revealed the other three steps; for we may not write about them. Only a trained mind can witness and understand the terror of love and law these states present to him. This is symbolised by the story of Moses meeting his Master Melchizedec.[1]

In the development of a nation the Transformation atoms have to be brought to birth in order to bring to man its periods of mental culture and enlightenment. It is through man's Master atom that the great literature of an age is produced: works the world proclaims as masterpieces. During the Elizabethan age in England we have an example of such a mind that drew upon its Master atom, and such was the supply of information that several writers—to whom he taught shorthand—even took down his table talk. This constant stream of illumined intelligence has lit the dark places of this world.

The Master with this development radiates these Transformation atoms of his Silver Shield into the atmosphere of his pupils who are in harmony with him. Many students have been awakened by the atoms of their teacher implanted within their aura. This cloak is often handed down

[1] The Comte de Gabalis

to the student when the teacher departs from his physical body. It can also be placed upon the student's shoulders for a moment when it is needed, and he will then know his teacher's atmosphere and intelligence. There is an old hermetic saying in our literature: "Love will take your atoms to the most distant star." For love is one of the greatest powers to direct a thing.

The Master's cloak starts this impulse to vibrate his student's body into greater activity. Students naturally think how happy they would be if this occurred to them; but this is really a most painful operation. The Master's love atoms radiate into the student and this is what he enjoys; then the teacher sadly smiles and he suddenly realises how heavy his teacher's burden is; a burden carried alone. The teacher often bears this in order that others may be free from those conditions that retard their development.

Ignorance has led people to think that a teacher can remove conditions that infect their atmospheres and "Bring their souls to birth," by the simple demonstration of his hidden powers. They do not understand that the teachers take on conditions and then clear their atmosphere of this debris. They demand everything, never realising that the teacher has his own work to do and that he does not always have the power to clear his atmosphere; for sometimes these forces do not manifest when called upon, and having a physical body he is often inflicted by conditions of others until he can adjust his vehicle to his own subtle, tremendous voltage.

In the history of the Initiates we seldom read of much sympathy rendered to a teacher's body and mind. People expect all and seldom think of him as a human being. Mary Magdalen was one who knew men. She recognised the human side of Jesus and ministered to His body and mind; for she had suffered and knew the evil of her day. Sometimes when out of the body a teacher will show the student the good in these women and assist them when they are in despair.

Mankind is generally cruel and selfish, and in their trouble and pain men call upon Jesus to relieve them of their burdens, and no just prayer remains unheeded. But they do not think of trying to assist the Master to whom they pray, to help him with his burdens. And this they can do by the pressure of their love.

The government of the Master atom's administration is similar to the government of a nation under the protection of a Master mind.

The following are some of the principles needed for a master mind:
(1) Be above the thoughts of the minds of men.
(2) Be above the mastering thoughts of evil and master the composite bodies of your own evil thought-creation.
(3) Be always master of your own mind.
(4) Be above the minds of the masters who create mastering thoughts of evil, and make your mind master of them; for above the minds of evil thoughts your master's stand ready to aid you.
(5) Be walled about by the good minds of the master's spheres.
(6) Attract about you men with master minds; their forces will protect you.
(7) Command the forces of your master's higher spheres, for they are able to master the minds of the men of evil who are ever near a master of magic; for these can dominate the minds above and below the spheres of man.
(8) Be master of your soul; for the soul has power over matter.
(9) Be master of your thoughts; for thoughts are mastering things.
(10) Be alert for your master's voice as he is alert for yours.

CHAPTER SEVENTEEN
SUBMERGED WORLDS

THERE comes a time in the student's development when he loses all desire for material things and fear of death, and goes into retreat under the care and observation of an advanced brother. Here he will enter his own submerged self and be suddenly confronted by animal-like entities to which we were once similar; and these he must eradicate from his nature. He will also face those who had tormented him in the past and those he had tormented; for he must now face his past evil as well as good.

He will feel that he has again become an animal without light. But the reason for the severance of this light is that if seen by the darker forces it would arouse their antagonism. Only afterwards does he realise that he still possesses it and can use it.

This world might be called hell; but it is not the hell of orthodox religions. We must study its various densities and atomic structures, its illusions as well as truths; for we are to descend still deeper until we reach the greatest depth of evil and intolerance.

As we review our animal past when we worshipped the forces of evil as our gods, we realise that intolerance affects us on the higher levels also, and that here we can attack the roots of this evil and destroy it.

In these hells we see how we worshipped the blood of our victims and sacrificed them regardless of their sufferings, how we in turn were likewise tormented. So we learn that we cannot inflict sufferings without paying the penalty.

These regions are easily charted, as one can chart places on higher levels, and many books could be written about them.

Unknown to the student, the Architect atom sends an intelligence from the Nous atom, when he is in these lower regions, to protect him from serious affliction upon his return from these depths when these lower conditions may attack him.

This intelligence is the student's guiding star during his pilgrimage and watches over him, allowing nothing to terrify him beyond that point wherein he would be injured. He is not aware of it until he is called upon to withstand this ordeal of burial in the depths of his lower conditions; it then appears before him, shining and protective.

The beauty of these lower spheres is intensified, for the denizens use their arts for the glorification of their own persons, and appear in an evil loveliness far beyond any ever witnessed in the pageants of the stage. They are robed in the evil of their spheres, and one can sympathise with the ancient anchorites in that they were probably tempted beyond endurance; for this evil encircles one in an atmosphere of intensified mental lust and passion.

The best we can do for those dwelling here is to encourage them and show them how to ascend to a higher state of consciousness. A great Initiate rules and seeks to direct them towards a higher level. He wears an iron band about his forehead and his face is unforgettable. He reminds one of an old Coptic legend about two brothers. One descended into the lower spheres to minister to imprisoned souls. The other came to Palestine to bring light to the darkness in man's heart. Hermogenes and his twin brother Jesus were the names given in this legend.

Thus one realises that, however low man sinks, there is always an Initiate friend sent to lift him when he aspires to ascend.

Here we meet great instructors who would enslave us and use us, if possible, in this physical world. They often unite into groups and show us their powers over people working on Earth, and how they can control events by impregnating courtesans with their properties of lust and use them for political purposes. Nations who use courtesans in this manner are usually under the elemental sign of a woman.

The elemental properties these magicians use have been cast out from the moon and inserted into the lower portions of their instrument's bodies. These magicians build up a period of greatness about these courtesans until their purpose has been accomplished. They are then dethroned.

Students can often see these elemental properties about a person; they look like a swarm of bees. One should keep away from such environments; for people can be inflicted with such qualities, as one can catch an impure disease of a Venusian nature.

The magicians of these spheres know all the things of our world, and several organisations have been influenced by them. As we have previously said, certain areas of the world are under the protection of hierarchal beings. The world is also charted and comes under the influence of these magicians; yet they are limited in their power for evil, as the white forces only allow them to operate in order to teach the foolish student to become wise. So that in their future studies they will not practise magic through curiosity.

These magicians have the power to intensify speech, giving it a hypnotic influence. Preachers often feel this, and this is frequently the beginning of a religious revival that often increases sexual attraction. This can be proved by the increase in the birth-rate after the emotions of the people have been stirred. These magicians always seek to bring about sex worship, and children born under such conditions are generally unbalanced; while, later in life, their astral bodies are more easily impressed by the lower entities.

It is well known that where the light is brightest the shadows are darkest, and we have seen, when out of the body, places where a thin wall separated a temple of great holiness from a temple where the greatest evil was worshipped.

When we enter these spheres of intensified intellect we are told that we shall be given great power and their highest secret wisdom if we will but surrender our souls to them. The student is probably aware that there are schools of mental Yoga on earth teaching systems of logic that will eventually impress and direct minds as they wish, and such schools are like the schools of these magicians whose processes of logic will prove that black is white.

We never discuss or argue over spiritual things on the higher planes, but the lower spheres bring us in touch with scintillating intellect—not intelligence—that is almost overpowering, and we feel drawn to this magnetism which these sadistic and brilliant schoolmen possess. By argument they will show how beautiful evil is, that the world is ruled by evil, and that eventually we must succumb to their master's direction.

The student is almost lost in the cruelty of these spheres and is given instruction, which, he is told, would shake the foundations of the mental atmosphere if applied to this physical world. But when he returns to normal conditions the Innermost will give him an antidote to balance him. This will be a sense of justice.

About this time a type of atomic substance brings a consciousness into the student's mind that has within it the "Precious balm of Gilead." It reaches far beyond what we would class as good or evil, for it contains, we are told, the source of what could be called the good of evil and the evil of good. But these qualities are equally balanced.

In our Transformation period we are intermittently given this "balm of Gilead," and some day, when we have evolved beyond our body and its structures, we shall enter this element and be beyond what is called good and evil.

This golden consciousness will then reveal to us our individual path and give us a period of rest, absolute in our own world and to all that is within it. Here we are given that peace and serenity called Nirvana by those Yogis who have breathed in its perfume. And we are greeted and recognised as those who have at last returned from a long pilgrimage of labour and experience.

During the coming century this bliss will be given to many.

In these submerged worlds the student reads his past records and sees when, owing to great evil and sufferings on his part, he began to seek an inner and higher security and prayed for such guidance. This then contacted him with the powers of good who instructed him regarding his daily life.

These Beings came to us in our Lemurian days; they taught us to build temples wherein they could place their teraphim and through them teach the people.

In those days we had skins like animals, with whom we could communicate as we possessed similar instinctive attributes. We also communicated with our own tribes by the aid of signs and symbols, and could utter sounds that resembled the cries of children and infants. We were also taught the use of sounds by the teraphims who could analyse our desires and project their intelligences into our astral bodies; for, though our mentalities were slowly developing, we could not convey our thoughts save through an astral consciousness. As we evolved we learned to converse by the aid of certain musical sounds.

In these submerged worlds swirling hosts of entities swarm about us and impart to us their atmospheres of misery and pray to us for help. Each entity would like individual attention and question us about the spheres above. They seem hopeless. Their light is shrouded and they have no power to levitate. They ask us to assist them to carry their thoughts inwardly.

At certain times these entities are driven into another sphere where they are assembled to receive two kinds of instruction: from their own evil intelligences, and from brighter Beings. We often see these higher Beings descend into these lower levels in order to raise the vibrations of these submerged people.

This descent into one's own past is symbolised in the task of Hercules cleaning the Augean stables.

When the teacher takes the student out of his body and has taught him to travel, he sometimes takes him into these lower realms to assist another student who has misjudged his powers and is in difficulty.

Many people when asleep pass unconsciously into these lower states and minister to those in distress. We have met several friends doing this constantly. We have listened to them in this dim twilight address countless multitudes, hoping that some would get a realisation of truth and aspire inwardly for their own star of deliverance.

Certain great intelligences who govern these lower worlds are past masters in dissimulation, and are interested in such work. Sometimes they will reveal themselves to us and we find them to be disguised saviours.

The student now learns that that which is called hell he himself has created, and only by nullifying and controlling his lower nature can he bask in the sunlight of eternal youth.

To bring the hidden lustre in man to birth he must be polished by the dust of the ages until his inner luminosity shines forth to ennoble a dark world.

In these lower spheres the student is often commanded to do things that will bring sufferings upon those against whom he directs his powers. This will make the student realise that if he is approached by a radiant Being who commands him to do things, this Being must be of an evil nature, who, if challenged, would be forced to reveal his true character. Moreover, he will break promises made to us: and this no Initiate will do.

In these lower spheres we can use the knowledge given us by the sylphs: the power of disintegrating a lower elemental substance, a secret power we often use when visiting the insane whose mental structures have been distorted by the hypnotic force of evil minds. Everyone has some kind of secret vice and through these evil minds direct their attacks. Vanity and self-esteem are the usual weaknesses that they intensify. The impersonal mind escapes such destructive forces; but not the mind arrogant and self-determined.

After the student has been shown the evil of this world, for several months he will feel that there is little to live for, having learned how the mind and body can be debased by animal natures and the seemingly innocent tormented.

This world can show little that can compare with the ingenuity in these lower spheres, where minds have a powerful mastery over others and can only be classed as demons seemingly beyond hope.

The law reads thus: "Man will reflect his own real character into the heavens as well as into the hells. He must choose his own future abiding place."

Fortunately for the world, these forces are divided into two opposing camps that wage war against each other. When one side has been able to hold the other in subjection, the victors slowly begin to approach the higher levels and in time appear in the atmosphere of the world. As multitudes pour forth this causes the defeated to rise again, and when a war ends on this earth it is because these atoms have to return to their lower spheres in order to retain their power over others.

Those leaders of a warlike nature governed by the Secret Enemy's atoms lose the intensity of direction they formerly possessed, are thus defeated.

In these depths can be seen a warlike nation with its great generals seeking to inspire war upon earth as well as in their own spheres; for there is never a truce between these demoniacal forces, and when approaching them we register their evil within our own structures, shudder in realisation of what war truly is as practised and understood by these gigantic forces of the underworld.

A dim twilight overshadows these regions, and they have a pattern world as in the higher spheres. In their museums are the latest developments in aerial and submarine armaments, including instruments dealing with astral and mental warfare. These models are minute, and could be placed in a wineglass. The reason for this is that the human mind can grasp them in their entirety if they are small.

On these lower planes are schools of trained observers who concentrate upon these images in order to visualise them. They then impress them into the sensitive membranes of the inventor's mind. When one observer gets tired another immediately takes his place, in order that the pressure should be constant.

These methods are also used on the higher planes; for good has to combat evil and invent instruments that will nullify its opponent's effects.

The Secret Enemy is using poison gas as one of its greatest inventions, not only for use against man but also against agriculture. In every field of scientific investigation the enemy seeks for mediums.

Here we can witness man's folly in creating enmity between nations and what methods are used to produce sudden outbreaks. Politicians are frequently used for these purposes.

The reader will now probably realise why Yogis seek release from further incarnations in this world.

The Initiates send us this welcome message: "In this new age many will follow the Law and keep it." This means that many will attune themselves to the energy of the Dayspring of Youth, and a nation's wealth will consist in its moral attainments; for they will have to choose their own paths: whether for good or evil, and history teaches us that they who take the wrong path are destroyed by Nature's upheavals.

In these submerged worlds we watch these brilliant and intense minds combine into a collective energy for the purpose of bringing disharmony into industry and commerce. These minds are great students and past masters in the laws of wealth. They devise ways and means of increasing a man's wealth in order that they can later use it as an instrument of destruction.

Plato has said: "The best government is that government that does the most for its poorest individuals." In the great international congress that we see assembling in the future great ideals will become laws, and several nations will unite to advance the prosperity of all within their boundaries. The nation that will seek to promote its growth at the expense of the weaker will in time be placed in a similar position.

In a book by an Initiate I have read: "As men will gather about their own doorways they will be placed within their own council chambers and be made to read their own laws." This means that when man is inwardly developed he will discover his own place and position in Nature. We also read: "As long as man is blinded by his own passions and desires so long will he be held prisoner."

The student now descends into still greater densities in order to recover his lost knowledge. Here he beholds the Great Intelligence who offers him its powers and reveals its truths. He shudders at its range of domination. It awakens within him memory of natural magic and his evil possessions of those days; for though he has suffered the penalty in his past evil he still possesses such atoms. Here he has to accomplish a difficult task, to nullify their mentality so that they can no longer operate within the lower centres of his physical body.

BLACK MAGICIAN

It is done in this manner: we first secure the information these atoms possessed and seek inwardly for the power to purify their atmospheres. But in seeking guidance we evoke their opposition, and this brings swarms of evil entities that hover and cling about us during this period, and these we also attempt to levitate to a higher plane.

When we bring light to our lower atoms they will serve us. Yogis call them the Informers; for they become instruments that will inform us about the operations of our Secret Enemy.

At this time we encounter their overlords, who to terrify us with their nocturnal atmospheres seemingly shout their desires with a deadening thud of positive power upon our Silver Shields; though behind them we feel secure.

When we encounter a magician, we use our own powers of magic in order to relieve them, for a time, from their mental agony—for these magicians suffer intensely however great their powers—and in gratitude they ask our pardon for having interfered in our work. We seek to heal their minds and raise them into clearer atomic atmosphere.

Thus do we learn a new law: that we can raise people from one vibration to another that will momentarily relieve them of their misery. We also find that whilst doing this work we are removing similar conditions from our own lower bodies.

This kind of work lasts some time, and it depend upon our service to others how long we are to continue in such work before we are freed from the strata of our lower nature.

In these hells appear people clad and engaged in similar occupations as when on earth. This is of an illusionary nature though very real to them. Here we see great agony; for people of a like nature are brought together and their earthly habits are exposed for all to see. The naturally secretive mind cannot hide, and as it realises this its sufferings increase.

The student witnesses the criminal mind brooding over its deeds, and countless beings who have to be classified and driven into compact sections under the guidance of Light Bringers whose work is to increase the growth of inner realisations. Many surprising things occur in the criminal sections, and one often meets people whom one knew when they were alive.

Priests, who have been destructive on earth, are also found here, as well as those who have given their souls into the keeping of others. Their features are moulded by the atmosphere of these places: elongated, fishlike eyes, and emaciated faces that always glance at one sideways as though fearing discovery.

Those who break physical laws are placed apart from those who break spiritual laws, and each type has its own particular odour. These two kinds are very destructive and can shelter themselves within the astral fluid of a medium's body. When using such for public work they can intensify the imagination of the audience and lead their minds into abnormal ranges of thought.

The religious section—though intensely intellectual and only meeting their own kind—live in such dullness that eventually they are forced to seek inwardly for the greater light that will bring them into incarnation. We have often seen noble priests clothed in their vestments surrounded by these types who try to argue against their teachings. They are helpers whom we aid whenever possible.

The method of conversation with these submerged people is through telepathy, and we are told that in the deeper states we have to use the ancient vowel sounds about which we have previously spoken.

No evil entity can attach itself to us unless we attract it by thought or by being negative in our actions. The negative medium, easily evoking these lower conditions, causes her astral body to become infected with these parasital forms that drain her vitality; these sap her life force and account for her abnormal appetite.

This shows the necessity for a clean body and mind and good health. Sick and sensitive people have more to contend with than is realised: for they attract the larvae of these submerged states.

In the new age we shall be afflicted with mental disorders, and because of this the Silver Shield must be developed in order to become immune from unnatural conditions. Surgeons and doctors of the future will have to develop themselves to understand such; for there are few in the Western area who can minister with understanding to these strange cases that are already beginning to manifest, as few of them have opened their third eye that perceives what the normal ones cannot register, though we have met some clean-minded doctors who are unconsciously clairvoyant and instinctively recognise such cases.

The student will now begin to analyse the forces of evil that work on earth, and he will often be in communication with adepts living in remote parts of the world. Here he will learn a system of Yoga that will hasten his lower development, and he will realise that he is being watched by many eyes; for, if he has been faithful, they will exert a united pressure to advance him as rapidly as possible. Western Yoga, being a method of quick development owing to the fact that we have not the leisure of the East, and there being so few workers in the West, it is necessary to prepare numbers of adepts in time for the manifestation of the Great Initiate, who has come, though he has not revealed himself. And, just as the great Nazarene had His seventy secret disciples who awaited His coming, so are there a number being prepared and awaiting in the West.

In the future humanity will be given information, now hidden, about the lamas, priests and prophets who had secluded themselves in order to aid man in his development. We will then learn that these great souls are a united power who advance the spiritual and moral welfare of the world. And the student must always be alert to receive communications from China, Tibet and other parts of the world; particularly from America, where there are a number of them. He easily receives such messages from these great distances; for thought exceeds electricity in swiftness.

Some of these teachers and their pupils may seem strange to us; for they do not conform to our methods of life, and at first may appear very simple-minded and childlike; yet within their own range of vibration they far excel those who are called cultivated and educated according to the standards of Harvard and Oxford.

It will probably interest the reader to know that neither the student nor his teacher know of their destined end until three months or a short time before.

The deeper the student enters his interior worlds and their opposition, the more latent becomes his so-called personality; for the knowledge he gains will not endow him with those qualities that the business man seeks to acquire, and one of the great arts of a Yogi is to withdraw his personality, though his words will remain for ever in one's mind. This power can be so far developed that he can almost eradicate memory of his personal appearance. This means that Yogis can manipulate their atmospheres so that the mind does not register their vibrations. This is a peculiar form of invisibility; though not dematerialisation. From experience we have known a teacher to appear at a great crisis and afterwards suddenly vanish.

As we enter the lower states we do not at first respond to their atomic conditions, our minds are apt to be confused, and our astral and mental bodies take on the appearance of the moon's elemental period, giving them an elongated shape, and we resemble the work of some of our modern sculptors who have been able to reach back to their primitive ancestry and attract atomic substances of such ages.

If we analyse the trend of thought silently working in the youth of to-day, we shall find rebellion against the so-called academic expression in art. For these men have awakened within themselves these faint echoes of a far-away past beyond form and its different attributes, and as they work from remote pasts, so do we hope that they will work from remote futures wherein the atomic substances of the sun will manifest.

When the discerning eye gazes at the modern works of such men, it will see that they have arrived at the realisation of things unnoticed by this age.

In the lower spheres as well as in the higher we find an intensity of expression that in the future will pass into the artistic expression of the world. Beauty is not called beauty here, but the symbol of what the Innermost desires us to respond to; it is the expression of the Reality manifesting through form.

The student will often seek among artists and sculptors those who have developed their Silver Shields: unfortunately he will meet but few who possess this development, and therefore that light comes from the Innermost.

In the middle period of the new age those artists who have missed their vocations and had to work for material things—not being able to express themselves creatively—will be given freedom to express themselves.

When evil artists work they sometimes unconsciously draw on a source that is beyond good or evil, and for this their evil genius punishes them.

Artists and sculptors are often natural Yogis; for when they lose themselves in their work they follow a natural direction wherein are three atoms that bring to a Yogi that state of unconscious bliss—a form of Nirvana—and at such moments a Rembrandt or a Velazquez will place into a work that substance that will make it a masterpiece and control the minds of those who study it. Whistler acknowledged that it was the last twenty minutes of unconscious work that made the portrait of his mother, placed in the Luxembourg Museum, a masterpiece. In such works we find that the imprint of the brush was seemingly done without effort, with precision and surety, making these pictures beyond price.

The world has treated our artists without regard to their sensitivity, and tries to corral them into their own planes of thought. Commercial and industrial minds have often enslaved geniuses in order, as they say, "To make a commercial bargain."

When the works of great artists are analysed, it is frequently found that they worked on a scientific foundation, and many of their discoveries were far ahead of their time. Claude Monet, whose theories of colour were first ridiculed and afterwards proved scientifically correct, is an instance. Michael Angelo, Leonardo da Vinci, Rembrandt and others can also be cited.

The student will discover that no physical or mental creation is ever lost, and he will find in the higher and lower worlds museums wherein they are still exhibited. Here we see bad as well as good art, and one is surprised at the evil creations left by the abnormal and perverted artists of Rome and Atlantis. Amid such creations the student is left alone, and he registers within his lower nature similar qualities possessed by these works. He would often wish to destroy these things created by ignorant and low minds; for they influence young artists with inferior atoms, who then multiply the productions of these evil works.

The Secret Enemy constantly attempts to interfere with those stimulated by the higher planes that give the artist a clarity of perception, and distorts their minds till they lose their contact and original purpose. Therefore an artist should not reveal his work until it is completed, as the Secret Enemy will use his friends to criticise and dishearten him. Some of the world's greatest masterpieces have been destroyed in this way by the intrusion of an outsider. Coleridge's unfinished poem "Kubla Khan" is one classic instance.

The Secret Enemy will attempt to impress creative types with the element of laziness, and those within its power talk with great authority about the arts but produce very little. Hard physical work is needed for all kinds of artists; for a sound body—as we have previously said—gives one a positive mind, and the weaklings of the artistic professions are seldom energised by their inner and higher systems.

We hope that these teachings will help youth to attain wisdom during their youth and strength—for art is an ideal carried to its completion—and youth frequently wastes its supreme moments dallying by the wayside.

There are different sciences taught by different systems of Yoga, and some deal with these submerged worlds. Students are taught to evoke these conditions and govern them, also clarify the atmospheres of people who have attracted them.

In all this work the student must not follow his inclinations but seek inwardly for right direction. He must not seek personal power; but if he is faithful he will in time be placed where he can aspire for power over Nature and serve her impersonally. Just as the carpenter has to learn his trade and the use of his tools, so must the student serve his apprenticeship under more advanced associates of his school.

The Western mind is a very busy one, lacking the tranquillity of the Eastern mind, and the Western Yogi must work out his salvation from within and not from without.

Passing into the lower spheres is like being buried; for the student enters an atmosphere foreign to his nature, and it takes him some time to awaken to it and remember his previous experiences in this denser region and the evil he did there. Yet, though this is all seemingly real, he knows inwardly that it is illusory.

The student meets an Instructor in these inner planes who asks him why he is there and what is his relationship to them. The student will then slowly realise that he possesses elements of an animal and evil nature, yet will also feel a binding cord connecting him to his Innermost, and this will give him a strong feeling of protection and faith. Then as he rises back to this physical world he will feel that he is constantly being reborn. In short: descent means death; ascent birth.

When people die they are still imprisoned in their astral shells. This is the fluidic substance that registers their passions and desires, and these elements hold them earthbound; for a thin cord connects them to their decomposing bodies. This is the apparition that haunts graveyards, and it takes considerable time before the soul can break from this astral connection.

In the early days of Christianity the elders or priests were able to pass out of their bodies and minister to a follower at the moment of death; they would penetrate the three belts of illusion—Purgatory—that encircle the earth, break this astral cord by a process of levitation or by a chant of a mantric quality, and take him to a place of awakening where he would be looked after by helpers of that plane. This is not always heaven, but those spheres that reflect the released soul's true character.

Many may wonder why people are buried near a church. The origin of this custom was that the tolling of the bell vibrated on the astral cord and snapped it. The ceremony of the Mass for the Dead was also to release the soul. Students are sometimes sent into churchyards to sever these cords through intense concentration, also to master fear.

Fear is one of the things the student must conquer; for in the lower spheres he will be brought face to face with things of a terrible nature, as the Secret Enemy uses fear as one of its weapons and will attack the student with apparitions similar to the Dweller on the Threshold.

The elemental forces easily reading our true nature will often seek to terrorise us if we walk into their territory. This is why so many sensitive people are afraid of the dark and do not like to walk at night through woods. The Yogi registers these conditions, analyses them, pauses a moment, then sends all his love into such places. The reader should try these experiments when he feels this fear. He will then find that this fear will be suddenly withdrawn, and when he again enters such a place he will feel a welcome coming to him; for he is recognised as one who would not destroy but love Nature. Gardens will also respond to one who sends them love.

The student is also instructed how to take entities that haunt places back to their own spheres; for they have generally been evoked from their normal conditions and must be assisted back. It is this desire for help that causes them to sometimes appear before a person. Magicians frequently use lower elementals to shock the mind of a sensitive.

Some old families who have been prominent in the history of a nation often have a composite elemental force of evil overshadowing them, and it sometimes takes many centuries to dispel such forces. In the old days magicians who had been ill-treated knew how to manipulate elemental powers in the form of hereditary curses.

There is more black magic going on today than people are aware of, and there are many organisations that worship evil deliberately and seek to destroy anything of a spiritual nature.

The people in the lower states who still cling to their worldly appetites are seemingly helpless; for they have not left a pressure of love behind them to elevate them to higher spheres, and love is one of the white magician's most powerful instruments to aid the evolution of man, and the love souls leave behind them is an immeasurable force that will assist them to regain their inner possessions. Some races knowing this teach their children to keep them in remembrance and pray for them.Those who do so should not seek to attract them back to the world, but should send them aspiration to rise higher.

The average man believes that when he dies he will have rest from all labour and enjoy himself; but he will find life active there as here. The atheist who does not believe in life after death finds himself within a shell that holds him prisoner for centuries.

When a person dies he is met by an angel who has recorded all his past inner and outer deeds, and he reviews and must judge and balance these deeds alone. This will cause him to gravitate to his own level. At the same time his Advocate will impress him to place his case in his hands and will seek to gain the notice of the Innermost and place the man's case before It. And if he earnestly seeks forgiveness he will be given justice tempered with mercy.

The Angel of Death does not possess the nature of the Secret Enemy, though he appears in a neutral grey garment, and he assists and guides the soul protectively through the densities of the physical atmosphere. The sensitive feels its presence by a rustling of wings in the air. This will undoubtedly sound imaginative, nevertheless it is true.

This Being is not elemental but belongs to a different order of intelligence that has accompanied each individual from a remote evolution. This angel was given us as a sign: that we are never without help from our Creator. It possesses the elements of all our natures and of the Reality.

There are different kinds of death just as there are different kinds of life. What is death for one person can sometimes be life to another. When one who is far above his fellows in development dies, his cast-off atmospheres can stimulate those possessing lower atomic structures. We breathe fine as well as foul matter, just as dead leaves nourish new life. This is why the relics of a saintly person are supposed to heal the body and illuminate the mind.

The realisation that comes to us when we are conscious of our Innermost's presence makes us look upon our physical and mental worlds from different angles, and we realise why we have incarnated in this age. This gives us the courage to pay off our karmic debts and inwardly seek for our release. Our Yoga practice gives us that determination to increase our inner relationship and work as our Innermost desires regardless of our surroundings.

This is why we have spoken so much about our lower animal spheres in order that the student should seek and aspire inwardly for his Silver Shield and bring to birth his own inner and secret power so that he might be beyond his own time and place.

CHAPTER EIGHTEEN
THE SILVER SHIELD

AFTER we have developed our power to attract the Aspiring atoms and have reviewed our past lives we begin to practise another kind of breathing to attract atoms that will protect our minds from outside interference: these are the Transformation atoms. They build about the lining of our mental body what is called the Silver Shield, formed from those atoms that in time will vibrate and immerse us into a higher wave-length. It is a mental atmosphere possessing the qualities of our wisdom experience, and when this is built up it becomes the temple for the Master atom of the mind-body, who ascends from the seminal system and there illuminates our minds. It is also a receiving station and condenser for the vibration of the Innermost and the higher counterpart of elemental Nature.

The quality and size of this Silver Shield depends upon the quality of the student's aspiration and his powers of attracting the Transformation atoms to his nasal grid and into his bloodstream. Later on we will describe the method of breathing to develop this shield.

The development of the Silver Shield is our real important work and needs time and patience; for such atoms are not easily attracted. These shield us from the interference of our submerged self and those conditions attracted to us the moment our atmosphere radiates atoms of an aspiring nature.

The calls of the past are difficult to eradicate from our atmosphere; for they contain atoms that would place the mind in their periods.

The new vibration of the Transformation atoms is very subtle, and one's sensitivity increases and is difficult to analyse. Though the student is not conscious of its approach after his first immersion in this wave-length, and though he will seem normal, this vibration will be difficult to bear and will cause him suffering.

If possible, the student should try to go into retreat in the country where there will be mental quietness and therefore little to interfere with his practice.

This is a period through which most of the ancient anchorites passed; for the conditions that infest the atmosphere repeatedly plunges the student into his own borderland, between his protective shield and atmosphere. This is like an army attacking a fortress shielded by an outer pallisade wherein swarms of evil entities hover, seeking entrance into the atmosphere of this powerful atomic substance composed of Transformation atoms.

The student is now a light in a dark world, and the mentally evil attack him whenever possible. This excites and disturbs the student very easily.

This struggle lasts longer than we desire; for, though shielded, we are not immune from thought-activity of a worldly nature. This is a period of instruction when we listen-in to the Master atom after it has entered the Silver Shield.

The student will now have to shoulder burdens others cast upon him. Before he can carry on his true work he is often plunged into the world of commerce, and, being very sensitive, this sometimes makes him unhappy. He will later discover how to help the people among whom he works; for he will be able to analyse what is needed for their betterment. Like a surgeon, he will discover what canker to remove in order to help the troubled mind.

We should remember that there are very few who can work consciously under the direction of their teachers, and there are students who assist in bearing the burdens of the Great Initiates.

Teachers will sometimes reveal their accomplishments and tasks in order that their pupils may realise their future possibilities, and show them that they are part of a great universal plan. Every man has his place in this vast scheme, even though he is ignorant of it. By Yoga practice we seek to work in harmony with this universal stream that creates, guides, and aspires all to become part of its intelligence. The seeker will attain to this does he but aspire; if not in this life, then in another.

Both the Aspiration and Transformation atoms have their own symbols. The radiations from an atom give it an apparent form; and this is often used as a symbol. The symbol of the Transformation atom is like a trident or inverted crossbow. This symbol is also used by the Brahmins, and the Silver Shield is known to them as the instrument of the mind-body.

The workings of the mind are not understood by Western psychologists. In their task of charting the brain and nervous system they have not yet discovered how thought acts upon the brain.

On our Silver Shield are a multitude of node points. When a thought is brought to them they transfer into the cell life of the brain their vibratory energy; this also brings to us information from other planetary systems.

The Silver Shield takes up a large area and upon it is the chart of our solar system. Its lower counterpart is the surface of the brain, but, being imprisoned within the skull, it has to be crumpled up. Hence the convolutions within it.

Each node on the outer membrane is attuned to its special kind of thought. If we send the thought of love, the node point of the receiver attracts it and sends it inwardly to the cell life of the brain vibrating to it.

The normal brain receives these impulses from these node points situated on the silken membrane of the mind-body.

Just as the physical body receives nourishment from food that causes atomic stimulation, so does the mind-body receive nourishment from its surrounding atmosphere.

It is interesting to note that when one fasts, after a few days one becomes mentally stimulated, for the densities of the body do not impede the mind by pressing on it.

The Master atom of the Silver Shield is a migratory atom of the seminal fluid. Its energy typifies the inherited strength of the student's ancestors, until over-shadowed by the energy of the Innermost. One often wonders why so few men have minds strong enough to begin and complete a thing of merit. If a man's ancestors have been dissipated and weak through un-natural lusts his Master atom is weak likewise. This is why the student is told to conserve his vitality in order that he may become aware of his mental strength.

We rarely respect minds enfeebled by dissipation; for as we develop into our secondary system we see the necessity for strength and vitality.

We have a reserve of nervous energy stored at the base of the brain; if this is wasted it is difficult to think with power and precision unless our supply of this energy is phenomenal. To succeed in this world we must retain sufficient energy to rise above our fellows. Heedlessly wasted energy shortens one's life considerably. Arabs possess a certain method of building up and conserving their energy when making forced journeys.

In various ancient books the departure of the Master atom from the seminal fluid into the Silver Shield is spoken of symbolically as man uprooting old conditions and transplanting the roots to the head. When this occurs we are given an intelligence that has been denied us for many lives, as our forsaken energies again begin to function.

The Master atom now halts us in our path and presents things from several unfamiliar angles. We begin to view conditions from within and the wisdom from our collected experience of past lives.

The Master atom attracts atoms that bring the exact record of our inheritance received from our mental and physical ancestors.

The Master atom teaches us that we possess unlimited schools of instruction, and from them we gain our ultimate wisdom. But this can only be revealed to us if we have attained a certain standard of purity in this and other lives. Nature's wisdom also gave us security and protection in our remote lives.

During the Atlantean upheaval they who had attained to this wisdom were preserved, and the future security of a race or person will depend upon the protective power of their Silver Shields.

Man is placed between two opposing densities of matter: one represents freedom, the other conquest. Freedom is enlightenment; conquest is destructive.

We have to be placed between these two atomic pressures, and the atomic energy of the sun attracts and unites these opposites.

The law of opposition is the law of attraction. The man who strikes you in a moment of anger has attracted a force from you that unites your mind to his. This is one of the so-called hidden laws of Nature. Opposition attracts two forces to unite their atoms. It is said that a "Soft voice turneth away wrath." This is the law: if one does not oppose a thing it is difficult for it to unite itself to one. Yogis have to learn this law in the jungles of life where each man preys upon the other.

There are many things humanity is not taught: simple laws needed in moments of emergency that those who pass into their inner barriers understand. Such are used for the protection of self and others. The human mind is easily illusioned by the atoms of the Silver Shield, evil is often prevented by means of illusion, and we have frequently read about adepts becoming invisible.

We cannot tell how long the student will have to remain under the instruction of the Master atom of the Silver Shield. This depends upon his own efforts, as he has to transmute the density of his mental atmosphere into its wave-length.

This Master atom can dispel the activities of the Secret Enemy at the base of the spine. It has many atoms under it that can instruct us.

The human body possesses many sheaths. In the lower sheath is a Master atom that can be called upon to perform miracles. Once we gain its instruction, we shall be under its authority for two or three incarnations. This was used by the ancients, for they understood the lower self and its surrounding sheaths of matter. It is not spoken about save by those initiated into its wisdom, and we only become aware of it through the teachings of the Master atom in the Silver Shield. But we are not permitted to write about it, as it will become known and analysed in the new era.

Among the esoteric Hebrews this was called the Manna of the desert, though not that which was gathered from the sands, and this knowledge is guarded in the Temple of the Sphinx.

When we begin building up our Silver Shield we worked under the Transformation atoms. Before that under the

Aspiring atoms and a sun influence that ejected from our physical body old particles of matter that absorbed our energy but did not promote our growth. But now we pass under the influence of the moon.

This moon force now takes us into its schools of instruction, and we pass beyond the range of our normal vision into periods of illumination that had been hidden from us. It has a different atomic structure from others; for the etheric currents flowing into it divide it into several streams of intelligence and we must unite ourselves to them. This will give us the perception to discover several kinds of animal entities, and realise that though we are human we are not immune from their astral activities.

Here it is that we can reach backward and forward into immensities of Nature and discover that wisdom we once possessed, also the ignorance of the beings found there. We now enter realms of unconquered darkness, as well as that supreme wisdom symbolised by the Sphinx; for this great elemental is the guardian of our ancient knowledge relating to natural law.

As the student enters this period of illumination he witnesses those great streams of intelligence that had left the moon aeons back to build up and work over our earth until it reached its own Transformation period: this was what we now call one of its golden ages. These Beings were similar to a nomadic chain, that is: an interlaced intelligence.

As we gaze into this vast depth of the past we wonder over and reverence the great commonwealth that is slowly being built up; we follow it into the future, and realise what wealth and prosperity is to be the portion of the Western area. But now we also witness those periods of darkness when a nation separates itself from its guiding influence; when it no longer seeks its Innermost but worships Mammon.

The consciousness of the Silver Shield gives the student a regal bearing. This comes when he contacts the atoms of the moon; for it is possible for him to possess the summit of its past wisdom; those qualities he had developed in its constructive and destructive aspects, and before he became imprisoned in the moist atmosphere of this earth. From this he will realise that in the past he had attained wisdom and power now denied him.

The moon symbolises man's own secret wisdom that will be revealed to him when he returns into his inner planes. When the student inhales the properties of the intelligence he will then find his own sacred and scientific literature.

This new kind of atom is, mentally, similar to the Secret Enemy but is beyond evil, though it can bring to us the Secret Enemy's powers and give the student part of its consciousness. The student now enters his underworld and meets two opposing forces: the wisdom of our Innermost and that of the Secret Enemy.

The light we receive from the moon also brings foreign atoms that disturb our atmosphere as they collect into clusters, and agitate the nerve cells that are under the jurisdiction of the sun. Thus sensitive people are nervous when the moon is full. These un-pleasant sensations cause the node points of the mental sheath to reflect their agitated conditions into us.

The moon influences us to deep inspirational tendencies. When this occurs it is well to listen-in; for its lunar atoms can impart their periods of instruction and assist us to revert to an ancient wisdom religion.

The human body is subject to two forces: that of the sun, and that of the moon. During the day, the sun's pressure holds back the germinating forces within us, and this preserves our vitality. The night current of the moon seeks to draw out this stored-up vitality. This is why animals, save those with a non-conductor about their feet, keep them off the ground at night in order not to be devitalised.

CHAPTER NINETEEN
THE ELEMENTAL ADVOCATE

WHEN we develop our latent forces and balance the solar and lunar circuits within our secondary or sympathetic nervous system, we come in touch with an elemental Advocate of whom we were unaware, and whose work is similar to our other Advocate. We created him when we were elemental in our nature and evolved him through aspiration of an elemental character.

When we bring these two Advocates into union we are surrounded by the atoms of the elemental worlds as well as the atoms of aspiration. As soon as this elemental Advocate manifests, we are given a sword—that had been locked within us—possessing administrative powers that will develop our possessions. With it we sever the Gordian knot that had held these secrets intact within our atomic centres.

Nature's sounding boards now begin to open, and we receive and sense the operation of her laws within us.

The science of Yoga determines our progress into Nature's secrets. When we enter her spheres we are bound to serve her: for she has a resonant voice that places us within her citadel, and with her at our back our progress is rapid.

There are many different systems of Yoga; but Nature's science is the one adapted for Western bodies; for the analytic and scientific Western mind needs demonstration and fact. We can devote our lives to meditation and prayer, and gain great purity of thought; we can sever ourselves through love from the activities of the opposition by taking the path of the mystic, but later we realise that we must build up our own framework and seek to erect our own temples in full consciousness of each step. The Western mystic seldom does this; for present-day conditions prevent him from retreating from the world to pass his time in prayer and devotion and gain union with his Innermost. We should also realise that the new hierarchal consciousness will not revert us to past methods of Yoga.

Just as within the lower spheres are helpers who have passed out of their bodies, so are there elemental helpers to assist those in whom elemental qualities predominate.

These realms are hard to reach, and little has been recorded about them in literature by the seers who generally record things dealing with the lower planes encircling the earth.

In the reign of the Emperor Charlemagne the elemental people entered our atmosphere deeply; from this period sprang the Romantic literature of the Round Table and King Arthur and his knights.

We are told that in the Dayspring of Youth, Nature will again reveal her presence and assemble her powers so that her elemental people will be seen. This means that the gods will again walk the earth and elemental Nature again be reverenced.

With the bringing forth of our elemental Advocate we can live within the vibratory orbit of our inner worlds and Nature's spheres, and thus register both systems. The Fatherhood and Motherhood of the Reality are expressed through these twin Advocates: the thought-creation of the best within us and that created from the best elemental qualities of our elemental nature.

There will come a time in the student's development when he will disintegrate his twin Advocates and return them to their own elements. Thus freeing them from further incarnations of service. The student always senses this longing to return to their true elements. As they say: "Our duties end when you return to your abode in your central system."

These twin Advocates have always served us regardless of our descents into the lower atmospheres and into evil. They have watched us through many distant lives as well as these later ones when we divorced ourselves from the sovereignty of the Earth currents; for these etheric waves of Nature are manipulated by these Advocates so that we can respond to their vibration. Thus through their aid we open Nature's store-house and read the records of an elemental world.

Ignorant psychics or seers often tell us that in some incarnation we were fighting in the Crusades; for they see a shining

Being clad in chain armour or bearing a shield with a symbol upon it. But this is one's elemental guardian and not ourselves in some former life; neither were we kings because the Advocate they see looks kingly.

In one's self-developed universe reside atoms of great power and endurance, possessing the nature of the elemental Advocate, and, like chieftains who observe those under their domains, they work unceasingly for their development. Such atoms serve us with their powers and they then direct us into our secondary system; they operate there as we do on this plane.

Our animal and human ancestors placed within us atoms possessing the characteristics of their seminal systems, and when we draw the filaments of our body together as we enter the womb of our mother, we find we possess certain hereditary traits that have been handed down to us. Several of these are unobserved: atoms that reach back to the beginning of our primordial creation, and when the student enters his secondary system he contacts these atoms that retain the memories of this remote ancestry. Thus we find within ourselves atoms that typify each past birth besides those of our fathers and mothers. These ancestral atoms wilt, if possible, revert us to inherited tendencies and make us express them. Anything that causes us to evoke them will cause us to resemble some characteristic we possessed in the past: just as an actor expresses a character in a play or scene. We can release ourselves from the domination of our ancestral inheritance only by entering our central system.

Ages ago we were elemental, but as we incarnated into the densities of matter we lost those qualities and lay in a state of oblivion regarding our past in Nature's consciousness. Our real instincts, buried beneath the ever-increasing energy of our atoms, could no longer respond to our own truth; and to-day we only intermittently and faintly remember such.

During the Atlantean upheaval our powers to revert to Nature's consciousness again dawned, and we were often guided by this ancient wisdom. We formed a system of Nature worship that was to help us contact her consciousness, and our ritual revealed within us a hidden sanctuary of a lost wisdom, and an understanding of our remote past.

The atoms that dispel our illusions are used by the two Advocates to keep our minds and imaginations balanced. Hysterical people are apt to dominate the mind-atmospheres of others, and distress them. People of a highly sensitive and emotional nature should aspire to their Advocates and ask them to distil their protective perfume into their minds.

The elemental Advocate is our instructor in natural magic. When we are guided by Nature we must sever ourselves from our old wave-length and begin to take on characteristics similar to the elemental Advocate who can then converse with us as the other Advocate does.

Many sensitives have felt the presence of two Beings within them. These are symbolised as the twins in the Zodiac by the third sign Gemini that contains the stars Castor and Pollux.

Some day, when man again obeys Nature's laws, he will have to re-establish the laws of this objective world. Man's own laws bring him destruction and unhappiness; Nature's laws take him into his own promised land where lies his forgotten inheritance. It is the duty of everyone to seek communion with Nature and aspire to again understand her laws. Instinct is Nature's memory. When we return to her rhythm this lost instinct will again rule our actions.

We are made from Nature's cast-off materials and we have little inner direction we can consciously claim as our own. We are told that if we submit to the teachings of religious instructors we shall gain an ideal existence; yet we are not given details as to what we are to do or to become after death.

The elemental Advocate possesses the supreme intelligence we attain to in elemental law and magic. It wishes to return to its own essence and bring into our normal consciousness its keynote, so that it can appear to us in this objective atmosphere. It has the sudden quickness of the Death atoms; for it can inflict death as well as restore what is seemingly dead. It can act both ways according to the nature of its master. But if the student obeys its governing intelligence and bids it to act, it will deliver many from their Death atoms and spread within them its elemental properties. The Advocate we have previously mentioned—its twin brother—will direct us regarding our proper relationship to our elemental Advocate.

When the Solar and Lunar currents are brought together in order to create a lightning conductor through which the Solar energy passes to liberate the Innermost from its prison house, we are then without any Advocates. The union of our positive and negative forces can bring about the disintegration of these twin luminaries when they have placed our karma before the Innermost's presence and have pleaded that our objective and elemental karma may be forgiven, and that we may now be placed within our tomb and be reborn without any stain of evil. This is the severance of those links that hold us to the consciousness of our own submerged animal spheres. This is what is meant by the forgiveness of our past sins; the severance of past conditions that still inject their waves of thought into our consciousness. These submerged animal pasts must be first nullified ere we can be prepared for rebirth by our Transformation atoms.

This elemental Advocate is the natural healer within us, a subtle power that will direct elemental vibrations to the six centres that will tune them to Nature's note. And the recovery of the patient will depend upon his response to this healing force.

When aspiring for purity of thought we contact our elemental Advocate. It teaches us the causes of many diseases of an elemental nature, and assists us to diagnose mental cases by relating us to the cause. It also helps us to heal them if the patient can respond and if his Innermost approves, though it will not allow us to work against Nature's laws.

When we do not respond to the direction of our Innermost it will refuse to interest itself in our lower nature; for we deny it the experience it wishes to gain, and when this occurs it will quickly allow the Death atoms to destroy the body. When we break Nature's laws and give way to lower desires our Administrator atoms rebel and cry out to the

Innermost to be relieved of the care and upkeep of the physical body that submerges them within a consciousness of hatred, lust, and anger; for they have to constantly combat such conditions, and are overworked beyond endurance, and as the Innermost has power over the body It will close it down and free them and Itself.

The elemental Advocate will often impress us to heal a sick soul, but this we must do impersonally. The patient's mind must be placed upon something the Innermost desires to experience, and when this is done It will immediately begin to build up Its body. Many Christian scientists and natural healers with lofty aspirations do this, though unaware that they are assisted by their elemental Advocate.

I have been told by my elemental Advocate that when I enter a sick room I should vibrate a certain centre; for one may not be rightly keyed to concert pitch. The doh note has fallen below the vibratory advance of civilisation, and is therefore below Nature's.

The East understands this thoroughly. Just as a student can be taught to see colour, so must humanity be taught to recognise modern music and not return to past conditions of melody. The student's notes will be a form of mantric music, and by these means he will learn how to open a centre within his body.

In order to radiate a positive atmosphere we must be very positive, and this will shield us from Nature's destructive forces. At this phase in our practice all the submerged rottenness of past generations will seek to rise into our normal sphere and destroy our mental and bodily health. If we then aspire we can gain the protection of our elemental Advocate; for when we ally ourselves to Nature's consciousness and seek her sovereignty the elemental Advocate will aid us, and its sword will be turned against our enemies. This sword is double-edged, and if we resist anything that manifests the character of our Innermost it will turn against us and give its allegiance to the Death atoms who will hasten our destruction. Hence, when we can contact this Advocate, it will help us in those things pertaining to our powers in elemental laws, and will teach us how to return to Nature's understanding and intelligence.

The prophets were men schooled in Nature's wisdom, whose laws became theirs. We shall realise that Nature's urge is her will seeking to manifest through us.

The student is shown the sphere where the prophets receive their swords of justice from their schools; the prophet being a destructive force whose laws are nearer to Nature than to man. Humanity has ever rebelled against their work, and has often crucified them; for they were many years in advance of their period. Those to whom this sword has been given on the inner planes have the power to direct their elemental Advocate to appear to their students when they are in need of protection from opposing forces. Sometimes the student will see this Being standing beside him clad like a knight in shining armour or an armed warrior of any period. At times he has appeared before martyrs to give them courage to meet their death, and teach them that beyond a certain range pain becomes pleasure.

Nature is a severe taskmaster; but if one aspires to regain his lost wisdom and understanding of her manifestations he is protected by his Advocate from the enmity of man in order to fulfil his mission. Thus he often dies without any recognition by the world till after death.

Humanity regards Nature as something that exists, though not as a conscious entity; but he should think of her as a just mother. One of the great principles Yoga has for man is that Nature is a great consciousness and that he should follow her laws and pass into her higher realms where peace reigns supreme. If Nature's higher laws were adopted by man he would have time and freedom to pursue the path of his individual development, and by so doing harm no one.

The king elementals refuse to descend into our illusion world; therefore we do not observe them working among us. Many people are very elemental in their atomic construction, and in their efforts to become themselves bring their genius to birth; but what they produce is seemingly misplaced effort, for it takes man a long time to recognise genius in their midst. When Whistler's painting of Battersea Bridge—now in the Tate Gallery—was judged by the Governors and hung at the Burlington Gallery, they did not know what it represented so hung it upside down: to-day any schoolboy could give an accurate description of it. Carlyle and Emerson were not understood save by a select few in their time, yet nowadays any educated person could read their works with understanding and pleasure.

The elemental Advocate watches over us in sleep and protects our bodies from outside influences that would wish to enter them. For we have often to travel long distances from our bodies, and the Silver Cord is stretched beyond its normal range. This cord—the higher counterpart of the Linga Sharira or astral cord—has to be loosened till it is only connected to the body by a fine atomic filament. If this is severed death occurs to our physical shell.

When we aspire to regain our lost possessions in Nature, her forces will at once begin to work about us and give us their shields of protection. If man would only ally himself to Nature he would reap the harvest of his own growth in her consciousness.

When we review our past we find that some races had not advanced very far beyond their soul-group, and we see how fierce and uncouth they were; for they had not yet arrived at the moment when their individuality was severed from their soul-group as it was among the Hebrews at the time of Jesus. Up to this period there were many tribes who were led and governed by leaders.

When man cannot think for himself he is easily led by other minds in advance of his development, whether good or evil. With the return of this new hierarchal cosmic stream, the Dayspring of Youth, the younger generation will become highly individualised and speak and think from within, and not from the intellectual debris of colleges. Our own experience should be our education, and not that gained from others. Books will no longer be needed when we can tap our own wonderful records stored within us. In the future books will be read for pleasure and not for learning.

It is a severe task to prevent our aspirations from falling into our personality and into objective conditions. There are times when a student seeks to enter his secondary system, that a helper, whose body is of a finer substance of mind-stuff, assists him by lending him the filaments of his own atmosphere to bridge the gap between his spheres and this world. But unless we aspire with purity these Beings will not instruct us.

I remember once when I had lived as a hermit upon a hillside far from man, and was about to return to the world, having failed to gain what I had been seeking, that a Being, clothed like an ancient Druid, stood beside me; and as I aspired he said: "I am lending you the finer filaments of my vesture to assist you to contact the planes you seek to enter." I afterwards found that when I was not strong in my aspirations I would lose contact with this plane. This Being had to descend and clothe himself in mind-stuff, so that I could register him with my sixth sense; for he lived in a sphere where man's mind can seldom enter.

There are many such advanced Beings who assist the student. They do not belong to the three belts of illusion that surround our globe, but to the areas of our secondary system.

When we return to Nature we are schooled in the lower elements, then work through them into the higher ones. Here we become bewildered at the immensity of Nature's workshops teeming with populations invisible to normal vision.

We are welcomed to Nature's consciousness when we are led by the elemental Advocate, and we learn how to pass into these worlds without endangering ourselves by her guardian watchmen; for Nature knows how to protect herself from destructive minds.

When we think of Nature the ever-present thought of beauty enters our minds; for the beauty of this earth cannot be compared with Nature's divisions into which the student passes. But with all her greatness of purity as well as beauty we also unfortunately face her submerged depths of elemental substances wherein all the impressions of horror and evil, comparable only to the hallucinations of the insane, are revealed.

That the human mind can create such elemental horrors is unbelievable to the normal mind. We learn of the depths to which the human imagination can descend in its distortions, and how they are seized upon by elementals who ensoul them and make them seem real. Evil forces often direct them to us with their thought pressure. We have dealt more fully with this subject in the chapter entitled "Submerged Worlds."

CHAPTER TWENTY
HEALING

HEALING by personal contact is apt to be looked upon by the medical profession of to-day as a superstitious belief. This attitude has been caused by many professed healers who know little about the true forces at work.

When we trace medical history we find that man has advanced but slightly in this science. Being prisoners in this illusion world, few men in the West have been able to receive information from Nature's consciousness to help the race.

The powerful Solar and Lunar currents that flow into us can be diverted into a sick section of a man's body. Health depends upon a harmonised and equal distribution of Nature's currents through us, and if we have a reservoir of energy we can use this for Nature healing.

Anything that blocks our life currents produces disorder. We should remember that our systems differ regarding the voltages passing through them, and if the normal energy is increased the body is subjected to an added pressure. Our bodies vibrate according to our relationship to our Innermost, and the natural healer is one who is more responsive to his. Our greatest healers have been in closest communion with their Innermost. Such are not the faith healers about whom one hears so much, but people possessing an occult knowledge of the inner forces of their being.

The healer locates the seat of discord within the patient's body by a system of analysis, registers it, then discharges into it atoms of a short wavelength that he slowly increases, and this disturbs the disease. Hence the method of healing is by manipulating Nature's wave-length. This is one of the secrets of healing.

When the centres of our secondary system are out of order the life currents are not registered and our physical energy is slowed down. When the healer sends his thoughts inwardly to the patient he usually finds that some basic trouble, such as hatred, envy, or lust, has been the cause of his disorganisation; for the powerful thought-wave he has sent out has evoked the opposition within his aura, and he has attracted and inhaled destructive atoms.

Mind-waves travel inwardly as well as outwardly, and impress us with their character. They can also inflict disorders within our atomic and cellular life. With good health and a sound imagination we do not usually do this, but if the imagination is distorted we also distort the effects of our secondary and central systems, that attempt to harmonise themselves to our objective plane. We are treated with reverence by our atomic centres when we are pure in mind and thought, no matter how highly they have evolved beyond our time. Though when we enter these inner spheres we are often called to account by the atom instructors about our attitude regarding our health, imagination, and social welfare; for we often inflict disorders upon these centres through the excessive use of alcohol and stimulants that disorganise our entire systems.

To aspire inwardly and build with reverence to our Innermost is an attitude that helps to keep us balanced, and several diseases are caused through lack of nourishment to the glandular system. Nature's method of drainage is interfered with when this system is blocked and unable to remove its impurities. This subject should interest the medical profession; for we think that many cases of cancer could be helped by the invocation of certain vowel sounds, as when these are sounded the glands must vibrate, which will give them the power to absorb the impurities that they have rebelled against. Let a person suffering from cancer sound a simple note of F sharp and give it the energy of a full breath. This will open the ducts within him and attune them to this note; for Nature's notes are the ones that really do the work for us in healing others.

On the higher planes we often meet schools or groups of physicians who are taught, when out of their bodies in sleep, the causes of certain diseases and who study prescriptions and memorise them. Such men are very intuitive on the physical plane, and can often sense and diagnose a disease when consulted. They have often asked me why they cannot recall on this plane the things taught them on the higher planes? The reason for their failure is that they have not studied Yoga, and therefore have not prepared an instrument to transmit their studies.

As we all know, there is a division within us that takes care of the physical body, but few people realise its importance as a unit of construction. For several years people have been experimenting upon animal life, regardless of its consequences to the human body, by transferring an animal element into it. It is important to know that a man cannot develop inwardly when engrafting within his system atoms of an animal nature. Already the animal in man has imprisoned him in this world of illusion.

The experiments appear to be of great importance to the world; for in some cases there has been a partial recovery of the sexual function. But the scientist is not aware of the disaster this will cause the human system; he does not understand that this infusion of atoms into a realm beyond them in development will bring harm to the patient; for it will produce an abnormal condition within the astral and mental sheaths after the patient has passed out of his physical body.

We have witnessed the disintegration of a man who had been given this animal matter and found that this brought about a compound fracture of his astral body. This means that in another life he will be deformed and disabled, since the animal atoms within him will be unable to conform to the direction of the Nous atom.

This after-effect upon the soul will be to divorce it from following its natural wave-length; for it has been animalised by this animal's wave-length that opposes the astral fluid, and the man's astral body will appear as the mind of the animal desires to those who have loved the man in his earthly life: the animal soul is divorced from its own soul-group and seeks to enter the human consciousness.

This, then, is what we have discovered: that when a man is engrafted to animal structures he endangers his soul and makes the animal soul-group refuse to receive its own member back; for it has entered the human kingdom.

I have been asked by those who work for humanity to give this information so that man will not permit the grafting of animal structures to the human body, owing to the terrible after-effects upon the Innermost.

Thus, besides the harm done to the soul of a man, there should also be considered the great injury done to the animal and the karmic debt the man will have to pay.

When building the human sheath according to the plan of the Nous atom, Nature works upon one form of development at a time, leaving other divisions of the body latent.

For instance, during the Hebrew, Greek, and Roman periods Nature built up the Causal sheath—that which registers the racial consciousness. For just as man is governed by his Innermost, so is the race governed by a directing influence in Nature. Nature uses the Causal body of a race as her sounding board or receiving station, through which the racial consciousness is impressed.

People often wonder why the above races permitted animal sacrifices. This liberated the blood of such sacrifices, and their atomic structures built up the Causal body; but when the Causal bodies were complete, blood sacrifices were no longer necessary; then Nature began to develop another section— that of our mind-world—and bring into it what the Christian would call the Christ consciousness, previously individualised in man's heart at the advent of the Great Initiate Jesus.

In this new age the ascent of the Master atom into man's Silver Shield will individualise man's mind so that he will no longer express the characteristics of his objective world, but his true individuality.

When we have completed the building up of our mental body the Reality will close down this wave-length of mental individuality, and we shall slowly create a vehicle for the expression of our Innermost.

CHAPTER TWENTY-ONE
YOGA TEACHINGS

THE Innermost will not reply to an ordinary question, for It does not interest Itself in the personality's world of illusion.

Probably it will surprise the student to learn that the highest within him is uninterested in his human and personal wants. It will work only for Its self-developed universe. If we wish to gain Its atmosphere and direction, this will only occur when we aspire to enter Its world. But we should not think ourselves devoid of the notice or love of the Divine Reality. We should always remember that our Innermost is our individual spark of God.

People with strong religious beliefs think that the highest within them will descend to their own level and awaken them into Its intelligence. This is not so from the experience we have gained in our practice.

The above might sound callous, but here is the reason. In our remote pasts we were directed by the consciousness of Nature and in moments of distress called for right direction; but later, when living in Lemuria and Atlantis, we became self-sufficient and began to break laws to suit ourselves and dominate our fellow beings.

We built our own world in thought and action and no longer appealed to our ancient guide, Nature. Our powerful egotistic activities in the realms of science brought about a period when we thought we could draw upon and manipulate Nature as we wished; we then made gods in our own image.

Nature always balances herself, and this brought about the great catastrophe that submerged Atlantis. Only those who appealed to and served Nature were saved. This is one of the great dangers that threatens man: Science versus Nature.

Therefore it can be seen that this world is not of the Reality or of the Innermost's creating, but the age-long illusions of man's mind, and if the reader will pause and gaze around him and ask "Where is God?" he will realie the profound saying and truth "That the kingdom of Heaven is within."

This is why Yoga is so very instructive. We have often prayed in moments of great distress for the things we need; but our prayers remained unanswered, for we were not inwardly evolved in the secondary system to receive an answer.

We ask the Reality to give us our daily bread, yet have frequently starved, and this will often shake our faith in a wise and powerful God. Still those whose prayers have been answered did not receive help from the Innermost or from the Reality, but from those myriads of atoms that we call upon by aspiration, who seek to show us the reason for our sufferings and who preserve the records of our pasts.

It is here that the Advocate comes to our rescue, for he presents our case to the Innermost, and, if we are truly repentant, these conditions end almost instantaneously.

The adepts say, "Think backwards and forwards to remove bad fortune." When we think for the well-being of others we utilise a reserve atomic energy, but only when we contact our secondary system, which we draw upon, as on a bank balance, to serve others and help them out of their difficulties. It is a most subtle stream of energy, and has a remarkable power of bringing things to pass, also happiness and good will into a person's atmosphere.

When we use this stream for others it removes conditions that have sought to imprison us.

The power behind this subtle force is the Nous atom, and we call upon it when our minds are directed towards others; often to people we have known but slightly, but to whom we are linked by this energy, though often unaware of the reason. Those who evoke this in us receive an abundance of these atoms and a sense of peace and prosperity.

In a remote period this subtle energy was called "The Energy of Perfection," but later, in this objective world, was called "Love."

The student will in time feel that an intermittent activity of this nature is going on within him. This force is a periodic discharge from the Nous atom's atmosphere, and is the cloak of love its atoms receive as well as those to whom it is sent.

These atoms will represent the normal conditions of Society in some future age. Many people receive only this wave-length, as they have not yet evolved beyond the intelligence in their heart.

The mental states are beyond those of the heart, and the atoms that bring love to the human intelligence are different from those that illuminate the heart.

.   .   .   .   .

Every man has what is called a "Pure Spirit." This is an atomic intelligence possessing the nature of our Innermost. People who aspire or are half asleep sometimes see a tiny mote of light—like a spark of dust floating in the sunlight—upon the retina of the closed eye for but an instant. This is the Pure Spirit, and we should attempt to commune with it.

If we can contact it, it will flash back to us, repeating its light a number of times. We should send it love. When it signals, it informs us that we can pass deeper than usual. Only purity of body and mind can bring it to us and contact us to its wisdom period. It has a wonderful knowledge of things, and what it communicates is of the truth.

This Pure Spirit has absolute authority over our intelligence; for it is of an angelic nature, and can bring our energies to birth or retard our growth. But generally only when we enter our secondary system and receive its wave-length can we converse with it.

It has been said that these stars of the Innermost have been used to give humanity a greater breadth of character, for they pronounce their edicts upon man and bind him to those laws that govern him.

The animal kingdom is also controlled by them. Different species are not allowed to transgress into other species, and these Pure Spirits keep them true to their type in evolution.

Man is also guided and repeatedly balanced by a certain power that constantly reverts him to his own natural wave-length, though he might incarnate into a nation foreign to the plan of his Innermost. The Hebrews are such an example; they cannot be diverted outside their own parent stream of energy. To-day many think it possible to pass out of its jurisdiction, but the spirit of the race will eventually cause an individual to revert to his original source. He might adopt another religion and live in its atmosphere for many lives, but in time he will again return to his own parental stem. Other races possess this permanent racial individuality, and though America and the Western areas seem to be a melting-pot for all races, yet in time, each one will re-assemble its own children and unite them to their own wave-lengths.

This mixture of different races and creeds and sex-inclinations to enter another race all have to do with a desire to return to their own true race; for once one has been an enemy to a race he will have to incarnate into it in order to learn toleration and justice. One may be a member of several racial stems, but this is only for a time. Later he will return to his true origin, and will feel a greater power of independence and authority. There also comes a time when a man attains a rounded consciousness that is above race, and he becomes the individual expression of his Innermost.

In our secondary system we begin to realise that we have often incarnated within a race upon whom we have waged war. When such experiences are reviewed, we learn that as we were once destructive to a certain class so will they in time destroy us. In this manner do we learn the necessity not to offend different classes and races, though they may sometimes be a trial. Many races are obnoxious to us on account of our persecution of them in other lives. It is important that we learn about the best in these races, though we should not be lost in them; frequently countries that have shown kindness to persecuted elements are overrun and the best taken from them. Kindness can often cost many a man or country more than they realise. Yogis do not accept gifts of kindness without thought, for they know that such have sometimes been bought at the expense of many weary minds and bodies. It may cost us little trouble to be kind to a person, but it may have cost others great sacrifice and endless toil.

. . . . .

There is a wise saying of a master: "We should only cultivate those who have been successful, and who are of a higher grade of intelligence than our own; for the forces that protect them will protect us if we associate with such."

This is the origin of the caste system, and was originally intended for the betterment of the races. But to-day the caste system has been adopted without the understanding that this law was created in order that man could ultimately unite himself to his Innermost.

The Chinese understand this, and know what happens to the mental atmosphere of a person who associates with lower intelligences than his own. Man chooses his own environment if he is free from material worries. Like attracts like, and it depends upon what his aura contains.

It is better for the student, in his early development, to live alone than mix with those belonging to a lower nature. "Always seek the intelligence of those above you on the Path," for they will assist you to gain your lost inheritance.

It does not matter who the person is, how he is clothed, or to what nation he belongs, if he possesses enlightenment beyond one's own. Customs differ in any land, and we should not judge one by our own customs.

In our higher schools we are not called by our Christian names, but are known by our symbols, that, we are told, were given to us by our Master atom in another incarnation. The sign we carry with us symbolises the kind of crucifixion we endured in the past, and means that we sacrificed ourselves for our followers in various ways. We also learn that a man's faith could have been an illusion as well as a discomfort to his followers. This is the explanation of the saying that "When we meet someone out of the body we can recognize his attainments by his caste mark."

.   .   .   .   .

Our hyperborean ancestors left us a book open for all to read, but to few is its meaning made known. It contains all that we can gain in instruction in this age, and all that we need for our development. It has a hidden science that can only be taught us from the inner planes; and though commonly called the Zodiac, it is but a fragment from a lost book in antiquity, and its missing fragments are to be found within our inner consciousness. We are told that only one-twelfth of its structure and wisdom is objectively related to us, and within our secondary and central systems are to be found the remaining portions.

The Zodiacal signs represent those states through which we have passed, and will return to us as we develop into our central universe. Although Astrology has not advanced much in the present period, yet in this new age this science will become respected and scientists will take it seriously.

.   .   .   .   .

The seasons change us regardless of our own will. The Reality does this in order that we may learn to follow this aspect of Nature's law; but we are unaware of this change of seasons occurring within our inner planes.

Four times a year, at the Equinox, there descends into our bodies a hierarchal current, and at these changes of seasons our bodies come under their influence. In Autumn and Winter the atoms of the seminal system are engendered and given nourishment; in other words, built up so that at the Spring Equinox they will be able to fertilise the brain cells with their energy. Similar to all life we answer the call of Nature. During this time the energy of the sun has been conserving our energy, holding it back so that we may have reserve power after the Spring and Summer months have passed.

When we have worked in harmony with Nature in all that we do and have learned when the seasons change, we then ask the Aspiring atoms to remedy our deficiencies. As the old alchemists say: "There is a place and a time when all such operative works should be begun." These men transmuted their own baser materials into their finer substances according to planetary influences. Within us there is also a planetary system corresponding to the outer system.

Astrology teaches us about the effects of the planets upon our physical body; but few know about our inner planetary system and its activities upon our finer bodies. The moon is most important to our inner systems; for its rays penetrate the mental bodies of the principal atoms so that they respond to its directing influences; for the moon sends into us its records of her wisdom periods, and it is from these Scholar atoms that we receive information relating to the different moon cycles of enlightenment. The sun and other planets do likewise, and through this we can re-experience all that we have learnt from such sources, for within us lie latent the atoms of the Reality's firmament.

When a planet comes directly into our range of consciousness, and this is easily noticed in the deeper states of Yoga, we hear an audible note emanating from the planet. This is the origin of the term, "The music of the spheres."

To synthesize the operations of Nature within us through our aspiration is to learn of the sun, moon, and planets that are nearest to us. In other words, we harmonise with Nature in order to become her instrument.

. . . . .

As our physical organism registers the forces of day and night and balances them, so does each force give it a certain nourishment. When women regain their memories of Nature's consciousness they will suckle their children according to Nature's direction, and give the child the breast through which the day or night current flows.

We find in Nature a quality of that Motherly love that relates us to all those who have been our mothers during countless incarnations, and as we review this attribute of motherhood we feel within us a power that evokes all our reverence and purity.

. . . . .

All people talk about art and religion with authority, and this is like discussing the nature of electricity when even scientists cannot analyse it. Yoga practice is far different: each step must be experienced before being spoken about, and in this manner we slowly climb a lofty summit where we are immersed in an atmosphere of a semi-divine nature. Until we do this we cannot gain any real information regarding religion. As we ascend from consciousness to consciousness we find that religion is like an essence emanating from one great source; though its expression varies according to the kind of cup that receives it, the student does not speak of it as the sole possession of any one caste or people, but as one essence permeating all things.

The Yogi will not discuss art or religion with people who only possess its fragments. These subjects cannot be analysed from the human plane of consciousness; but the sincere seeker will be helped in such problems by the Yogi turning the seeker's mind inwardly to self-thought.

CHAPTER TWENTY-TWO
SUMMARY OF THE SILVER SHIELD

THE mental body will not be given the power to overcome its opposition until we can direct our thoughts inwardly. When we aspire we slowly cover our atmosphere with a silken lining far different from the mental lining we possessed before we began this practice. This new envelope protects us from our objective thought-world. We rebuild this lining by the aid of the Transformation atoms, and when the Silver Shield is constructed we have erected a temple for the Master atom. This enters this sheath from a period in advance of our time. The coming of this Master atom gives us, for the first time, a directing intelligence that enables us to draw from self our own knowledge and wisdom.

The first instruction we receive from this receiving station has to do with the perfection of the body; for it must be prepared in order that the Solar force within us may be liberated. This is a process of adjustment of the body to its current. Then the Innermost is released from the prison house of the body.

When the Innermost entered matter we began to clothe ourselves with the objective atmospheres of this world; this finally shut us out from our divine inheritance: the powers and wisdom of the Innermost.

After the release of the Innermost the Solar current circles about our body and can be heard at times by its swishing sound; we then get the sensation of a rotating current so strongly that we feel we want to rotate with it.

Though in this book we do not deal with the liberation of the Innermost, we have attempted to show the student how to be brought in touch with that inner intelligence—the Master atom—and, through its agency, with the Innermost.

When the student can receive his inner instruction he will then be brought into touch with those who will give him personal attention.

In Yoga the student should remember that it is always well to remain silent after he has attained unity with his secondary system, or he will be an object of derision to those ignorant of the importance and aim of this profound science; for what is food for the Yogi is not nourishment for the many blinded by this world of illusion.

. . . . .

It should be realised that man uses only a small area of his physical brain, and an Initiate is one who has developed these areas which are the receiving stations for the entire universe of man.

These large areas are not brought into activity until we have developed our Silver Shield, and when this is constructed its node points begin to agitate the latent cells within these disused areas, and thus link man's inner consciousness to his objective mind. He will then begin to view things from a different angle.

When we have built up this Silver Shield and formed a temple for the Master atom, we do not have to go for instruction to the centres of the physical body that have enabled us to re-experience our past lives, but are now taken into the mind-world to meet intelligences called Scholar atoms, whose work is to instruct us to regenerate our objective nature and help us aspire towards our central universal current that flows into our Silver Shield. The nodic poles we have built up will transmit the learning of these Scholar atoms, and the student must bear in mind that all this is within his own self-created universe. This central current flowing into our consciousness by way of the Silver Shield brings us the higher elements of the moon that is symbolised by the planet Neptune.

CHAPTER TWENTY-THREE
DETERMINATIVE ENERGY

THE Dayspring of Youth has several strands that run into us as a stream runs into the ocean, and each strand is the manifestation of some attribute of the Innermost. Though at first we cannot register these ever-increasing waves of energy we can tune our own wave-lengths by aspiration. We then bend these waves into our secondary system by attracting their atoms into us and gaining their intelligence.

Every new age brings another form of enlightenment and instruction to man.

When we determine to do a thing it has already been accomplished within our secondary system, and this gives us a determination to work and accomplish this on the objective plane. But we generally fail if we do not consciously or unconsciously draw upon the determinative energy in Nature. If we use this principle we shall complete our determined work in this life or in our next incarnation. For we all incarnate to gain certain experiences, and we cannot be happy if we fail in this.

The density of the world's atmosphere revolts against us if we desire to complete anything, and we are immediately attacked by the Secret Enemy and the Opposition atoms of the atmosphere, who hamper our work so that we are unable to accomplish it. We also find that the moment we begin to do a thing an opposition energy will weaken our interest, unless it possesses the nature of our determined plan, and discourages us in our work. Literary and artistic people realise this more than those of the scientific class; in comparison with those who deal in objective things such as metal or wood they are whirls of atomic energy.

Just as there are certain centres for instruction within our secondary system, so have we centres that register Nature's movements. When we learn to harmonise ourselves to these we can gain information. This is how we begin to raise Nature's veils and learn about her forces within us. This gives us the power to ascend into her spheres and commune with her in-telligence and inwardly sense the workings of her will.

We have spoken about Nature's will; it is this that precedes the thought of our universal centres of consciousness. Before thought breaks into sound and colour it is preceded by something; for the indwelling consciousness determines our thought. When we go inward we find this determinative principle at work in our different systems, and always preceding us. Hence there are two things that erect as well as destroy thought: the indwelling consciousness—that Genius of Perfection whose energy precedes all thought—and the objective and destructive energy of the opposition in the atmosphere of this world.

In our deeper consciousness we meet streams of energy leaving our Innermost; these are atomic waves of sound and colour, and the light they create, when viewed from the objective plane, is like sunlight illuminating a dark avenue down which we are travelling.

These currents that precede thought energise the Silver Shield, which then seeks to focus our thoughts of the objective world towards it. It will then attract atoms and forms that will collect our thoughts into the Silver Shield. This means: the Innermost sends its energy into the Silver Shield and energises it. The Shield then directs it to the Master atom, and this seeks to unite us to its intelligence by sending before our thought a wave that will link us to it.

Unknown to our personality, the Innermost seeks to revert our thoughts to Its source.

Determination is a positive force acting in one's mind. The occultist will learn to determine a thing and carry it out. This is a process wherein one inwardly completes a thing, then determines to materialise it.

We all possess undeveloped hidden forces, and this determinative faculty is one of them. In the secondary system there are atoms who call up the powers latent in our central system, and these collect about a plan that is given the power to overcome all obstacles. The plan to be completed is withheld from the objective planes until we are informed by those atoms, that call up this determinative energy, that the time is ready for its birth.

We are sometimes impressed to do a thing regardless of anything else occupying us at that time. We do not always sense the source from whence this impression comes, but when we enter our secondary system we can then be instructed by those atoms who work according to Nature's plan. From these atoms we derive the determinative energy of Nature's plan that is withheld from this world, and here we use what scientists term "Will," used on earth for personal aims regardless of our Innermost's desires.

Self-determination will enable a student to give his powers full action, and he will grow and flourish like a tree in Spring if we will but draw upon its energy. This is a powerful as well as a subtle force all possess, though few often draw upon. It comes from elemental Nature and has nothing to do with individual will. Incidentally, Initiates seldom use the term "Will" in their teachings. They say: "Let Nature do it."

When we aspire we forge links that brings this determinative principle over to us, though only after we practise Yoga are we aware of it. This power holds Nature true to her plan.

When we feel inspired and an added strength is given us it is this force that we call Nature's Oversoul. The white magician, who is Nature's disciple, uses this when registering the different states of density in the mind-world's atmosphere.

Man registers what he perceives through the organs of the senses, and if the atmosphere is changed and the material world vanishes, another form of contact is opened to our senses. Thus Nature's subtle force can alter the mind of a person to whom it is directed. This power is used by certain great Yogis when they wish to produce objective phenomena. This is not illusion, but the functioning of the mind within a different wave-length. When we can bring this finer energy into our atmosphere it will give us power of direction—that power that will carry a thing to its conclusion.

Thus the student attains the power of Nature's will to run parallel with his personal will, and he has the consciousness of a thing completed ere it manifests upon the objective plane.

This principle will be one of the new forces to be drawn upon in the coming generation.

As we have within the body latent organs that are healthy but unused, so are there many unused divisions within our mental screen. When we use this subtle force that runs before a thought, we begin to clothe our thoughts and provide an instrument through which Nature can render to us her seven mental attributes. When these attributes become active within our mental atmosphere we possess an instrument that will clothe our thoughts with sound, colour, and energy, and return to us our lost possessions in Nature's mind.

With these attributes a positive mind need no longer send into the atmosphere thoughts that sway like broken reeds before the opposition winds of this illusion-world, but thoughts of a nature hitherto unknown to us—thoughts that can gather their lost energies. Before this we directed our thoughts by our personal will—an instrument previously used to project our thoughts into this objective world.

We use personal will without understanding it—a power to dominate ourselves and things. This will possesses intelligence, and is a motive force of the objective world, like the steam that drives an engine; but we are unaware of it when we enter our secondary kingdoms.

When we seek union with our Innermost we return to Nature, but certain entities, elemental, physical, and submerged astral—the world of our Secret Enemy—cannot ascend into the inner spheres of being; for they are not given this power of Nature until they renounce their personal will. That is why many people, when they pass over, are earthbound.

In short, this means that just as we have prepared, through Yoga, our physical body to receive Nature's finer vibrations, so must we likewise develop our mental screen, or Nature's sounding board within us, in order to register her finer movements in thought and clothe our thoughts with her essence. This is one of the reasons for the construction of our Silver Shield.

Our Master atom represents not only the wisdom intelligence of our myriad lives, but those lives wherein we clothed ourselves with Nature's filaments, and from now on our thoughts will possess a double quality. Thus Nature armours our thoughts so that they will penetrate any opposition. This is one of the powers of a Yogi hitherto kept secret.

People often wonder why occultists of all ages are told to renounce everything. This has been misunderstood. What they renounce is their personal will.

Many occultists are told to conserve their creative energy: to master their lower sex nature. Atoms always find their own level. It is the vapour that rises from the surface of our seminal fluid that gives us this determinative energy in Nature. The demand for personal power will not bring these higher forces into operation. But we can evoke a force that binds us to our lower animal nature, and this gives the black magician his power.

As the manifestation of the Dayspring of Youth becomes more pronounced we should seek to become its instrument, and Nature will implant her ideals and instruction within us, and we shall no longer regard the personal opinion of the world. The old inheritance of illusion must make way for this force of the cosmic hierarchal energy, and humanity will be ruled by this parent of our creation and not by the experience or intelligence of this world. As man is but a fragment of the Reality, he must seek to recover his own lost inheritance by aspiring to regain this consciousness when he responded to this determinative energy of the Reality—God.

The more the Yogi develops his instrument, the more can he record the atomic powers of Nature; but before he can do this he must aspire and seek the instruction periods of his secondary system, and fertilise his brain with Nature's atoms of aspiration and intelligence. Thus "Know Thyself," written at the entrance of the temple at Delphi, means to know the Innermost. For it possesses all the accumulated wisdom of all man's experience since his entry into matter.

This is the only system of Yoga suitable for Western bodies that will unite us to our own supreme power and the Dayspring of Youth.

To work under the protective cloak of the Innermost, free ourselves from the forces of this abnormal world, work out one's own experience, gain the activity of the Innermost, and give to others that which we possess and redeem them, is the deeper meaning of emancipation.

When we ascend into the finer states of matter we are again organised into Nature's determinative energy. As we are prisoners in an illusion world and in bondage to the atoms of the Secret Enemy, we have to be re-called to Nature's consciousness and given that true inheritance to which our personal will must be subservient. This emancipation from the physical world becomes permanent.

The student must not forget that this energy also works for the well-being of his physical system and instinctively impresses him as to what he should eat and how he should express himself.

He will now discover that his body's desires will deal with elemental food values and not with the physical food values he used to eat.

Elemental food values are those that nourish our intestinal tract and furnishes it with its desired atomic structures that will give this part of the body a sudden energy. Many kinds of food only encumber our intestines with a multitude of atoms that disturbs its organisation, and hence we must only take nourishment that will act upon this tract, for the stomach is but the simple reservoir that holds, prepares and churns our food into its different densities. And as the intestines supply us with our inborn energy, we must take this system into account and give it necessary intestinal strength we denied it ere studying Yoga.

If the system is choked by refuse, it is difficult to deal with; for constipation causes the atoms of this refuse—as such atoms are of a death nature—to seek to re-enter the seminal canal and evaporate their atmosphere into a cloud of depression, and the mind impregnated by such moods and anxieties is not the type chosen by the Yogi for a pupil. The Red Indian as well as the Eastern Yogi knows what causes this depression and has a simple remedy; but this method is almost unknown by the so-called civilised West. It is an invariable law that constipation causes depression.

The lower part of the student's trunk should be elastic; for when he meets a teacher he has to stir up his Solar energy—the Sleeping Serpent—by physical exercise as well as by Yoga practice. He should place his hands against his lower ribs and rotate his body from right to left. This will also keep the stomach and intestines in proper condition. And we should remember as we have previously said, in our efforts to keep the body healthy we should drink as much water as possible. It is often thirsting for it, as it cannot always clear itself of its impurities. We should drink fresh water between meals and keep a pitcher where we can see it. Whenever exercising always feel that your strength comes from your abdomen.

Besides this being necessary for the normal man, it must be far more so for the student, as he must be alert and sensitive to respond to any current that Nature may suddenly release. Conquer your trouble of constipation, and you will be able to conquer your lower sex-nature and command it.

In the seminal tract is a centre of atomic intelligence possessing the nature of the Silver Shield; its atoms cluster about their own individual seats of consciousness. These centres impress us with a veneration for all creative effort. This means that if we are as moral as they, we shall receive instruction regarding our moral welfare; the Jews have this strongly in their race; for they venerate the worth of moral things such as holy books, traditions, and so forth. Just as the Chinese poet will bow in reverence before a great book ere reading it.

This character of veneration that these atoms possess will, if we possess them abundantly, cause us to reverence holy things, and if a person does not possess these atoms we do not reverence him. Thus the holy man in the East is recognised if possessing this quality by invoking in others their spirit of reverence. If our parents do not possess such atoms we do not reverence them, though we may love them. It is an unconscious quality that a student feels without being aware of its significance: but later, owing to his association with such atoms within his seminal tract, he will realise why he reverences holy things.

People who do not reverence others do not possess "Manners of distinction," or any manners worthy of note. They will rush in where angels fear to tread, and are lacking in courtesy or discretion. Reverence to those who possess these atoms is most common in China, and they who possess them leave a chain behind them that never severs them from their descendants. This is another angle of ancestor worship unknown to the West.

It is not until the student possesses this quality that he can reverence Nature—besides appreciating her beauty—and enter into her consciousness as though he entered a holy place.

When this spirit of reverence has been born into our consciousness, we become natural and courteous to all with whom we are in harmony; if we are not in harmony with a person's atmosphere it is because, unconsciously, we do not reverence that person's understanding and wave-length. Sometimes when we meet a person of another race we do not feel reverence towards him, for we do not harmonise with his racial individuality, and we are often unconsciously harassed as our own wave-length is disturbed, and such vibrations, being strange, shake us. If we begin to analyse this disharmony we shall often discover things that will become important to us; for we do not harmonise with those races in whose atmosphere we have in the past been subjected to persecution; but we must also realise that we ourselves in a still remoter day had caused suffering and misery to them. This is Nature's method of adjustment.

If we fathom this mystery, we shall seek to harmonise ourselves again and be just. When we feel this antagonism towards a member of a different race we must analyse his atmosphere, and we will find that the pressure comes not from the personal side but from his thought-environment; elemental and earthbound entities that will always seek to communicate with a sensitive person.

CHAPTER TWENTY-FOUR
AN ARCADIAN CONTACT

THE student is contacted to the different elemental divisions by his teacher through the proper use of a symbol, and if the person has a strong creative nature he can, after his first steps in Yoga, intermittently contact Nature's spheres of inspiration.

A student has permitted me to include in this book a fragment from an unpublished work. He had the necessary persistence and faithfully observed these occult teachings. He worked hard at his breathing exercises and developed his physical body, and, though for some time he had to be left to himself, he was able to develop his latent forces and was easily taken into his inner planes. Afterwards he was taught the use of symbols and was able intermittently to receive inspiration from the elemental hierarchies; the source of inspiration for those able to gain the interest of these spheres of majesty and beauty. Here follows the fragment wherein the goddess Minerva relates the Sad History of Arcadia.

Minerva speaks: "When the world was young this land was the cradle of Spring. As she grew her breath gave fragrance and coolness to the air and became the sylphs. Wherever her sandalled feet trod buds uncurled and hills and valleys shone. Whenever she sang birds were born and fluttered over the land; and whenever she spoke the waters unwound their silver tendrils and followed her. When she sat and thought the little people were born, and when she prayed the gods were created. And the flowers and birds, the naiads and sylphs, the little people and the great gods worked together and designed man. And when man stood upright and his eyes were lit with divinity, he gazed at the beauty of this land and the spirit of Poetry inspired him to name it 'Arcadia.'

"This was the age when man was stately in thought, childlike in desire, and lovely to look upon. His eyes shone clearly and shadowed forth the width of his wisdom, and the gleam of that age still glows within the lambent minds of the poets, and within the fiery hearts of the prophets. This was the

Golden Age; the age that flared from music, from poetry, and from the lover.

"Man's needs were simple, his wishes few. Life did not run on steel legs and roar from brazen throats; the world did not move by the muscle of the machine and fill each minute with the weariness of monotonous labour. When the mornings rose they unfolded joys and not sorrows; when the evenings were born and the dews fell his slumbers were untroubled and deep. Happiness ran through him as a stream runs downhill: leaping, singing, flashing. Love burned like mellow sunlight and thoughts darted as swiftly as leaping hinds. For man honoured a simple creed: that life was given for joyfulness; that he dwelt within the radiance of the heroic light of the gods; and that their protective and strong fingers governed his destiny and understanding.

"Ah! the gods, the gods. The high-born of Arcadia, whose cymbals are the thunders, and bright spears the lightnings; who once ruled man with a gay enchantment. Ah! mighty Jupiter, judge of all things, when will you return to breathe justice into the minds of men? The world needs a new mantle and a new majesty, for her garments are threadbare; her queenliness has been dethroned. The creed that had the note of the faun's pipe in it and the serenity of a Summer's dusk has vanished.

"We treasured the music of the winds blown through the locks of the world; we treasured the lyrics of the birds and of the streams. We believed that Beauty was the gem that clasped all things together and that wisdom was the fire that flowed through this precious stone. We held that the blood of the gods enriched and ran through the veins of man. He who played with skilful fingers upon the lyre; he who chiselled marble and drew loveliness from it, and he who shook flame and dreams from words, were the princes of Arcadia. That was a great age; but now only a whisper from it, only a forlorn chord, sighs through the darkness, and the birds and the winds hear, and occasionally the dreamer.

"For Winter withers the petal; the soul becomes silvered as well as the head. Man grew old; but without the hope of Spring. The beauty that lay within marble was no more unsealed; the music that slept in the trembling lyre no more awakened; and the wisdom cradled in the lyric no more spoke. For eyes lacked clear sight, fingers lacked tenderness, and minds lacked depths. Darker and darker grew the years overshadowing the spirit of the people till they felt and thought greyly. Till their backs became bowed and their limbs slow, and their voices quivered thinly as the voices of the old. Their memories grew dim and faltered; and when we wandered amid them they gazed at us without understanding. And sometimes I would strike my shield at the birth of a great one, but they would not hear; and the gifts of the great one would often die with him. And sometimes Mercury would place a wreath about the brow of a favoured one and they would strike and stone him. And when Jupiter placed a sword into the hands of his servant they would mock him and deny his just sentences.

"And Apollo mourned: 'I wandered among the ruins of Arcadia—the land that held the first fruits of the world—and saw that Spring and the rose had withered. The marble statues had fallen, the lute of Orpheus lay broken upon the temple floor. Alas! the beauty of man shines no more; he has forsaken our temples; dust lies upon our altars. His graciousness has flown, has crumbled as a flower. Fair as the morning on the waters was he, swift as the flash of spears; but now bitterness is within him, and greyness in his heart and hair. Were our temples not beautiful for him? Our groves fruitful? Our world stately?'"

Minerva ceased abruptly: John waited. When she resumed it was in another strain: "As you walked with me through the town you saw the degradation of its inhabitants. Those in whom beauty shimmered were beggars and persecuted; insensitive egotists who knew not the delicate tremors of inspiration were applauded. Men, who were once human, had become automatons, and we, who once ruled them, have been compelled to hide. But when we disappeared the realms of enchantment also disappeared; we wove a veil over the roads to magic. Sorrowfully we closed the doors to Wonder. But when we hid, man created other gods; for man must worship, if not a god, then a dream, a machine, a hero, a woman; for all that he worships is an echo of his lost splendour. And it is this that must be recovered ere we can reveal ourselves again."

She ceased and held up a warning forefinger as John was about to speak: "Hush, can you hear? There is singing; so elusive and wild, so poignant."

John barely breathed as he tried to hear. For some seconds there was silence. Then he heard; but it was so remote that he thought he imagined it. Then swiftly rushed upon him and swirled and beat into his ears a music of such forlorn, such despairing sweetness, that he almost wept. It evoked images of mountain peaks, cool, quick winds, and torrents of foaming waters. It was a singing that swept the mind clean and made it spacious; as though the brain had suddenly grown into a vast hall through which lovely oreads swept; and with it came the sense of the beauty of naked things. He was whirled into a storm of pagan freshness and wildness till his body felt clean and splendid. Then the voices dwindled as rapidly as they had rushed upon them, leaving only an echo of melody and an intense regret that he could hear no more.

After some moments' silence he huskily whispered: "Oh! how beautifully they sang. It hurt. Tell me please. Who are they?"

The goddess replied: "They are the sylphs lamenting over the sorrows of this world."

A melancholy silence fell upon both, whilst he listened to the fugitive chords that still haunted him with their ghostly sadness.

Again Minerva continued: "They weep because we have hidden ourselves and man has lost his freedom. But when Arcadia is set free and the spirit within man is released like a freshet, beauty will be revealed anew and not mocked; and inspiration will awaken within him like a sunrise. The mornings will unveil things fairer than light; and the evenings more joyful things than love. The forgotten majesties that slumber in the quietness will awaken and enfold man, and bring to his eyes a loftier glow; for he will be as lordly as a forest in Spring. But this will only come when he will be freed from the steel clasp of the machine; from the oppressors of this realm who have manacled his divinity, and will return to the simplicity of Nature. But his new wisdom will be nobler than his past wisdom; for it will be as wise as that wisdom that dwells behind the brows of the gods."

Her voice rose and its silvery quality became golden: "Then he will enrobe himself in our meditations; tread our halls of crystal, and walk within our gardens of fire. Then Tempests will kneel before him, and he will clasp the quivering lightnings and unshackle the winds and make them carpets for his feet. The pulse of the Universe will shake through his heart and he will know the secret reveries of the star and the flower. This is the promise I make for him when he arises and throws off the rust of the ages and becomes young and clean again."

CHAPTER TWENTY-FIVE

MANTRAS

WHAT do we know about Nature behind her veil? Everything in Nature has its keynote, and if we use the proper invocation we receive an immediate response. Place two pianos in a room, strike the G string of one and the other will vibrate in harmony. This is one of the secrets of Nature's magic: when one gains a response from a thing one is attuned to its consciousness. In this manner Nature operates and we relate our mind to her thought. The murmur of brooks, the sounds of winds and spray, are classed as sound-waves of a similar notation, and before we hear those sounds we will hear Nature's keynote. When we use her magic we first tune ourselves to this note, and this will unite us with that particular stream or waterfall we wish to hear though it may be far away. This is another example of the determinative energy of Nature preceding sound as it precedes thought.

To wait upon a Master is to be his disciple, and to be his disciple is to become an instrument of his energy. The law of the magician is not easy to learn; for it is very exacting and no one can gain such knowledge without careful and difficult training.

Just as we aspire to become the instrument for the Dayspring of Youth and manifest in its intelligence, so must the magician be immersed in his own individual Dayspring of Youth before he can make anything obey his direction. That is, he must do two things: be a ruler in Nature's consciousness and still remain her pupil. In everything in this science there is a definite bridge to be crossed before one can gain the approval of any power.

Masters of the Masters of magic renounce everything and retreat from humanity. Then they fast and curb their desires until they are conquered. They no longer impress their wishes upon their navel tract, for in it lies the instrument for magic, and the strength of the entire system is drawn from it. There is also an element that can be used for the greatest evil as well as the greatest good, and the magician has to choose between these two principles. The good hastens us to our godlike destination, whereas evil hastens us into the depths of our Secret Enemy where we become its instrument. If we wish to develop our magical powers we place ourselves within this energy and use its governing force as we direct it: be it for good or evil. The object in magic is to overcome any force that opposes us. People who aspire to their Innermost are not greatly interested in phenomena of this kind; for they realise that such manifestations do not hasten them on their Path to their Innermost.

In our central system we observe a thin membrane covering the organs that intermittently registers the finer currents of Nature that pass through them during day and night. These organs are sounding boards held together by their atomic structures. Each one registers a different wave-length and their vibrations emit an audible sound. Our different physical nerve cells are similar to these and are also attuned to receive certain vibrations. To evoke the activity of our latent atomic centres we use the seven vowels of Nature, called mantras.

In the future the physician will use these in place of his usual pharmacopoeia. We begin by sounding our note in Nature, and learn to vibrate each centre within us. For instance: if our atmosphere is dormant and sluggish we awaken the centre at the base of the throat, and feel a big inrush of atoms that clarifies the atmosphere and places us in contact with the elemental Lords of the Mind. This is a form of physical culture for the mind's atmosphere, and the most insensitive person should sense this clarification of his atmosphere. Sometimes an actor, when unconsciously liberating this force, will succeed in attuning his audience to his mind. This is what he calls "Getting over the foot-lights."

These mantras are secret and taught only to the sincere seeker. After calling up a centre by sound invocation, we listen-in, and, if our aspiration is pure, our Watchman or Advocate links us to that centre we wish to contact. All the different spheres of elemental nature are called up by this method. We can also evoke any condition of a lower nature much more easily than the higher; because it is easier for us to think outwardly than inwardly.

We cleanse our mental atmospheres by sound mantras; also when we leave our bodies on a mental flight we bathe our atmosphere in Nature's finer element, and this cleanses us as water cleanses our physical body.

No matter how great the tumult about a Yogi, he can easily shut off all outside communications by listening-in.

The primitive man understood these mantras and some of the Indian tribes of America chant the same mantric sounds that we hear in the East. The Zuni Indians use the same Eastern mantric chants to the Sun.

At a certain period in a student's development he is given a sacred word to meditate upon and sound its invocation, though this would be useless if written down. There comes a time when a student is given his real name. This is his key to his attained states of consciousness and unlocks to him his lost possessions in Nature that, through magic, he has sealed up before incarnating and which was to be opened on his return to his consciousness in his secondary system.

When the sincere seeker after truth passes over, he gravitates to his own higher level and his great recreation is to reopen his lost possessions in Nature. He collects this material and seals it by magic so that no one can tap his treasure save himself. Knowing of its great worth to humanity, he seeks, during his next incarnation, to contact his inner spheres and reveal these treasures to the world. It is by the use of this key— his real name—that he unlocks these.

When the student wishes to vibrate his physical, secondary, and central system, he calls upon the super-Solar force— the determinative principle in Nature—Sol our physical sun, and upon Mercury—the Lords of the Mind—by sounding their notes. This harmonises his bodies to receive their streams of atomic energy and the vibrations of his Innermost.

The Early Mass in the Roman Church was supposed to do this, but, if you asked the Church authorities, they would reply that as far as they knew the celebration of this was in memory of events that happened in the past. Singing in churches is but the reflection of an ancient ceremony of mantric invocation.

When entering a village compound the Yogi generally produces some phenomena to attract the crowd. He chants a mantra to vibrate the physical, psychic, and mental bodies of his audience, then expounds some simple text from one of his sacred books. Vibrating, his body vibrates the bodies of his audience and allows their higher selves to be impressed by his discourse; thus his hearers will remember what he has said.

When we enter our secondary system we hear Nature's note: a theurgic wave of sound inaudible to normal senses. This is called upon when the adept wishes to produce natural phenomena; for if we take an energy into ourselves, and entwine it about our own wave-length, we have a keynote that may only be used as Nature wishes it.

Nature's notes increase and decrease during the day and our centres respond and change over in harmony with them.

Viewing the world from an inner state man sees this world as an illusion of his own creation. Change the mind into Nature's vibration, and Earth will be seen as a vapour. The hills and mountains disappear; the surface of the world passes away and through this mental change Nature reveals her secrets and we seek to obey her laws.

The reader might say: "But how I would hate to lose the beauty of this world." Nature's recompense is threefold, giving us three attributes that are so much more wonderful that we shudder when we return to her outer veil. These three attributes are: wisdom, virtue, understanding. Not the wisdom, the virtue, or the understanding of this world, but their higher counterparts.

When we enter our secondary system we are told to sense what we have gained from our objective education. Passing through life to life and re-experiencing them on this plane, we find that only that which we have experienced and learned to GOVERN in ourselves was our true education. Later, when we enter our Transformation period, we REMEMBER the wisdom gained from each individual life and see how often we missed the true experience for which we had incarnated.

We witness our failures and see how difficult it was to regain that experience we had determined upon when incarnating. Certain well-known figures in history remembered their past lives and places they lived in. Pythagoras is a good example.

Knowing some of the incarnations of a friend, a man of great distinction, I took him to an out-of-the-way place in Paris and stood him over the floor of a dungeon wherein he had been confined and died in another life. I then asked him if he received any sensation, and he suddenly burst out crying; for the remembrance of this past life returned and he re-experienced his torment.

It is not pleasant to go through such experiences, such as remembering having been burned at the stake. One sees the excited mob, and the mind travels across the river to the palace where the despot lived who gave the order for this execution, that one knew was watching from his terrace, and the buildings loom up again as they did in the past.

Students are sometimes taught a process of ordeal by fire, so that later they no longer fear it. This is used by the Zend priests of Japan for the cure of disease. The fighting classes of Japan are also trained to endure pain, and this is why the West wonders over their fighting qualities.

· · · · ·

We do not believe that the real knowledge regarding reincarnation will be given forth for some time, though it has become common talk among occultists and students of Buddhist philosophy. The Sufis, beside other mystics, understood this; but did not dwell very lengthily upon this subject. Later we hope to publish a pamphlet upon the esoteric side of it.

There are questions man has never asked himself; secret questions that the Innermost could solve. Like children in a dark night of existence, we wander about seeking to find for ourselves a way out of this darkness. Yet we never ask ourselves those questions that would bring a response from our Innermost. It is generally towards the end of one's life that one asks a CERTAIN question which, if put in youth, would have been the means of changing one's entire life, and one realises how many years of fruitless effort one could have been saved had this been done.

How many people in meditation have ever asked themselves questions as though speaking to their Innermost? They will ask the Reality—God—for things, and they speak to Him; but do they ever receive a direct reply? The way to the Reality is through our Innermost—that part of the Reality within us—and if we aspire, and ask a certain question, when our Innermost replies a problem every serious seeker asks will be solved. This is symbolised in Wagner's *Parsifal*.

CHAPTER TWENTY-SIX
TRANSFORMATION BREATHING

AFTER the student has inhaled into his system the Aspiring atoms, he begins another kind of breathing to attract atoms of a higher voltage known as Transformation atoms. These will complete the Silver Shield that all have in embryo, though few rarely develop and bring into conscious manifestation.

The first exercise is to aspire to the Innermost—for the Transformation atoms are of Its nature and the Builder atoms of the mind-body, as the Aspiring atoms are of the physical body—by inhaling through the right nostril and exhaling through the left; then inhaling through the left nostril and exhaling through the right.

This alternating breathing brings the Solar and Lunar currents into opposition, and opposition, being the occult law of attraction, causes these two currents to bring to the magnetic field of the nose these Transformation atoms of protection and security. In time this kind of breathing forms a nasal grid or screen at the entrance of our nostrils—a rotating mass of atoms that alternately swings from right to left—and rejects the impure atoms and debris we naturally inhale, permitting alone the entry of those atoms that possess the qualities of the Innermost and the higher states of atomic energy. This nasal filter is easily sensed and felt when it has been formed; for it has the tendency of causing us to lift the nostrils when it is in operation. In time we also develop the power primitive savages possess of sensing things by quick intakes of breath when we enter the atmosphere of any person and "smell them out," as to their position in the densities of matter about them, and thus recognise their qualities. The student can also smell the odour emitted by the astral fluids of discarnate people, and can sense entities and grade their status without using clairvoyance.

PRACTICE

Sit erect with the chin in and chest brought forward. Hands resting naturally on thighs, with palms upwards and forefingers and thumbs meeting to form a circle. It will be necessary at first to press the middle finger against either nostril when changing over each breath. Later, thumbs and forefingers must be kept closed throughout exercise. At the end of the sixth breath, hold it easily and aspire to seek the approval of the Innermost for this new undertaking. Seek to listen-in, to sense an atomic atmosphere within and record the impressions it reflects into the mind. After the screen grid is formed, and this should be easy, the student should not spend more than five minutes at this exercise at first; then he should increase the length of practice. Be natural and alert, and do not strain or exhaust yourself in any way whilst doing this. After you have completed your exercise aspire and write down the impressions you receive. In time you should receive a short sentence that you should memorise and constantly repeat before practising; for this is a secret mantra that the Innermost will reveal to the sincere student, and should not be told to anyone. It is a precious possession and will not be revealed to the seeker until he has developed his nasal grid.

After each practice the student should clear his brain. This is done by kneeling and placing the palms of the hands upon the floor with thumbs touching, then placing forehead upon backs of hands. This washes the brain cells of their impurities. The younger student should learn to rest upon the back of his shoulders and support his body in an upright position. This will drain impurities from the digestive tract and flush the glands.

CHAPTER TWENTY-SEVEN
COSMIC RAYS

THERE are atoms that bring what is called "sunlight" to this Earth; if we did not receive this atomic rain we would live in semi-darkness. What we think is light from the sun, is the sun's energy that burns them up and creates daylight. But for these atoms we should be covered beneath a kind of volcanic ash and life could not exist.

When things are viewed from the inner spheres we see a light about us that creates no shadow. If a Yogi brings his inner light into a room, this produces a similar effect: an equal distribution of light without any shadow. It is this inner atomic substance that the teacher brings into his student's atmosphere.

There is also another kind of atomic rainfall castoff from planets more evolved than our own that do not resist the sun's energy. These interpenetrate the interspaces between the atoms of the world's sheath and illuminate the minds that can register them. The Dayspring of Youth is of this nature, but from the Sun behind the sun. This is mentioned in the Commentaries of the *Comte de Gabalis,* and scientists are beginning to learn about this force.

From *Washington Evening Post,* October 15, 1931. "Rome: Myriads of cosmic rays pour down upon the earth from distances hundreds of millions of miles farther away from the sun, each ray carrying energy of 786,000,000 volts, four distinguished scientists reported here to-day.

"Robert A. Millikan and Arthur Compton, American scientists, and Professor Bruno Rossi, of the University of Florence, reported on the rays to the congress of physicists meeting here. Mme. Curie, co-inventor of radium, corroborated their statements.

"The two Americans told the congress that experiments conducted this Summer disproved theories that such rays proceed either from within the Earth's atmosphere or from the sun or visible stars. The place of origin, they said, is interstellar regions unknown even to astronomers.

"Thus far, the scientists said, the experiments have been in the field of pure science. When utilitarian science takes a hand in the researches, they have indicated that the tremendous energy contained in the cosmic rays may be harnessed and converted to man's use.

"Professor Millikan, of the California Institute of Technology, reported he had divided the cosmic ray into four substances: helium, oxygen, silicon, and iron, containing 27,000,000 volts, 100,000,000 volts, 260,000,000 volts and 443,000,000 volts. Professor Compton, of the University of Chicago, carried on experiments in the Rocky Mountains at an altitude of 13,000 feet.

"The two Americans told how they had arrived at the conclusion that the rays had nothing to do with the Sun by observing their intensity day and night when the Sun was of different strength, and finding the intensity invariable.

"The same observations, they said, proved that the rays did not come from stars visible to astronomers.

"The rays vary in intensity according to altitude, they said. The rays on Pike's Peak were four times stronger than those at sea-level. At a height of 46,000 feet, reached by a captive self-recording balloon, the rays were ten times stronger, while at 245 meters underwater the rays were almost entirely absorbed.

"Mme Curie described experiments in Paris in the passing of rays through iron and a magnetic field measure their energy."

Sometimes when lying down we gently massage the eyeballs; this agitates the ophthamic nerves for a moment, and the pineal gland, sympathetically reacting, becomes energised, and one perceives a radiation similar to diffused sunlight. This is the light the Yogi radiates. The Yogi says that if one atom can be illuminated it will illuminate others. By concentrating upon a flammable substance a Yogi can cause it to burn.

As the earth rushes through space it constantly picks up atomic clusters—many of these were dispersed into the atmosphere at the time of the destruction of Atlantis—and some of these clusters provided the Atlantean robots with an intellectual force.

In the deeper states of our secondary system is an intellectual principle. This is not intelligence, but mind-stuff material that will seize and enslave the brain. From intellect we gain nothing that would advance us to our source. As we are ignorant of the true definition of these terms, we speak of great souls as great intellects, whereas they are great intelligences.

We can learn parrot-like and bathe in this illusion of intellect, memorising what other great minds have experienced; but what intellectual discussion has ever brought man nearer to God?

In an ancient Chinese painting one division shows the student carrying his soul on a lotus leaf into a group of learned men, where he listens to their discussion. After he has left this group he is seen alone with Nature studying the lower activities wherein he receives his first contact with the consciousness of Nature, and later we see where he unifies himself with the consciousness of the cosmic ray.

These hierarchal forces possess three distinct attributes: creative, destructive, and protective. Mantras also possess similar qualities.

CHAPTER TWENTY-EIGHT
NATURAL MAGIC

KNOWLEDGE of natural magic came to us in the early Lemurian days. This was handed down to Atlantis and from there to the Initiate priests of Egypt. This power caused animate things to respond to their invocations, and in this manner they carried on interesting conversations with their sacred animals. They could also interpenetrate substances with atoms and place records within them, so that later adepts could contact this atomic substance and read its message.

The Master atom within the Silver Shield can instruct us in this ancient science.

Egyptian statues impregnated with such records were immersed for several weeks in a substance that imprisoned these atoms; for they believed that in a future life they could return and reveal what they had hidden. It should interest the student to know that perhaps he himself has sealed up, by the use of elemental magic, his own records that he might release in some future day. This, as we have previously written, is his own birthright.

Many Atlantean records sealed in this manner were possessed by the Egyptians, and we have been told that future scientists will invent instruments whereby much of Egypt's hierarchal wisdom will be unlocked.

In ancient Atlantean days the well-being of the community was vested in a small body of Initiates. They were united to their Innermost, and for some time their enemies were slain by the sword of Justice. Their atmosphere was completely different from that of this age. They formed a sacred college wherein they passed their wisdom down to their disciples and brought about a golden age of intelligence for those under their Shekinah before great destructive wars overwhelmed their civilisation.

Their method of instruction was to return to a disciple his own knowledge of Nature's laws, and they also taught about the future, and, knowing what kind of future atmosphere was to surround this globe, they created what are called Teraphim, or speaking idols, that could be adjusted to a future age.

A student was immersed in liquids of an alcoholic nature: the atmosphere that was to be; then a seated image was placed in the bath, an element of the student's Nous atom being transferred into this image. When this occurred the atmosphere of the Nous atom followed and formed within the Teraphim a composite atmosphere similar to the Nous atom. This process usually took several weeks, and an instrument was used for the purpose of transferring this atomic element. This image could then impress its mental activity into those minds that contacted it; for now a powerful intelligence was imprisoned in this image.

Ages later one of these images was placed in the Ark of the Covenant that then delivered its oracles.

A certain brotherhood possesses a means of receiving information from their Teraphim when permitted to consult it.

To enter the consciousness of Nature and gain her determinative energy one becomes schooled by her teachers in this elemental or natural magic. We all possess these substances composed of the elements in the ether surrounding us, and we can draw upon what our physical body has reserved.

If we are healthy we always have a reserve of these elemental atoms, and the Yogi seeks to build up a huge reservoir of this force that is responsive to Nature's will. These reserves are similar to an army radiating about our nerve centres and can be drawn upon in moments of great strain or anxiety. It is this that we have attracted to each nerve centre that determines our strength and power of resisting the opposition atoms of this world. If our reserves are exhausted we easily succumb to evil and disease, if not we can live to a long age as well as enjoy health in all our organs.

In the golden age of Egypt the average age of a religious man was 120 years; for their religious observances dealt with the proper sanitation of their environment, and the cleanliness and purification of their outer as well as inner bodies.

In the future, scientists will discover that our supply of energy is within the keeping of elemental Nature, and if we disturb her functions within our system we shall not be assisted unless we are ignorant that we have broken her commandments; for Nature, the great mother, tempers her justice with mercy.

If we insist in doing things against our health, Nature will refuse to give us the use of her reserve energy stored for critical periods.

The Master atom within the Silver Shield determines how we should protect ourselves in cases of accidents or infectious diseases, for it controls this reserve energy, and if we can call upon Nature's determinative will we shall then possess a great reserve of this elemental vitality. When we come under the directing intelligence of the Master atom, it often calls upon us to spray this power into diseased bodies, and this assists them to return to a normal state.

It is interesting to note that the Master atom can sense the abnormal conditions of people about us, and to protect its own instrument it will seek to assist the Worker atoms in the bodies of others within its vicinity. When a student sprays a person's atmosphere with this healing force the person on leaving will sometimes remark how much stronger and vital he feels. This is also why sick people like to bask in the atmospheres of healthy bodies. But selfish people can never draw upon this energy from the Master atom; though they often vampirise others.

Man little realises how great this latent reserve force is and how seldom it is drawn upon. When we serve Nature, Nature will serve us fourfold.

There is a plane in the inner spheres called "The World of Secrets." Strange to say, it is the Mohammedan Initiates who know most about it. But there are rules to prevent them from revealing this knowledge.

Here the student can see those inventions that will be used by man in the future, and sometimes, if he is worthy, and the time is ripe, he will study an invention and be allowed to bring it to the world.

Early Rosicrucians in Europe taught their students the method of leaving the body and entering this secret plane, and they kept many inventions hidden till the world was ready for them. Their power to transmute base metals to gold was common knowledge to the initiated, but this was only used to favour certain causes; such as the endowments of hospitals, asylums for the poor and aged, and seats of learning for the young.

Scientists are not permitted to go beyond a certain point. Nature then steps in and for a time closes down the activities in certain fields of science. If one seeks to reveal that for which the world is not ready he is warned three times, and if he persists he is removed.

This once happened to a great soul I was privileged to know, though I was ignorant of his name at that time, or the great work he did for his country, till after his death.

He met me apparently by chance in a foreign country, and only afterwards did I realise that he travelled a long distance to meet and welcome me. One evening returning to my room I found him seated in my armchair, and this seemed strange to me, for I had not told him my name or address when I met him; but before going out I had ordered a fire to be lit. Why I did so I did not know, for I was very poor and living the life of a student. Yet whenever I had ordered a fire to be lit that winter, I found him in my room on my return from an evening class.

Before he died he addressed an audience of scientists and told them that in his next lecture he would reveal a great discovery he had made, after eighteen years of research in deciphering an ancient Arabic alchemical document, that would place chemistry upon a new footing. But this was not to be, and he died; for the world was not yet ready to receive this knowledge.

In this plane of secrets can be seen models of aircraft and locomotives entirely different from those now known, and engines of destruction carefully guarded from those who would inflict them upon the human race. There are also methods that would wipe out a famine in a short time and eradicate carriers of disease and obnoxious germs over a large area. I have seen solidified liquids that can retain their shape without any mould or dispersion of their properties, and germinating fluids to produce longevity for several hundred years. Also books that will enkindle the minds of future generations.

CHAPTER TWENTY-NINE
EGYPT

THE great teachers frequently delivered their messages to meet the needs of the people of their day and not the future generations. When entering our secondary system we learn that the prophets addressed distinct classes of people who often represented certain organisations.

If we read our history carefully we shall learn that the people who brought light to their world were fostered under the protective wings of elemental Egypt. Solon who gave Greece its great laws, Moses the Lawgiver, Apolonius of Tyana the great magician, and Jesus who sought to fulfil the Solonic laws and organise the oppressed castes, all received their instruction from Egypt, guardian of Nature's laws.

The foundations of Egypt's great period were based on elemental laws that sprang from a remote Neptunian activity the Egyptians called Amenti. From this consciousness the Egyptian's Innermost built up Its lower sheaths as we to-day are building up, under the manifestation of the Sun, our lower sheaths.

In the past, Egypt reached a degree of development that will take us several centuries to attain, and the Yogi reverences and aspires to its golden age, and often contacts the atomic centres within him that unites him to this great civilisation and ancient wisdom.

As Egypt worked under the aegis of the higher counterpart of the moon—known to Astrologers as Neptune—and therefore being exceedingly elemental, the Pharaoh Akhenaten, aware of the deficiency of the Sun's positive nature in his people, endeavoured to re-establish sun worship in its purity; but in this he failed, for the elemental wavelength of the Egyptian consciousness was far stronger.

When the student travels in the inner spheres and visits Egypt he enters an elemental realm, and in initiation he is often brought in touch with these elemental gods who directed Egypt's higher attainments. These gods are terrible to behold, especially Horus, and on his forearm he wears massive golden rings. When he gives one to an Initiate, as he did to Moses, he becomes a people's leader.

The characteristics of this Neptunian-Amentian consciousness gives one the power to penetrate deeply into any problem, solve it, then cast it out of one's consciousness. This is a power many business men possess.

The depths of the Neptunian consciousness are far greater than we can know, and as we enter its activity it gives us a powerful current that helps us quickly to complete a thing without any apparent effort. It has a healing effect upon those who suffer mentally, if they can contact its consciousness, also repair and seek to re-establish those souls who have lost contact with their directing purpose. An employer possessing this consciousness would know the possibilities of his workers, and would never place square pegs in round holes.

Within the Egyptian soul and atmosphere were opposition atoms of the Secret Enemy that would have imprisoned the Egyptian mind as they imprison the mind of to-day in this world of illusion. To escape this dark period that the great Initiates of Egypt knew was coming, they embalmed the bodies of their dead and thus protected their atoms from the destructive force of man's thought. This shielded them until the out-pouring of the new hierarchal cosmic energy—the Dayspring of Youth, that they called the coming forth by Day—released them.

This did not mean that their mental bodies lay in a comatose state; for these evolved through Amenti, and arose from the depths of their Neptunian consciousness to become enlightened and purified beyond human conception.

In our inward journeys we have seen these Egyptian souls, though minute, in their myriads; for out of the body a soul is a shining atomic substance about the size of a thumb. They emanate a powerful mental atmosphere, and constantly ask us when we will give them the signal for the release of their Ka's from their tombs, which would give them complete freedom of movement.

We are told that when a great Initiate returns to Egypt the mental pressure of these millions will be evoked, and will flock to his banner and shield him with their atmosphere from the destructive forces that will shortly appear at a great crisis in the world.

Many students have within them their old Amentian consciousness, and the Master atom within his Silver Shield will sometimes link them to this. They will then learn about destructive as well as constructive phenomena by the use of sounds and colour and the formation of sentences that will call into activity the elemental nature about them.

There are certain schools on Earth that use the dark side of this Amentian magic. The one nearest to Europe is in the Balkan regions and is a disturbing factor in the world's atmosphere. There is also another school, but constructive, as far North as the edge of the Mongolian desert. I am only speaking about the great schools of these forces, for the world is full of men trying to disturb Nature's laws, and these lesser schools are not so important, as they deal with ceremonial magic and do not know much about the deeper side of these good and evil forces.

There is an Amentian school of white magic, using Nature's determinative energy, in Asia where resides a great Being called the "King of the North," though the real title should be the "King of the Northern Latitudes." Ossendowski, the traveller, has written about this Being, whom he called the "King of the World," in his book *Beasts, Men, and Gods*.

The entrance to this secret place is guarded by a great elemental whose mental pressure and glance is enough to terrorise the untrained mind; but the Yogi can enter this subterranean place if his passport is correct.

Amenti was the submerged Neptunian sphere where the Egyptians and Greeks were to perform heroic deeds in order to regain their inheritance known as the Dayspring of Youth. The Greeks called this Hades; but this was not, as some people think, a mythological hell, but a region wherein they gained certain defined ranges of experience.

This descent into Amenti-Hades is symbolised by the story of Proserpine, the daughter of Ceres—Nature going into this world. And when Hermes-Mercury was sent to guide her back, this meant that the Lords of the Mind assisted Proserpine—the Daughter of Nature—to return in the Spring—the Dayspring of Youth.

Though this myth has been taught us to symbolise the return of Spring to the Earth, in the deeper occult schools it symbolised the return from a remote voyage of experience of these Amenti-Hades souls into this new age.

The Dayspring of Youth is also symbolised by the Egyptians as the time of deliverance of those atoms preserved to this age by the mummified bodies in Egypt. This means that the Ka's of these bodies—or astral entities—will be delivered from their period of seclusion and work to assist humanity to regain its severance from the lower animal nature within them.

These atoms were prevented from returning to their natural elements, and are held prisoners until this new hierarchal energy releases them. We are told that in some remote day those atoms that cannot be freed from the illusion world will also attain their deliverance.

Many people have pondered over the mystery of the Sphinx. The defaced image we see is the physical symbol of a great elemental Being of a hierarchal order. It is the sole guardian of ancient periods of Nature's elemental wisdom, and within a finer atmosphere there is a secret temple where instruction is given to those who have attained to Nature's consciousness; though here it is not easy for the student to enter the College or stand before the Sphinx. If he only passed the barrier he would have to be free from evil and respect this science.

When the student demands admittance he is measured regarding his fitness by a Warden. In occult terms this means that the spinal column is measured, and if the Warden or Tyler permits him he will then enter a new world of development.

In this College of the Sphinx the Tyler is seated on a cube-like throne. He was a great Initiate Pharaoh who taught his Egyptian disciples elemental magic. This Initiate remains behind until the last magician of his cycle has attained to his level of consciousness.

This Tyler's arms are crossed, holding his sceptre and flail or scourge of Justice, and is the real administrator of this hidden science of Nature's determinative energy. Should he admit us to this College, he will challenge us and give us, if worthy, the power to overcome any opposition any guardian may have against us as we pass into higher levels.

The ancient Masons were acquainted with this College, and came under its administration, and their names were inscribed upon its scroll.

In this College the student will be united to his own wisdom experience of elemental Nature.

The Temple of the Sphinx is the repository of Masonry in its purest form, and the Chinese Masons have attained to a singular purity of its expression.

Here is a note that should be of interest to the Masons. In ancient Egyptian Masonry it was the elemental Tyler who examined the aspirant regarding his elemental fitness, besides those others who examined his physical and moral fitness. It is this lack of Nature's support and wisdom that modern Masonry seeks, for to-day no Brother Mason is aware of being challenged by an elemental Tyler. Yet, in every true Lodge one stands at the entrance, and a Mason, initiated when out of his body in sleep, knows of Nature's place in his ritual.

All the secrets of Masonry are found within man, not without; when Solomon's Temple was built it was erected by the alliance of Nature's finer forces with man and symbolised the human body.

The great elemental Sphinx is Nature's Advocate, and its energy is only intermittently brought into humanity's atmosphere; for as we have been working under the Solar forces, she will not take us under her direction until we contact our elemental Advocate and the Dayspring of Youth sends its consciousness into us.

As above, so below. As we have written elsewhere, we cannot contact our own elemental Advocate until we bring our Master atom into our Silver Shield.

In our practice we have built up our Silver Shield and provided a temple for the Master atom of the mind. This Master atom is like a pendulum, swinging intermittently from the Solar atmosphere to the Lunar: for we have within us an alternating current that carries the Master atom backwards and forwards. This current opens and shuts out different centres, and because of this we have often to wait patiently for the opening of a certain centre from whence we wish to gain information. But if at times it is necessary to quickly obtain information from a closed centre we can approach the Wardens, for each centre has two Wardens—one of the sun and the other of the moon—and if we are deemed worthy we are passed through.

From the Egyptian records we are constantly referred to the attainments of the great Initiate Jesus; for when He came to Egypt after his return from distant lands one of the initiated took down His words and from these hidden books we receive a great deal of information. Though this will probably be challenged, yet these records are preserved intact, and in some future day the archaeologist's spade will reveal them.

The records used by the religious sects to the work of Jesus are but fragments of His teachings. In the Egyptian soil are the real records. When they are revealed we shall learn how man can be illusioned by a religion that is but the fragment of an Initiate's great work—how a religion can become partly destructive by those who hold it sacred when it is incomplete.

Within us are those Elder atoms who have recorded the teachings of the great Initiates, and the student reverences them; for they work obediently to natural law, and reveal their possessions to those alone who respect their authority. Thus the student can contact within himself the essence of any Initiate's teachings whose cloak once protected him in past lives. But only when he has attained his own central system will the fullness of an Initiate's teachings be revealed.

There are several places in Egypt where records relating to Atlantean history are hidden: also those dealing with America after Atlantis, and the coming of a great Initiate to the Red Indians on the Eastern coast; who taught them agriculture and gave them an alphabet, leaving two books that are still in the possesion of an initiated Indian.

The Indians at that period possessed a code of morals and social laws undreamed of by those who came after, and in the future, when the Red Indian has established himself within his own territory, they will be brought to light. In those days these Indians were living simply, without destroying animal life unnecessarily. They cultivated the soil and the tribes lived in harmony. But a little later a foreign people swarmed in from the Caribbean Sea and forced them to take up arms, and ultimately severed the tribes from their previous unity.

In the future, America will have to bear its karma regarding its treatment of these people, and they will increase until they will be powerful enough to demand their own provinces and hold them. Then the American Federation of States will reach to the Arctic Ocean, and these people will extend their territories Northwards and live at peace with their neighbours. For the great Initiate will shield them and return them to their inheritance.

Yogis are often instrumental in holding a force in check that is destructive to others, and in the College of the Sphinx they will remember how this is done.

When the student bathes in the atmosphere of this elemental Sphinx, he remembers the time when he was androgynous and was conscious of his elemental and physical nature. In this manner he regains his knowledge of elemental law.

In Egypt's early days the hierarchal energy of Nature entered its civilisation and prospered its development. Afterwards a small body of disciples of the Sun-God's Initiates, whom to-day we call the Great Atlantean, blessed them with his Shekinah and this now rests upon the shoulders of a small group of men who have preserved intact the instruction that is to be used in the Dayspring of Youth. The well-being of Egypt lies in the hands of a group of impersonal men and women.

Over the altar of their hidden temple hovers a pulsating monadic substance that symbolises the Illuminate Crown of Victory. This Monad has often left its altar, and once it moved itself to Glastonbury in England, during the age of sun worship. But opposing forces later disintegrated it, and it returned to its original shape and place high above the altar of its ancient sanctuary.

In the remote past, the Egyptian priests came to Glastonbury at the Spring Equinox; as also many of the initiated from Greece, Rome, and the surrounding countries. At the moment of the solstice, when the hierarchal earth-current entered the earth, the High priest of its cult delivered the oracle for the coming year, and the initiated returned with their messages to their countries. During the Autumn Equinox this current passes through Tibet.

To-day this monadic substance pulsates to the great theurgic rhythm of the universal consciousness. We believe there will come a time when this Monad will return to Glastonbury, be enshrined there in a temple dedicated to the Sun. For it was foretold that it would move Westward, following the path of the Sun.

In a remote place in America there is a Teraphim that contains an imprisoned atomic atmosphere that predicts the future prosperity of the great American Federation of States. These future states, extending North to the Arctic Ocean, will be under the care and observation of the Great Atlantean Initiate. There will be a division of territories best adapted for the many races to enter their fruitful inheritance, who will work in harmony and union for the betterment of its poorest individual.

America's future prosperity will depend upon its response to this new cosmic energy now pouring over several sections, and if we aspire to the intelligence within its several rays we shall become part of its manifestation. So that everyone will in some degree be able to acquire a directing impulse. For the Atlantean has been for some time planting into the subsoil of this commonwealth those atoms that will give the younger generations the new impulse—that consciousness that will unite them to Nature's law, so that they will instinctively obey it regardless of outside conditions. We see that scientific minds will also work under this new energy.

Each person has an individual atmosphere, and in all occult work we have to be guided by our own intelligence; for as we awaken into the energy of the Dayspring of Youth we are also individualised as persons and will have no strong affinity to other minds. This the student will observe in his relationship to others. We receive their ideas and give forth our own; but we do not possess their intelligence, neither do they possess ours as formerly: we become foreign to their atmosphere. This separation will cause many students some difficulty, at first, in understanding other people easily; for the world of the past with its decayed influences no longer stimulates them. All old thoughts, conceptions, and ideals have passed away; the mind is nourished upon the foods of a new age. The student becomes as a child entering a new world of experience, and is protected by those powers he has awakened.

.   .   .   .   .

Moral standards differ in every country, and we cannot judge them until we know what standards we have attained to within ourselves.

The Great Initiate, under whose care the West area is being developed, does not tell us what should do, but implants into our mind-atmosphere those atoms that will instruct us about our future welfare. And in our efforts to recover our high standards of living, we also find in this substance love and appreciation of our faulty efforts. As far as we know, we are never commanded to do this or that unless it is to save life.

CHAPTER THIRTY
CHINESE CONSCIOUSNESS

WHEN we are united to our secondary system we pass into an advanced period of experience and slowly gain a rounded consciousness of intelligence. As the Chinese adepts say: "When several of these states or atoms, that have preceded us, unite into a central unit, then the adept has regained his rounded consciousness." The secrets of these Chinese adepts have never been revealed, and to-day several schools work under the direction of this consciousness.

The history of the Chinese mind has yet to be written. Those foreign to its consciousness have endeavoured to enter and understand it, but they who have accomplished this are few. Only one, we are told, has attained this in the West. Several Western people have gained a knowledge of some of the secrets of its artistic expression, but if we wish to fathom the integrity of this race we must apply our own integrity towards understanding it. A Chinaman once said: "When our own ideals are exhausted then we will adopt those of the West."

I have been told by a great Tibetan magician that the Chinese language signifies more than is known to the public. That within it are keys revealing hidden meanings, and that the composite body of its language will be disclosed to the world at some future period. Their systems of education—now lost in antiquity—were the means of preserving records of events now only known to those initiated into its secrets.

The English vowel sounds are not related to our inner energy, and the secret of the Chinese vowel sounds lies in that they vibrate to the lost chords of Nature. This is why the best Chinese and Indian music is considered, by those who understand such things, to be superior to ours; for it relates us to these lost chords. Some day we shall learn how to pronounce such sounds and draw upon this hidden energy, that reacts upon magnetic fields within our nasal organs, and attract the different atomic energies diffused within our atmosphere.

The occult student who is in business can put into practice, if he will but realise it, those teachings he receives from his secondary system. Delay regarding a thing we should do at once, and do not do, inflicts the mind and troubles us. Successful business men—and they are philosophers in their own limited range— attend to a thing at once. What the student should learn is: not to fear a thing. The Chinese understand this, and talk a thing over immediately before a misunderstanding can gather headway. The reason for this is that the Secret Enemy can then gain no loop-hole and so bring about a greater disturbance. By such a method the student teaches himself to abolish fear.

The greatest tyrants in business have their good side, and the student can, by proper use of the imagination, generally evoke this by sending his best qualities into the man's atmosphere. As a teacher once said regarding a man who was trying to ruin him: "I have sprayed his atmosphere with my best atoms." Strange to say, six months after this man returned begging for instruction. A seed-thought planted into a person's atmosphere takes six months to germinate. This is why students who apply for assistance are seemingly neglected; for the teachers say, "We await the time of their healing."

In these instances we are dealing with normal people; but there are people in whom it takes far longer to bring things to flower. The egotistic and showman type of student, who has gained a little and begins to build a school about his personality, takes a long time to grow spiritually. Seeds will not be distributed into the minds of unjust men, no matter what their rank and position in the world; for this is something that can neither be bought for gold nor title, but by faithful service to one's fellow-man.

Moral worth does not come from handed-down tradition. It enters the world from its own secluded systems of intelligence, and often a man who has been unfortunate or fortunate enough to have been born in degraded conditions has an intelligence to guide and direct him that can be of a high standard of moral worth, and he will unconsciously radiate this atmosphere into all who come into his presence and purify them.

I have known a worldly man to suddenly leave a room wherein a great soul was seated, and as he passed into the hall he was heard saying to himself: "Unclean, unclean, so unclean." Afterwards, when asked to explain his rude behaviour, he replied: "I could not stand that man's atmosphere. I felt my mind was unclean as well as my body, and in need of a bath; so I went and had one."

The deposit of filth that a mind can carry cannot be too greatly exaggerated. The sensual type is full of such atoms, and these attract atoms of a like nature.

In a Chinese work dealing with the Solar force we read: "In our Solar force are many Disciple atoms possessing the greatest intelligences. But if we only pursue worldly things, they will not record their knowledge within our Silver Shield. Only when we rise above our worldly appetites and desires will they take us into their confidence and teach us their wisdom, instructing us in the fulfilment of the law of the Innermost. If we are backward in our development, these atomic intelligences will dissipate our ignorance in this life as well as in others; they will place within the silken membranes of the Solar body's envelope their own atoms to remedy our faults, and permeate our intelligence with their illumination."

CHAPTER THIRTY-ONE

THE ELEMENT OF FIRE

THE element of fire now begins to manifest within the student, and he will work for a long period in it. This slowly consuming fire will now gravitate into the atmosphere of his mind-body, and he must welcome it, for it will destroy foulness and disease. He will now constantly drink water, as the nervous system will need it to extinguish the grosser elements of fire and make room for its higher counterpart. This higher vibration should pass through him without resistance. It is the density of matter that rebels against it.

He will now breathe in the Solar force atoms, and this will mean spiritual rebirth; for he must leave his ancestral inheritance and teachings of a religious nature, and seek the religion he has created within his own central universe, wherein are stored fragments of each dynasty through which he has passed. Here he will discover what he has experienced of the Reality, and what he knows about truth and justice in their higher as well as lower aspects.

To evoke this flame and be reborn into its atomic structures is the great step he must now undertake. He must pass into its nature and succumb to its desire.

The Sun has the power to transfer us into a substance similar to its elements, and this brings us deeper realisations of what our physical and mental bodies can become. In the East this sun element is called the Lawgiver, and again we repeat our previous exercises to bring these Solar atoms into our bodies.

In the beginning we aspired inwardly and breathed atoms that repaired our physical structures, and revealed to us our undiscovered areas and past experiences. We now enter into the activity of their higher counterpart.

These Aspiring atoms built new elements within our organs and remedied them as much as possible. This cleared us, in some small degree, from the atoms of destruction. We then begin to increase our Solar energy and seek to become ennobled by its powers.

These new atoms—atoms of abundance—have come to us from a distant past, and they represent a type of activity foreign to our body; for they represent periods when we were similar to the elements of the Sun. But at first we cannot recognise what they symbolise. In our practice we again breathe them in as we did in our early days, when we were intermittently immersed in their consciousness. This also brings the energy of the Dayspring of Youth.

We now seek to unite ourselves to this new energy in order that we may become its instrument; it contains the message and power of deliverance for humanity, and we must develop our bodies to become its sounding board whose surface can be attuned to any consciousness that the earth-streams may press upon it. The earth-currents are not the hierarchal streams, but bodies of atoms that flow into us and inspire our atoms to build up their structures regardless of our own personal feelings in the matter.

The earth-currents are similar to the ebb and flow of the tide, and within them are atoms of an instructive nature that stimulate our lower sheaths.

The hierarchal streams are similar to the sun's positive nature. We now come under its jurisdiction—that is of a father consciousness—instead of being nourished by our mother atom under whom we have been working. Here we will be taught regarding our true destiny and plan and the kind of body we have to build up.

We owe a debt of gratitude to mother Nature who brought to birth our systems of natural law and our moral and scientific characteristics. We now enter the positive side of things, as we had previously entered the negative or feminine side where our emotions and sympathies for humanity were awakened.

From these inner observations we discover a wonderful law of order and design, and this ever impresses us; for we realise that the Creator's thought is directing and guiding all things, and the minuteness of our own Solar system becomes apparent.

The element of fire has nothing that is dangerous in itself, nor will it harm us if we apply its energy correctly by listening to our Advocate's directions. The danger lies when it is used for personal power.

To develop this energy depends upon our power to inhale atoms of a like nature. These are within our inner besides outer atmospheres, and they will bring to us teachings regarding the Solar force. We must aspire for this; for the element of fire has the keynote of this universal substance, and of all our past lives united into one composite note. And those atoms that cannot respond to its note are disordered. Hence the resistance of the physical body to its vibration, and the student becomes strongly aware of this power within him. Slowly it will begin to rise and straighten out its coiled substance, awakening when it hears its keynote.

This energy, beginning at the base of the spine, will rush through our central nervous system and seek to leave the body through the top of the head. We must not be afraid to impress its forces within us and engender its living flame with that which we ourselves have stored up in our physical body. It is enclosed within a sac-like sheath, and when evoked will pass within our generative organs and remain there if we allow it; but if we do so, it will turn us into beasts and be used by the Secret Enemy. But if we aspire to evoke it to control our nervous centres and the sun centre within us, it will use its force for our development and enable us to attain intermittent teaching from a great and wise intelligence: a Nous atom belonging to the energy of the Solar system, and we must be strong and bold if we wish to control it, for its nature is foreign to us.

When we unite our Solar and Lunar currents at the apex of the spine, the Sleeping Serpent no longer receives its usual nourishment, and, being hungry, stirs within its sac. The watchman then pours forth the seminal energy; this awakens it, and it begins to uncoil and seek nourishment by trying to enter the door leading into the seminal tract. Here it changes its voltage, and this gives it the power to pierce the opening into the spinal system; it is now fed with a kind of static electricity: the seminal system's higher energy. This force quickens, and it tries to pass up the spine.

It is here that the greatest caution must be observed, for it depends upon us as to the kind of energy it will receive: whether of our higher or lower nature.

This energy has several strands similar to the positive and negative poles of electricity, and these must be severed from the base of the spine and united at its axis; this will then bring up through a third strand the coiled serpent force that will open the nasal organs to its stream of energy. From this third strand the Great Liberator comes to birth; for the third strand is similar to a lightning rod, and about it streams up the hidden fire from our navel tract. This energy will then open our principal centres as we direct them, and the organs of generation will not be able to hold it prisoner. This power will give the student the greatest intelligence he can possess: a lost power long denied him.

This is a gift to humanity from the Innermost; as we develop it we rise above the Secret Enemy's power and possess a substance of the more developed Initiates, who are of its nature.

The Sun atom is similar to the Egyptian scarabaeus, save that it is rounder and consists of two opposite forces—positive and negative, with a wall dividing both. It extends two feelers, like crossed swords, and holds a minute atom—of which it is parent—and from these feelers stream two forces. This is called the winged caduceus of Mercury. The minute atom contains all the elements of fire, and draws the fire nature from the different planets. It possesses an intelligence that is beyond good and evil, which is neither destructive nor constructive; and into such a consciousness the student must not fear to enter. This is the normal state of the Innermost. Here, beyond good and evil, we reach a state of constant bliss, and do not register the sensations or burdens of our human body. This state is the goal of the student.

The Sun element will not instruct us until we are in the boundaries of our Innermost; it will then hasten our development.

The doctrine of the Innermost has to return to us; for we must perform our own ritual and service towards the Supreme ruler of this Solar system and its different densities of matter.

. . . . .

In the human atmosphere there are Sun elementals who have retained the wisdom of the moon. They are far in advance of our day, and are beyond good and evil. These are used in what we call higher clairvoyance. We can attract these atoms into our nodes of thought, and make them communicate with us. This is an instrument that will collect and deliver our messages and send them inwardly to any sphere, as well as to any place on Earth. The method is to impress a thought-wave upon our Silver Shield.

These atoms have their keynote, and the student must aspire to hear it; for by its use it evokes the Sleeping Serpent. This method of using sound-waves to evoke the five systems of atomic substance within us has been hidden from the West. Although the East possesses this knowledge, the West cannot use the same sound invocations, as we live in a different period from the East.

An American entering another country cannot understand why everything seems so slow. He represents a swifter vibration, does not realise that he should adapt his own wave-length to the country he visits. The student should always endeavour to do this, in order not to cause unnecessary annoyance; for his atmosphere can often be offensive. It takes many years before a member of one race can harmonise himself to that of another.

There are many misfits in humanity, and such people, though similar in appearance, do not feel at home or in harmony with their surroundings. Each race has its tribal mark upon the soles of their feet, and in Tibet a scholar will ask his pupil to show him his feet and will then know the parental stem from which he has descended. Sometimes an Eastern teacher will arrive in the West to claim one who seemingly incarnated into the wrong race. This will sometimes cause Westerners to revert to Eastern teachings. If the soles of their feet were examined, the people would be found to belong to a different race. When the seventy disciples of Jesus were sent into their different countries they were led by the markings on the soles of their feet.

The moon current keeps the body moist, the sun current dries it up, and when these currents are controlled the nourishment that the Sleeping Serpent depends upon is denied it; this will cause it to move and open the centre about which it was coiled, and seek to enter it. As it is enclosed in a tissue of membrane, it will seek to break out and pierce the sacral plexus or lowest centre.

When this Serpent begins to move about it will often cause severe pain; for the sensation is similar to a ball of quicksilver moving and tearing its way between the tissues.

When this occurs one must be patient and aspire, for the pain is very severe, and this is apt to last several months; neither should one feel excited or nervous. A steady stream of minute particles are now being energised; these are forced along by the Solar current, so that they can open the centre towards which they are directed and revolve about its axis. These atoms are a combination of sun and moon atoms, and unite into a mass.

The Solar flame is united to the flame of the Innermost, and as we release this flame we are taken from our own sphere and transmuted into the atomic substance of another world period far different from this present one. This new world has no conditions of sadness and misery, and is an intermediate station; for we would perish if we entered the sun's energy suddenly. Here we are called upon to serve its errands of justice, to work in our objective world as it will direct us; and we are also subjected to a severe schooling by the Elder atoms.

We learn that we had attained to this instruction in other lives, and are reminded that we will not gain our source unless we are willing to renounce all things of the Secret Enemy's nature. We are now constantly reminded of our past transgressions, and slowly build a barrier between this past and the Innermost.

In the school of the Elder atoms we have to learn about the trinity in Nature, as well as the trinity within man. These atoms possess the consciousness that was of our Advocates—that have now returned to their own elements—and stimulate us towards our Innermost.

In this intermediate state, that is beyond good and evil, we receive that illumination that will make us harmless to our neighbours, harmless in that we will neither oppose them by force nor by argument. This is the wisdom that some of the great Masters use when dealing with humanity. This consciousness makes us indifferent to people and things. This is not a callous state, for we are more sensitive to their pain and sufferings than ever, but we can see deeper and help with greater understanding; for, if we would be of use to this world, there comes a time when we must detach ourselves from it.

This intermediate state shows us how to work with multitudes instead of individuals. When we work in this consciousness, we feel that we are standing thirty feet above the crowd. Many occult students have unconsciously felt this state working through them.

About this time the student becomes aware that many eyes are watching him, and that unseen help is being sent to encourage and assist him. He also feels that these people have awakened their Solar force.

This force comes suddenly to birth; for we have been building up this power of fire. If we have worked at this science in previous lives it will awaken more easily and quickly.

It is well to send a silent prayer inwardly before beginning our practice, and this will harmonise us to our Innermost. A prayer will sometimes evoke something within us that will operate a centre which begins to teach us. When the student is alone, and will not disturb anyone, he should pray aloud with strength and vigour; this vibrates his mental body, and will pass more easily and clearly through the three lower spheres of illusion and contact spheres of worth.

The shaft of light that we send forth in prayer interpenetrates into the higher as well as into the lower planes. The mind should therefore seek purity and not invoke the animal entities of the Secret Enemy that will attempt to control our thoughts and envelop us in harmful conditions.

We are held responsible for our prayers, and as we have not learned how to pray we often inflict our conditions upon those for whom we pray. A group of people praying about a sick bed can sometimes drive out the real personality from the body and allow an obsessing entity to enter.

When we pray we often visualise the person for whom we pray; but we fail to realise that we send our own atmosphere to them as well. This can frequently bring greater disorder than ever.

There are many religious organisations that pray at mass meetings for individuals that they may be converted to their beliefs. They imagine they are helping them, but are on the contrary similar to highwaymen on the mental plane; for they seek to dominate them regardless of their liberty of experience. This can often shut out the true light from those sincerely seeking it.

When the Yogi wishes to assist a person, he first seeks union with his Innermost and asks It for direction; he then contacts the Innermost of the other person and receives the information best needed to help the individual.

In a book previously mentioned by us, *The Comte de Gabalis,* we have written this passage about prayer:

"When you pray, think. Shut out all lower thoughts. Approach God as you would the entrance to a holy place. Ask if it will be well to demand to be given wisdom according to law. Be strong in purpose and firm in demand; for as you seek power of a spiritual nature you will balance that power in self on the lower planes. It is to penetrate beyond these lower planes or spheres of illusion that Jesus said: 'When you pray, SAY these things.' You have by a direct and positive effort to reach the higher spheres of consciousness, therefore let your thought be clear and precise, for a sincere, positive, and well-defined prayer harmonises man with God. On the other hand, an idle or unthinking prayer without definite expression becomes an infliction to the mind and destroys the receptivity to the light. A fervent prayer to the Deity crystallises the mind so that other forms of thought cannot enter, and prepares it to receive a response from the God within.

"Prayer of concentration on the Highest Source man is capable of imagining is a path to Wisdom found."

The use of prayer wheels in Tibet are treated with contempt or merriment by the Western mind, but if we had the graciousness of heart to enquire the reason for this we would be given an interesting and occult explanation that in the light of this book would be easily understood.

These wheels are used in hundreds and thousands in their country, and are turned by hand as well as by water power. They are covered by written layers of prayers and are the sincere appeals of the writers to their deities. These papers are impregnated by the atomic atmospheres of the devotees, and then placed upon the wheel that is set in motion. The result is that these atmospheres form one composite body that attracts atoms of a developed nature that works over this atomic mass and increases and stimulates its spiritual power. The Lama then steps into and collects these developed atoms into his own atmosphere.

In the West we have not been taught the reason for Eastern postures in prayer. These are spiritual, mental, and physical exercises that tend to bring about a union with the Innermost. The Yogis also divide man into three types, three general diseases, and three cures.

CHAPTER THIRTY-TWO
THE SOLAR FLAME

WHEN we evoke the Solar force and send it into the central system it floods each centre as it pierces it with its power. It is then under our domination, and this places within our administration a university that represents a defined period in our evolution. Each centre has that experience stored up for our use and reverts us to its period, whether past or future; for the history of the world when viewed inwardly represents but a moment. Each centre symbolises a round of experience: this means a series of incarnations for a definite purpose.

Each centre has seven doors, and each door unites us to one of the seven attributes of the Innermost.

In time man will fully realise the hidden meanings behind our great religions regarding our inner spheres of being.

The outer man can be best described as an engineer working to produce a mighty atom that will develop the wisdom of his own creation.

A feature of this new age will be to show man the other side of his character: that of his secondary nature.

When our Solar force is awakened it permeates each atom and cell of our body as it rises. This brings new life and vitality to all. In Christian mysticism this is the meaning of the descent of Christ's consciousness to man. The Yogis reverse this term and say that we must rise to it.

The early mystics constantly speak of having had great illuminations; they gave one to understand that they had moments when everything about them radiated light and love. One can ask mystics many questions, but one seldom receives much information. They may get momentary states of bliss, in which a Yogi can remain for hours, and this stimulates them to pray for this visionary state. St. Augustine speaks of having attained this three times.

Just as the student is taught what to expect when he enters the consciousness of his secondary system, so must he be taught what to expect when he enters his central system; for the Solar energy has its own sheath, as well as that of several other Solar and Lunar systems, and it is necessary to contact their intelligences; for the student must learn to analyse the subtleties of their vibrations and immerse himself into their atmospheres.

We have not perfected a substance that can vibrate to the consciousness of the Innermost until we have developed an instrument that can register it and relate its consciousness to our objective plane. For when we enter our central system we can only contact its lower division and awaken our lower centres; not the highest one, called "The Thousand-Petalled Lotus," by Eastern Yogis. When we can evoke the atoms of the Innermost by the use of the Solar force we can attain its consciousness.

Through the wrong use of sound invocation, and during religious revivals of an emotional nature, people have unconsciously evoked the response of several types of atomic energies within the seminal system, and especially in Voodoo rites we know that these people speak in many tongues. Even among the more sophisticated Shaker communities of New England, members in their religious ecstasies would simulate Red Indians and speak their language. This is sometimes a kind of obsession, though not always, and we have witnessed similar things with trance mediums; but there is a demarcation between the utterance of different tongues and obsession.

With the occultist this power called "The Gift of Tongues" is often developed, though at first seemingly subconsciously. A great Initiate can bring this power to birth in his disciples. This is latent in the seminal system and operates the organs of speech. The distinguished members of the great Atlantean chain of illumined minds possess this gift and speak to anyone without the slightest hesitancy. But we have not the consciousness to recollect our past days and tongues; though we are told that when we are developed this gift will return to us. Hence the student must acquaint himself with these atomic structures that possess this gift of returning to him these hidden possessions; and the gift of speech will be essential to the student when passing through the different stages of his development.

Nature has a common language spoken by the Initiates, and in time all humanity will revert to it. When we no longer build up our towers of Babel but seek to regain Nature's response, we shall speak her language, and, like Apolonius, converse with animals. The magician of the finer planes uses one note that sounds like a terrific roar, as if the whole universe vibrated. The din then ceases and he plays upon this note accentuating certain vowels, and in the silence there echoes a metallic sound. This shows us how Nature audibly responds to the magician; but if the note is not sounded correctly then Nature will not respond.

These magicians teach us how to pray with power, and we can see how a thought or word is built up into a composite body, how it emits its note and colour and vibration. In this manner we learn how a thought sent out is like a germinating seed attracting other thoughts of a like character about it. If we can prevent this image from disintegrating, it will return us that substance of intelligence that our thought expressed. In this way do great aspiring minds like Professor Einstein and others receive an answer to their questions. No man without a lofty spiritual ideal can receive information that is of worth to humanity and stimulate other minds.

The nearer one can approach his Innermost, the greater is the expression of his teachings for man. Emerson and Carlyle, whom we again mention, for they were of the few who worked from the inner planes, often brought their torch of divinity within other minds. But to-day the atoms of the Secret Enemy are so powerful that few minds are strong enough to think; for their thoughts are immediately disintegrated by this outer atmosphere. He who can gain the virtue of a thought places it in his secondary system, thus it escapes the illusion of this world. Where people look, there they place their minds; their eyes being usually on this objective world, their thoughts are easily disturbed.

In our inner schools we realise why Justice is symbolised by a bandage over her eyes. We are told that in a remote future our judges will be men who were born blind.

From the *Atlantean Testament of Learning*, we learn: "As you plough it will come to you to sow for those who cannot work and furrow the ground."

The atoms within the seminal fluid are of different types, and these represent a distinct world evolution or development. In ages past we evolved through other Solar periods, and these other energies are added to the composite energy of the Solar fire, that, when awakened and freed, also awakens these far different Solar and Lunar periods now beyond the range of normal consciousness. When, through our practice, we are united to their vibrations, we direct their power into the seminal tract and from thence into our central spinal system, and feel overcome with joy when we do this; for we have freed the imprisoned Solar atoms that can now return to their own source.

When we can bring the element of fire into the atmosphere of the Nous atom's workers, who have served us faithfully, we raise their consciousness.

There is an atomic watchman in the seminal system who registers our thoughts towards our Innermost. When the Secret Enemy seeks to pour through its interspaces a collective silver fluid that causes us to become conscious of its evil activity, he guards us against contamination from the servants of this evil power. He also uses this energy to open the door leading to our central system. This energy is the higher counterpart or distillation of our seminal power of creation, and this is also the energy that protects the Sleeping Serpent with its atmosphere. This shields it from being directed by the Secret Enemy, though this atomic watchman will obey the student whether it is directed for good or evil.

All this should be done under the tuition of a teacher, and not for selfish gain. Unless he aspires to the highest it will make him a beast instead of a god-enlightened man. The seminal system possesses our holiest atoms and atoms of a most debased and destructive nature. Hence the old Hermetic saying: "Where the light is brightest, there you will find the deepest depths of the shadow."

The lower intelligence within the seminal system has the wisdom of the foulest nature that human ingenuity can conceive, and if this is developed it will engender us with its passions and desires; for we can inherit the foulness of our ancient days when we were ignorant and uncouth and lower than the present animal kingdom. The higher side of this energy must be aroused. When this is done we can command the lower side of our intelligence and wisdom, also a period of consciousness when, angels devoid of any moral nature, we subsisted upon the sidereal universe and were not subject to incarnation. These were the angels mentioned in the Bible, who came over to this Earth and became conscious of its beautiful women. This does not mean that we were Luciferian beings who ruled over the lower kingdoms; but angels led to observe the conditions of the Earth and help it. These "Married the daughters of men," and taught man the arts; for "There were giants in those days."

Before we can use our Solar energy correctly we must go through a preparatory course of Yoga, about which we have already written. We must re-experience the merits and demerits of our past lives. As we aspire, this watchman will help us by assembling to its atmosphere atoms of the highest nature; these release within us the power to enter a trance state of bliss, in which bliss we gain the sacred vision.

The zodiacal signs of Cancer and Capricorn represent the first manifestation of our material universe before we evolved through the breath-world, then the form world, and afterwards the physical world. It is to return to the first manifestation of our universe that we aspire for those pure atoms that will ultimately help us to re-enter it; the world of our Innermost or breath-world.

Through the practice of Yoga we can consummate and bring to birth within us those atomic substances that, through failure, were removed from us when we developed our sex body. This is represented by the lowest sign in the zodiac.

When we enter the breath-world of the Innermost, we find ourselves without form, beyond life as we registered it, without a sex body, alone and yet not alone, within a vapour of fire and radiance. This state of bliss is beyond any human comprehension, and here the student is given the understanding of his Innermost. This is called "The flight of the Alone to the Alone."

In this seminal system, the advanced atoms migrate into the blood stream and are caught up into the Silver Shield. These having the atmosphere of the Innermost can, in response to its intelligence, form a channel through which our Architect atom manifests its plan to us. We can attain union with our Innermost through our Solar energy; but we must provide the means for this attainment. This is done by raising our hidden energy to its true pitch, and when this is directed upwards, it is given additional energy as it pierces each centre and releases their latent properties. Thus from centre to centre its voltage increases, producing for us a hidden subtle energy that is unequalled by anything scientists have yet discovered. This is the Innermost's energy that later we seek to unite to the cosmic consciousness of the Reality. And they who have become one with this greater consciousness—the Christ consciousness in Nature—are the great Initiates.

If we become at one with Nature's determinative energy, we can then DETERMINE the activity of thought; and thoughts are THINGS we can use in relating ourselves to our Innermost. Nature has her sovereigns who will obey us, and when we aspire for our own kingdoms in Nature we can, we find, command great administrators whose work is to obey us; and, if we employ them as the Law demands, we can use certain powers. If our thoughts are preceded by Nature's determinative energy, they will become powerful and vital entities; for we have protected them with an elemental shield, and the opposition will be unable to disintegrate or hamper them from attaining their aim. This is known as determined thought.

The cosmic energy entering the world to-day has this determinative element. This we seek to gain in order to become its instrument, just as future generations will.

The determinative energy that precedes a thought is that current that gives a thought its objective appearance, which a developed student can see and analyse. This thought can only be seen when this energy precedes it.

Thoughts rapidly disintegrate unless held together by the positive power of the thinker, and many people do not know their powers, or that they possess this determinative force; that their thoughts can penetrate our illusion world and implant a thought-image into our seminal system. This thought is then analysed and sent to our brain cells, and we can then see it as it has been sent to us; for in the envelope of the atmosphere its elemental impression is left, and the atoms of the Secret Enemy and the opposition of the world atmosphere cannot prevent this thought-wave from sounding its character and expressing itself on some sounding board tuned to its vibration. Thus we have the power to clothe a thought with an energy that cannot be disintegrated by the opposition of this world. Until we have built up our Silver Shield we have no transmitting instrument to relate Nature's determinative thought to the brain, therefore the Transformation atoms in our seminal tract register their vibrations to the brain. But when the Silver Shield is built, we open a receiving station that can register Nature's intelligence.

Hence we find that when the seminal system is clogged or diseased by atoms of an animal nature, or that we have infested this tract with venereal diseases, the disease will be driven from the seminal tract to the brain fibres.[1] These diseases appear almost simultaneously in the brain and in the sexual organs. Hence the necessity to have a pure blood stream by cleanliness and bringing in of atoms of a higher vibration. The evoking of man's Solar energy can cleanse us from all these diseases; for its fire penetrates every element in our body and keeps the blood pure.

Portions of our interior body do not have to incarnate for earthly wisdom and experience; they have already attained it, and the student has to enter their consciousness. To gain this knowledge we become subject to that flame buried within us,

---

1 The Japanese scientist, Noguchi, was the discoverer of this particular fact.

and to its parent: the Sun behind the sun. Within us are several suns similar to our own sun, and when these are united they bring to birth a master Sun—the summit of our cosmic plan.

Up to now we have been developing under two forces: the Nous atom and the Master atom of the mind. They have carried us into our inner worlds and by their aid we evoke the energy of our own Solar force that unites us to our central system of intelligence. The forces of the sun and moon now run parallel, and if we balance these energies we can pass into our inner stream that awakens when these two energies unite.

There are two nerves on either side of the spine: one carries the sun force, the other the moon force. Both are of a physical nature. These currents are electrical and, when united, bring to birth in our consciousness a third energy that links us to our central system. It was normally in a semi-latent state in our physical body, but the positive and negative forces awakened it. These energies unite at the apex of the spine, and there the third current is brought to birth. These three forces give us the power to evoke the Solar flame.

This science may be new to the Western world, but it is a very ancient science known to the initiated.

When we attune ourselves to this Solar energy we rise far beyond what the world calls thought; for here the Silver Shield becomes radiant with this energy and its atomic consciousness is raised to the level of the Master atom within it. When an Initiate appears as though "clothed with the sun," this means that his Silver Shield radiates this inner light.

The student now approaches the summit of his inner world that possesses the static energy of the super Solar force that he draws from his generative organs. For within our seminal tract lie seeds of power and nobility possessing the nature of our Creator. These seeds are the conserved energy of the sun's radiance, being placed within our physical body where they can create or destroy.

Restraining and conserving this force into a powerful energy will ennoble the student, and it will when drawn upon evoke within his body the Sleeping Serpent about which we have written.

When this force leaves the body through an opening in the top of the skull man is no longer a prisoner in this illusion world, but is united to his own central universe, and here finds that he is but a fragment of the Solar system's energy.

This consciousness is difficult to describe. Here we do not communicate by means of speech, but are taught by sounds possessing thought, colour, and emotion. For example: give a blind man a rose. He will only know it by its perfume. This will then bring to his mind the colour and image of a rose. On these planes the soul of a thing is first seen, then clothed in its form, colour, and intelligence.

There is in the semen a distinct essence that, when leaving its sheath, is like vaporous sunlight. This is the energy of the seminal tract that is released at the death of the body, and its Transformation atoms have the appearance of a trident similar to the Neptunian sceptre. We have spoken of this elsewhere.

This emblem is the symbol of life as it is known in other spheres; for it symbolises the destruction of matter and the clearing of illusion from the mind, and also man's Solar energy that he uses to energise his own powers of creation. These atoms can deliver him from this illusion world.

This vapour of Transformation atoms, in conjunction with those Transformation atoms attracted to the magnetic field of the nasal organs, produce a combination of physical and mental attributes to the semen and provide us with a nourishment different from that which we receive from food. It is by means of these Transformation atoms and a third kind that we attract into our system that the Yogi is able to fast and live on but little. This product of the seminal system gives the mind its illuminative powers; for we draw upon it for support and mental stimulation regardless of our other functions that give us energy and sustenance.

Too much drain upon the seminal system exhausts the mind. Life will be greatly changed when we learn to live by this powerful force.

It has been stated by the great Initiates that in time man will subsist without partaking of any animal or cereal food, and that he will draw upon the essence of the Silver Shield when desiring nourishment. The West has never followed the East regarding their conceptions of life. When visiting these Yogis out of the body one feels their powerful vitality. They subsist upon this hidden energy that stimulates their organs, and they are alert and active and do not consume in a week what the normal person would consume in one meal. I have often visited such ascetics and found their auras swarming with an atomic vitality that can prevent one from coming into their presence unless directed by them.

There are many places on Earth that remain to be discovered: cities into which few strangers have passed, often underground and screened by forests, and guarded by these Yogi's atmospheres.

One cannot enter such places while out of the body unless one discovers the method. There is a concealed city in South America that is only revealed to the observer by means of those great adepts living in Central Asia, and one has to gain their permission before one can pass these watchmen in South America.

These retreats are in constant communication with several centres in America, Yucatan, and Southern Mexico. When the world is ready to be told about these underground places it will be astonished at what has been concealed from its knowledge. Those who live by the labour of others, and have commercial interests in these countries, would fight like Cortez or Pizzaro for these treasures if they were revealed to them. The Atlantean secret records have been placed there; records of people who have walked over American soil and who have passed away long before American history began. We are told by the great Atlantean that "During the reign of justice these records will be revealed."

These places have a most interesting way of communication. In Southern California they have a method of sending messages through the earth. When scientists discover this secret our countries will be swept clear of telegraph poles.

In our practice we constantly make new discoveries. We seldom realise how greatly we depend upon the unseen and unsensed forces within our Silver Shield and our physical body: things that do not agitate our brains or carry us within the realm of this objective world.

At first we know little about our silent sentinels who work for our return into our central system. These inner states have atoms that watch over us and seek to deliver us from our objective illusions, and these great intelligences adjust their consciousnesses to ours in order to rebuild us into their world.

These sentinels are permeated with the consciousness of the Innermost; but we are so far beneath them in consciousness that it is rare for us to contact them. But if we are accepted by such high atoms it will take much energy as well as patience on our part to command their respect. Though, through Yoga, we learn to harmonise ourselves with them, we must learn how to transmit their thoughts into our seminal system that is then reflected to our brain. For the greatest atoms in our seminal system respond to the direction of the Innermost just as the Sentinel atoms respond. Thus later in our practice of listening-in to our atomic centres we become aware of the atomic consciousness of our central system: the higher counterpart of our secondary system. And here we will speak of the still finer atomic substance that we all possess though seldom contact.

Within our seminal system dwell those sacred atoms that can relate us to our central system by contacting the student to its poles of instruction. These are large centres about the spinal nerve current that instruct us through the agency of the Solar atoms in the seminal system.

The instruction the student receives from them is similar to that given by a great Initiate, and when he contacts this first centre he finds he is passing through an initiation similar to a physical plane initiation. An initiation means that one is stamped with the approval of a Solar intelligence. This also means the permanent attainment of another consciousness, hitherto unknown, that the student can always contact. An initiation through ceremony does not always mean the attainment or rebirth into another consciousness.

These Solar atoms ennoble us by their mere contact. We have been accepted and feel exalted and strong; for this means we have been observed by a great atomic consciousness within our central universe. It is the greatest teacher the student has so far contacted, and he feels the reverence and respect returned to him that he sends to it. This is done in order to train the student and build a bridge between the two. Thus creating an ever stronger bridge.

These Solar atoms preserve our wisdom records of previous instruction; for some students in their past lives had been accepted into their inner universe, and here is found that wisdom they collected after death sifted down to its finest essence. Those men who have attained this wisdom knowledge are called the Wise Men, and they walk the earth to-day as they did yesterday.

The student's return to his wisdom poles of instruction depends upon his Innermost's power to manifest within this dense atmosphere of matter. This means that there are highly developed and lesser developed students according to their Innermost's response to Its Reality.

Nature's currents are not continuous, and our centres react alternately as her voltage increases and decreases. Thus we are subject to different activities of which we are unaware. Certain sections open and work for several seconds only. This also occurs on the other planes. In our practice we gain information from these currents, just as we gain instruction by wireless when we tune into different stations.

We have passed through Nature's divisions as symbolised by the lower half of the zodiac. When we pass into her higher spheres, we find that we are born to command Nature and learn of our past developments within her area.

In certain divisions of our secondary system we find atoms that have preceded us in our objective development. These enlighten the student regarding their periods and give him food to hand down to his followers. They also decide the type of instruction he wishes to receive for use in his everyday life.

In order to gain an inner receptivity, we must accustom the body to a higher voltage. If we did not use this process of condensation these higher voltages would destroy us. Nature's currents have voltages that scientists have not yet been able to register. And when we are told that it only takes three seconds for a thought to reach the planet Venus, we shall realise what great powers lie dormant within us. We do not know how the body adjusts itself through the terrific streams of energy Nature pours into us, just as we do not think about atmospheric pressure. If we were to block these waves of energy we would be immediately killed; but as Nature adjusts us to our environment such forces pass through us without any resistance beyond our own ranges of normal receptivity.

Yoga teaches us how to acquire a higher voltage, and how to resist it and leave behind our old wavelength as we accustom ourselves to the new. This makes us more powerful and generates in us the protection of the Silver Shield: the sounding board that radiates the intelligence of this new energy known as the Transformation atom. These pour into our nervous systems a power we did not recognise till now.

These processes of resisting these powerful currents eventually awakens the Solar force.

Our response to an ever-increasing higher vibration attunes the objective body to our secondary and central nervous systems. This means that our inner worlds will slowly manifest through the physical body, and the greater our resistance to this vibration the greater will be the response from our Innermost. It is well known to scientists that tremendous electric voltages can flow through the body without harm, yet the moment the subject touches anything connecting him with the earth he will be immediately annihilated; for he has then resisted it.

There is a wise intelligence within us who will not permit the Yogi to resist this voltage beyond a certain range, and if he aspires for guidance he will be protected.

When these higher voltages displace old conditions, the Solar and Lunar currents of our secondary system combine their forces to produce a third: a combination of both qualities, the lightning rod that receives a latent energy we have to evoke after having tuned our bodies to the higher voltage.

Failure to attune the body to these currents will bring disaster and misfortune upon us.

CHAPTER THIRTY-THREE
CONCLUSION

WE all assemble ourselves about our central Sun of experience, and as we develop the central system within us it begins to give us power to bring to birth our hidden possessions. As we advance we realise the importance of our Innermost, and aspire to gain its commanding intelligence; for we must become the real intelligence of the Innermost, as it is the evidence of our inner world; and while we are engrained with the substance of our physical world we cannot assume the operations of the Innermost.

When we return into our physical body, after leaving it, we are impressed with the lack of reverence we had given to our Innermost; for we are again severed from its attributes and govern ourselves by the laws we make in this objective world. Hence the Dayspring of Youth is to give us the power to assume our own individuality and become a secondary being under the united protection of our Aspiring and Transformation atoms who respond to the direction of the Nous atom and the Innermost.

If we are to be secondary people—that is, people with atoms composing our two natures, the secondary and physical—we must obey the laws and edicts that the hierarchal energy will pour forth. This is what we mean by the union with the intelligence of our secondary system and the energy of the Dayspring of Youth, that is a flux which binds these two bodies. This will cause us to live within two worlds at the same time, and our secondary nature will slowly begin to be operative within our mental and lower bodies.

This union with our second self will begin to change the appearance of our physical body; for when we begin to receive our education from Nature and respond to our highest, we then begin to shape ourselves into the image that is the plan of the Nous atom's body.

We have often spoken about Nature working intermittently, and the Dayspring of Youth represents Nature's activity manifesting upon our objective bodies.

The interlinking of these two bodies will cause a period of intense activity within the seminal system and bring to birth the highest form of creative ability as well as the lowest. It will be for us to choose; whether we clothe our bodies within higher or lower atomic substances, and work and aspire towards our secondary system, or develop and evoke our submerged animal nature into our objective atmosphere. This union with the development within our seminal system will produce a human physique similar to the hunting type of man; the hunter who will do so for the pleasure of slaying his own kind and seeks to exterminate all who oppose him.

This period was written about in the ancient Atlantean books; for they have analysed their own hierarchal outpourings and can thus read the records of the future. What we read regarding this future period makes us shudder and recoil; for we read not only about the godlike man, but also of the brute. The reason being that where the light is greater, there the shadows are darker.

It will be for the youth of the future to determine their own attainments in their secondary systems, and these two new caste types will easily recognise each other.

The advanced man will be conscious of possessing two personalities manifesting simultaneously on two planes. To the aspiring student this is symbolised by his twin Advocates, or Castor and Pollux.

The student should constantly bear in mind the saying "as above so below." When we introduce into our bodies atoms of a higher voltage we are slowly immersed into its wave-length. In this manner we are related to our own parental energy. Though the Innermost descended and clothed Itself in matter, It is still related to Its parental stem; as far as we know, this stem is the individual expression of the Reality from which the Innermost sprang. Though we have formed about this, and have changed the nature of its substance, in our practice we try to express and regain Its own true individuality; for we have introduced elements far different from our original pristine substance; and this diffusion of matter hampers the Innermost from relating its intelligence to our mind.

If we study the formation of crystals this will explain what we mean. In the researches of Mitscherlich, 1918-1921,he says:

"The law of replacement of Elements by others of the same group was found to explain the differences of chemical composition observed in minerals which in other respects appear to be the same kind.

"Or again, substances of a crystal may be changed, but so slowly that each particle of new matter takes exactly the position of one of the original particles. As a final result the new matter resumes the form characteristic of what it has replaced."

In the body there is a portion that adheres to its own seat of instruction. These atoms congregate about this seed germ, which is similar in shape to its own Nous atom's image. Each centre within us has become infused with foreign matter, therefore it cannot conform to its true elements.

The opposition atoms have introduced this foreign matter, and it is this cleavage that opposes the Nous atom's plan. Here we find a different atomic energy at work; for as we are divided into several groups that rotate about the Innermost, we cannot reflect Its intelligence within us on account of the infiltration of foreign densities, and so are unable to carry out Its purpose. We find our atoms massed about a general parental stem, but cannot relate them to their original stem until we unite them by Yoga practice. For when we evoke our Solar energy we unite all our centres to their own parental stems, and then unite them to the central system of the Innermost.

The minor parental stems are those that come from the Innermost's parental stem; but they manifest their own individual expression.

It is interesting to note how the Dayspring of Youth is manifesting within the auras of our younger composers, though they are unconscious of this. Man's nerves are all being pitched to a higher key, and a crystalline element is slowly reverting them to their parental stems and conforming them to the image of the Nous atom.

Advanced youth will think for himself and seek to demonstrate his own individuality, and the past that has moulded the youth of our generation will no longer manifest. They will band together and refuse to be dominated by past political or social conditions. The world will be changed by their combined thought; for as one thinks, so he becomes, and the very atmosphere of this world will alter as the Dayspring of Youth forces its way into its consciousness. This will bring to birth in their instinctive nature new laws that they will use to meet the needs of their time. Ancient laws regarding property and incomes will be discarded.

This new force will make their minds analytical, and bring an intensity of expression that will help them seek their Innermost and not rely upon outside creeds and codes. In the Western area the great Initiate has been sowing our subsoil with atoms that will bring to life an intensity of individual experience, with prosperity for our great commonwealth.

Those students, placed upon the Path of activity, and whose symbol is the sword of Justice, have to work in an advanced period when practising; for it fits them for coming events, and a student will often go to a foreign country in order to be at a certain place when that event he has foreseen occurs. For a simple event can sometimes swing countries into a chaotic state. This also happens when a student is being trained by his teacher, and he will learn to act at once by their system of communication. Great sacrifice is sometimes made on the student's part in time to prevent a calamity. The student is not schooled as to what will occur, but he feels an intensity of impression, and he will know what to do. Great craft is often needed, for the black forces are as observant as the white, and a student carrying such directions in his mind has his atmosphere easily read by these darker forces. Thus a second degree in a student's work is to meet craft with craft, and not think about the danger that may threaten him. The student who is under observation will know it; for he registers their thought pressure and sees them clairvoyantly. The advanced student will discover that there is a method of seeing through the back of the head those who seek to track him down, and the more evil such people are, the more clearly are they seen.

During the great war, several nations made the mistake of making their couriers memorise their messages; for when they awakened they were sometimes aware of their messages having been demanded from them and freely given to a magician working for his country. To the occultist secret diplomacy is a farce, and we should therefore realise that no mind is safe with its materials in its objective atmosphere. If you wish to prevent your creative thoughts from being stolen, do not distribute them in your outer atmosphere.

In the future we will wear natural and not artificial clothing, in the form of an atmosphere that we will create. When we can develop this, we shall no longer have recourse to artificial needs. This will be an atmosphere of radiation drawn from one's own inner universe; this will also warm us when we are cold, and make us immune from the attraction of beasts and insects.

This natural state will produce a purity in thought and action, and man will no longer burn up his system with the passions and desires of a dark age. This method is used by Yogis when they wander through the jungles, and this also shows why they can live above the snow-line clad in but a single garment.

The younger generation responding to the Dayspring of Youth is already unconsciously beginning the slow development of nudity in various parts of Europe.

A pupil once taken on a trip out of his body to America, suddenly exclaimed. "He's an Adamite man and wears nothing but a loin cloth." This was his first visit to a great Initiate.

For several centuries the great Initiates from all over the world have attracted to the Western areas, including America, those bodies possessing a particular type of atom. These are now to be assembled to their own parental stem—Atlantean in consciousness—but at the same time there have also flocked into the country opposing forces: types who work against law and order. For the Secret Enemy always seeks to destroy the ideals of Justice whenever possible, and to-day we can see how Justice is mocked and that the freedom of an individual is being moulded by the engineers of social disorder.

The forces of good and evil have their deposits in man's nature, and each will give of their wealth to the mind that appeals to their various centres.

They who fear God and seek to abide by His commandments will prosper in this coming new age; but if a nation will not seek God to manifest within their courts of Justice, such will have to bear the Scourge of Affliction. If the true members of this Atlantean stem will unite and sweep the forces of the Secret Enemy from their threshing floor and set their barns in order for a great harvest, then America and the Western areas of Europe will achieve their ancient inheritance: the illumination of the Dayspring of Youth. The student should remember that the sub-soil of these Western areas are impregnated with the atoms of the Atlantean civilisations.

We have constantly dwelt upon the power of the word: "Aspiration," and we hope that it has created, strange though it may sound, a complex in the reader's secondary system, so that this word will be held inwardly and not outwardly.

To have a mental complex is not good; but to form an inner substance of an atomic group of Aspiration atoms will give the student an added power; for such atoms promote the growth of aspiration, and this shelters one's thoughts beneath the protective Silver Shield. In short: we must develop the habit of constant aspiration.

· · · · ·

I am one who has been privileged to study and reveal this science of Yoga adapted for Western bodies, and I trust that others will also profit from these instructions.

I hope that later I shall be permitted to write a work on the development of the American Commonwealth from its hidden side.

I have endeavoured to give the reader a slight understanding of an unlimited science, an enlightenment that will unite the sincere student to the joyful Dayspring of Youth and give him an intensity of beauty far beyond human speech—that may advance him into a knowledge of his own being. One can spend an entire life in practice and find that one has journeyed but a short way along the Path.

I have sought to adapt this work to the intensive culture of this age, so that neither the body nor mind may be held prisoner, and that every person may manifest according to the wisdom of his Innermost.

Index

Abdomen 111, 183
Abstention 102
Actor 155, 192
Adamite 251
Adept 30, 48, 54, 87, 194, 219
Adepts 72, 89, 137, 149, 168, 203, 219, 242
Adeptship 120
Advocates 153-154, 156-157, 228, 248
Aegis 209
Aeons 150
Aerial 133
Agriculture 133, 214
Air 35, 50, 52, 65, 73, 97, 107, 110, 114, 144, 185
Air elementals 50
Aircraft 206
Akhenaten 209
Alchemical 206
Alchemists 172
Alcohol 164
Alcoholic 204
Alert 15, 18, 40, 71, 77, 126, 138, 183, 198, 242
Alertness 10, 16, 114
Aloud 229
Alphabet 23, 214
Altar 37, 60, 65, 215
Altars 187
Amaranthine 65
Amber 43, 63-64
Amenti 209-211
Amenti-Hades 211-212
Amentian 211
America 1, 45, 121, 138, 170, 193, 214-216, 242, 251-252
American 3, 45, 199, 215-216, 227, 242, 252
American Commonwealth 252
American Federation of States 215-216
Americans 199-200

Analyse 5, 7, 9, 16, 32, 40, 56, 97-98, 103, 111, 131, 137, 139, 145-146, 173, 184, 234, 238
Analysed 48, 68, 81, 140, 149, 174, 239, 248
Analyses 98, 142
Analysing 9, 51
Analysis 163
Analytic 153
Analytical 250
Anatomists 99
Anatomy 71, 89
Ancestor 184
Ancestors 22, 37, 103, 147-148, 155, 171
Ancestral 22, 99, 155, 223
Ancestry 32, 139, 155
Anchorites 128, 146
Ancients 149
Androgynous 215
Angel 83, 89, 143-144
Angel of Death 143
Angelic 169
Angels 41, 82, 184, 237
Anger 24, 64, 149, 157
Animal 4, 21-24, 29-30, 32-33, 42, 51, 88, 91, 101-102, 123, 127, 132, 141, 144, 150, 155, 157, 165-166, 169, 181, 212, 215, 229, 237, 239, 241, 248
Animalised 165
Animal-like 127
Animals 23, 26, 32, 42, 88, 101-102, 131, 151, 203, 235
Antediluvian 32
Ants 35
Apollo 54, 187
Apparitions 35, 142
Appolonius 32, 43, 209, 235
Apprenticeship 88, 141
Aquarian 47
Arabic 206
Arabs 148
Arcadia 185-188

Arcadian 48, 50, 185, 187, 189
Arcady 61, 65
Archaeologist 214
Architect 82, 87-88, 127, 238
Architects 7, 14
Architectural 47
Architecture 7, 45
Archive 39
Arctic Ocean 215-216
Areoplanes 67
Aristocracy 99
Ark 204
Arm 64, 77
Armaments 133
Armchair 206
Armed 121, 159
Armies 13
Armour 52, 154, 159
Armours 180
Armpit 76
Armpits 77
Arms 62, 72, 212, 215
Army 146, 204
Art 23, 48, 70, 72-73, 139-141, 173-174
Arterial xii, 99, 101
Arteries 99-100
Artery 37
Arthur 154, 199
Artificial 251
Artist 7, 51, 140
Artistic 50, 122, 139, 141, 177, 219
Artists 14, 23, 48, 68, 115, 139-140
Arts 43, 68, 70, 72, 128, 138, 140, 237
Ascetics 242
Ash 21, 199
Ashes 37
Asia 211, 242
Asleep 131, 169
Asphyxiate 110
Aspiration 2, 8-9, 11, 14-15, 32, 35, 68, 78, 85, 93-94, 108-109, 119, 143, 145-146, 153, 168, 173, 177, 181, 192, 252
Aspirations xii, 8, 27, 49, 53, 55, 69, 83, 98, 158, 160-161

Aspire 2, 4, 9-10, 21, 29, 35, 56, 67, 77, 79, 91, 95, 101, 109, 131, 141, 144, 146, 156, 158, 160-161, 164, 167, 169, 175-176, 179, 181, 191-192, 196-198, 216, 225, 227-228, 237-238, 247-248
Aspired 161, 223
Aspires xi, 2, 80, 128, 146, 159, 209, 236, 245
Aspiring xi-xii, 1, 5, 8-9, 11, 13, 15-17, 24, 27, 35, 69, 76-79, 81-82, 88, 93, 95, 98-99, 119, 145, 149, 157, 172, 181, 197, 223, 235, 247-248
Aspiring Atoms xi-xii, 8, 11, 13, 15-17, 24, 35, 69, 76-79, 81, 88, 93, 95, 99, 145, 149, 172, 197, 223
Astral xii, 17, 26, 29-37, 52, 56, 95, 112-114, 123, 136, 142, 165, 197
Astral Body xii, 29-30, 32, 112, 137, 165
Astral sheath 26, 29-32, 34, 37
Astrologers 209
Astrology 172
Astronomers 199-200
Asylums 206
Atheist 143
Athens 7
Atlantean 7, 45, 55, 89, 119, 148, 155, 200, 203, 214-216, 234, 236, 242, 248, 251-252
Atlantean Testament of Learning 7, 89, 236
Atlantis 45, 90, 140, 167, 200, 203, 214
Atmospheres 8, 16-17, 22, 39, 56-57, 71, 113, 117, 119-120, 122, 125, 131, 135, 138, 141, 144, 154, 175, 193, 205, 225, 231, 234, 242
Atmospheric xii, 37, 39, 67, 94, 102, 107, 109-111, 245
Atmospheric Screen xii, 107, 109, 111

INDEX

Atomic xii-xiv, 1-2, 4, 6, 8-11, 13-14, 17-20, 23, 30, 35, 67, 74, 78-79, 81-82, 84, 91-93, 98-101, 103, 117, 122-123, 127, 130, 135, 138-139, 144, 146-148, 150, 153, 159-160, 164, 166, 168-169, 177-178, 181-183, 192-193, 197-200, 203-204, 209-210, 216, 219, 221, 223, 227-228, 231, 234, 236-237, 240, 242-243, 248-249, 252
Atoms xi-xiv, 1-11, 13-17, 19-27, 29-30, 32-36, 45, 47, 51, 68-69, 71, 73-74, 76-81, 83-84, 87-91, 93-95, 97-102, 104-105, 107-108, 110-112, 117, 122, 124-125, 133-135, 139-140, 145-146, 148-151, 153, 155-158, 163-165, 168-169, 172-173, 175-179, 181-184, 192, 197, 199, 203-205, 210, 212, 214, 216-217, 219-221, 223-225, 227-228, 231, 234-239, 241, 243-244, 247-250, 252
Attach 20, 137
Attached 30, 33, 45
Attachments 35
Attention 114, 119, 131, 175
Attract 2, 5, 13, 21-22, 24, 26, 34-35, 49, 72, 76, 90, 97-98, 103, 107-108, 117, 122, 126, 137, 139, 143, 145, 178, 194, 197, 219, 221, 227, 241
Attracted xiii, 9, 11, 26, 55, 68, 107, 141, 145, 149, 164, 204, 241, 251
Attracting 2, 145, 177, 235
Attraction 47, 111, 119, 123, 129, 149, 197, 251
Attracts xi, 1-2, 19, 33, 35, 94, 97, 103, 147-149, 171, 231
Attune xiii, 13, 16, 67-68, 78, 92, 112, 134, 164, 240, 245
Attuned 6, 87, 147, 191-192, 224
Attunes xi, 87, 245
Attuning 192
Audible 23, 114, 173, 192

Audibly 235
Augean 131
August 45
Augustine 233
Aura 1, 88, 98, 124, 164, 171
Auras 56, 108, 242, 249
Austerity 54
Author 94, 121-122
Authorites 193
Authority 13, 27, 29, 56, 140, 149, 169-170, 173, 214
Automatons 187
Autumn 172, 216
Autumn Equinox 216
Awake 18, 45
Awaken 8, 10, 24, 99, 105, 111, 141, 167, 188, 192, 216, 229, 234
Awakened 75, 87, 124, 139, 187, 217, 224, 229, 233, 236, 240, 251
Awakening 37, 54, 88, 112, 142, 225
Awakens 24, 37, 56, 81, 134, 225, 236, 240, 245
Awaking 95
Aware 1, 9, 15, 34, 39, 45, 80, 83, 128-129, 143, 147, 149, 165, 179, 183, 209, 213, 225, 229, 243, 251
Axis 29, 226, 228
Aztec 112
Bable 235
Babylon 61
Balance 7, 9, 20, 71, 80-81, 119, 130, 143, 153, 168, 230, 240
Balanced 24, 27, 103, 105, 130, 156, 164, 169
Balances 120, 167, 173
Balkan 211
Bath 204, 221
Bathe 75, 193, 201
Bathes 215
Baths 73
Battersea Bridge 159
Beast 236
Beasts 4, 34, 211, 225, 251
Beautiful 16, 44, 51, 55, 95, 130, 187, 237
Beautiful Greek 55

Beauty 5, 8, 23, 41, 44-45, 59, 62-65, 83, 101, 115, 128, 139, 161, 184-188, 194, 252
Bees 21, 62, 129
Being 1, 4, 8-11, 20, 27, 30, 32, 37, 41-43, 49, 53, 59, 67-68, 70, 73, 77, 80, 82, 84, 88-89, 96, 109, 112, 120, 123, 125, 132, 137-139, 141, 144, 146-147, 150, 154, 159, 161, 163, 173, 180, 183-184, 197, 204, 209, 211-213, 217, 224-225, 228-229, 233, 235-236, 240, 247-252
Beings 4-5, 17, 23, 33, 36, 39, 41-44, 47-51, 53-55, 59, 83, 91-92, 97, 101, 112, 114-115, 129-131, 136, 150, 156, 161, 167, 237
Bible 237
Bibles 47
Bird 60, 64
Birds 185-186
Birth xiii, 1, 17, 22, 61, 74, 80-81, 84, 87, 95, 117-118, 123-125, 132, 141, 144, 155, 159, 169, 178, 187, 224, 226, 229, 234, 237, 239-240, 247-248, 250
Black 20, 23, 26-27, 30, 42, 71, 129, 135, 143, 181, 250
Black magician 30, 135, 181
Blessed 215
Blessing 70
Blessings 11, 45, 65
Bliss 87, 111, 130, 139, 226, 233, 237
Blonde 49
Blood 13, 15, 23, 97-99, 101-102, 127, 166, 186, 238-239
Bloodstream xii, 13, 78, 97-100, 145
Blue-blooded 99
Born 40, 43, 55-56, 73, 89-90, 103, 119, 129, 184-186, 220, 235, 244
Brahma 87
Brahmins 147

Brain xii-xiii, 15-16, 42, 60, 109-110, 147-148, 172, 176, 181, 188, 198, 201, 239, 243
Brains 242
Brazen 186
Bread 23, 72, 168
Breast 62, 173
Breasts 117
Breath 13, 77, 111, 164, 185, 197-198
Breathe 13, 15-16, 73, 76-77, 90-91, 97-99, 107, 110-111, 114, 144, 186, 223-224
Breathed 130, 188, 223
Breathes 37
Breathing 2, 5, 8-9, 35, 73, 76-78, 82-83, 90, 97, 99, 107, 109-111, 145, 185, 197
Breath-world 237
Brothels 49
Brother 23, 40, 80, 123, 127-128, 157, 213
Brother Mason 213
Brotherhood xi, 23, 204
Brothers xi, 7, 23, 30, 39, 55, 71-72, 74, 128
Buddha 6, 87
Buddhist 48, 195
Burial 36, 90, 128
Buried 36, 90, 107, 141-142, 155, 239
Burlington Gallery 159
Business 42, 74, 138, 210, 219-220
Caduceus 226
Calf 77
California 200, 242
California Institute of Technology 200
Cancer 164, 237
Candle 33
Capricorn 237
Carbon dioxide 110
Caribbean Sea 215
Carlyle 160, 235
Castor xii, 156, 248
Cathedral 8
Causal xii, 94, 166

Causal Body Sheath xii
Celibate 75
Cell 16, 110, 147, 233
Cells 15, 99-100, 151, 172, 176, 192, 198, 239
Cellular 164
Central Asia 242
Central System xiii, 10, 17-18, 29, 32, 94-96, 154-155, 178, 192-193, 214, 233-234, 236, 240, 242-243, 247, 249
Central Universe 5, 90, 172, 223, 240, 243
Cereal 241
Cereals 102
Ceremonial 47, 211
Ceremonies 67
Ceremony 142, 193, 243
Ceres 211
Chain 61, 65, 150, 154, 184, 234
Chain of Initiates 65
Chalice 60, 63, 65
Change 5, 18, 44, 76-77, 99, 119, 172, 194, 247
Changed 3, 179, 241, 248-250
Changes 17, 32, 172, 225
Changing 99, 195, 198
Channel 238
Channels 71
Chant 142, 193
Chants 193-194
Charlemagne 154
Chemical 249
Chemist 5
Chemistry 206
Chest 77, 197
Chicago 200
Chieftains 155
Child 37, 43, 59, 74, 87, 90, 105, 173, 217
Childhood 19
Childlike 59, 95, 138, 185
Children 21-22, 27, 40, 43, 45, 54, 65, 67, 73-74, 95, 108, 129, 131, 143, 170, 173, 195
China 72, 138, 184
Chinaman 219

Chinese 14, 23, 37, 48, 70, 171, 183, 201, 213, 219-221
Chinese Initiates 70
Chinese Masons 213
Chord 186
Chords 56, 188, 219
Christ 6, 43, 123, 166, 233, 238
Christian 43, 158, 166, 171, 233
Christianity 142
Christians 37, 121
Church 142, 193
Churches 193
Cigarette 21
Civilisation 7, 17, 37, 68, 73, 112, 158, 203, 209, 215
Civilisations 48, 107, 252
Civilised 182
Clairaudience 93
Clairvoyance 98, 197, 227
Clairvoyant 30, 137
Clairvoyantly 98, 250
Clarity 8, 115, 140
Claude Monet 140
Clean 15, 26, 42, 45, 54, 69, 74, 76, 98, 113, 137, 188-189
Cleaning 131
Cleanliness 43, 85, 98, 204, 239
Clean-minded 137
Cleanse 16, 76, 193, 239
Cleansed 32
Cleanses 193
Cleansing 22, 102
Coiled 225-226, 228
Coinventor 199
Cold 73, 75, 251
Coldness 64
Coleridge 140
College 56, 71, 203, 212-213, 215
Colleges 160
Colour 7, 29, 42, 49, 56, 61, 72, 140, 158, 178, 180, 211, 235, 241
Coloured 62
Colours 87
Column xi, 71, 212
Coma 37
Comatose 210

Command 5, 13, 19, 40, 56, 126, 183, 237-238, 243-244
Commanded 72, 132, 217
Commanding 247
Commandments 205, 252
Commerce 62, 122, 134, 146
Commercial 69, 74, 140, 242
Commonwealth 150, 216, 250, 252
Communicate 44, 67, 74, 76, 131, 184, 227, 241
Communicated 131
Communicates 169
Communication 2, 10, 34, 49, 67, 78, 81, 93, 137, 242, 250
Communications 15-16, 88, 138, 193
Communion 156, 163
Compassion 43
Composers 249
Comprehension 84, 93, 238
Comte de Gabalis 50, 54, 124, 199, 230
Concentrate 1, 24, 68, 84, 122, 133
Concentrated 69, 84
Concentrates 85
Concentrating 68, 77, 200
Concentration 1-2, 84-85, 142, 231
Conjured 117
Conquistador of Love 65
Conscience 105
Conscious 3, 53, 74, 123-124, 144-145, 159, 197, 215, 236-237, 248
Consciously 10, 32, 121, 146, 156, 177
Consciousnesses 243
Conserve 77, 147, 181
Conserved 240
Conserves 87
Conserving 148, 172, 240
Constipation 73, 182-183
Construct 120
Constructed 30, 175-176
Construction 10, 44, 159, 165, 180
Constructive 13, 19, 24, 45, 47, 78, 87, 101, 150, 211, 226
Constructively 88

Coptic 128
Coral 48
Cord xiii, 30, 33, 80, 141-142, 160
Cords 142
Corinthians 40
Cortez 242
Cosmic xi, xiii, 1, 50, 56, 160, 181, 199-201, 210, 216, 238-239
Cosmic rays 199-201
Countries 8, 55, 68-69, 72, 170, 215-216, 228, 242, 250
Country 13, 26, 45, 65, 72-73, 92, 107, 114, 118, 123, 145, 170, 206, 217, 227, 231, 250-251
Courage 9-10, 40, 80, 109, 144, 159
Courtesan 59
Courtesans 128
Covenant 204
Cranium 96
Create xiii, 47, 68-69, 81, 92, 126, 157, 161, 166, 178, 240, 251
Created xii, 17, 23-24, 34, 45, 49-50, 69, 92, 95, 101, 132, 140, 153-154, 171, 185, 187, 204, 223, 252
Creates 23, 54, 70, 146, 199
Creating 35, 50, 133, 167, 244
Creation 7, 18, 20, 42-43, 56, 68, 84, 88, 101-103, 123, 140, 155, 181, 194, 233, 236, 241
Creations 5, 68, 84, 140
Creative 18, 26-27, 29, 68, 92, 95, 122, 140, 181, 183, 185, 201, 248, 251
Creatively 139
Creator 69, 89, 122, 144, 224, 240
Creators 20, 68
Cremate 36
Cremation 37
Cross 69
Crosslegged 73
Crown 65, 92-93, 215
Crowned 60
Crucified 69, 118, 159
Crucifixion 69, 121, 171
Cruel 42, 125
Cruelty 51, 65, 130

INDEX

Crusades 121, 154
Crystal 59, 61-62, 64, 85, 189, 249
Crystalline 65, 96, 249
Crystallises 230
Crystals 85, 249
Culture 8, 35, 107, 124, 192, 253
Cure 195
Cures 231
Curie 199-200
Custom 142
Customs 40, 49, 171
Daemon 81, 83, 92
Daemon of Socrates 83
Danger 24, 51, 225, 250
Dangerous 21, 224
Dangers 167
Dark 18-19, 24, 27, 36, 59, 83, 120, 123-124, 132, 142, 146, 178, 195, 210-211, 251
Dark Angel of Destruction 83
Darkness 3, 33, 65, 68, 80, 90, 117, 128, 150, 186, 195
Daughter 211-212
Daughter of Nature 212
Daughters 61, 237
Dawn 1, 72, 81
Dawned 122, 155
Dayspring of Youth xi, 1, 3, 7-8, 22, 61, 70, 78, 109, 134, 154, 160, 177, 181, 191, 199, 210-213, 215-216, 224, 247, 249-252
Dead 26, 36, 107, 117, 142, 144, 156, 210
Death xii, 23, 36-37, 50, 61, 64, 74, 101, 103, 110, 113, 121, 127, 141-144, 156-160, 182, 206, 241, 244
Death Atoms xii, 156-158
Deaths 114, 121
Debt 105, 166, 224
Debts 104-105, 144
Deeds 17, 27, 33, 123, 136, 143, 211
Degenerates 27
Degradation 33, 187
Degraded 220
Degree xii, 6, 52-53, 110, 118, 209, 216, 223, 250

Degrees 21, 113, 121
Deities 231
Deity 230
Delphi 54, 181
Delphic 54, 122
Delphic Oracle 122
Dematerialisation 138
Demoniacal 25, 133
Demons 82, 132
Dense 8, 14, 17, 39-40, 244
Denser 35, 141
Densities 8, 20, 30, 104, 113, 127, 134, 143, 147-148, 155, 182, 197, 227, 249
Density 21, 47-49, 55, 108, 114, 119, 149, 177, 179, 223
Depressing 35
Depression 24, 27, 35, 92, 108, 113, 182
Descend 17, 33, 91, 127, 131, 159, 161, 167
Descendants 184
Descended xi, 14, 69, 128, 227, 248
Descends 134, 172
Descent xii, 123, 131, 141, 211, 233
Descents 154
Desire 2, 23, 26, 28-29, 50, 117, 119, 127, 142, 146, 170, 177, 185, 223
Desired 182
Desires xii, 13, 15, 27, 30, 34, 40, 42, 67, 83, 89, 101-102, 118, 123, 131, 134-135, 139, 141, 144, 157-158, 165, 179, 182, 191, 221, 237, 251
Destiny 93, 186, 224
Destroy 16, 24, 52, 55, 57, 87, 92, 101, 109, 111, 118, 127, 140, 142-143, 157-158, 170, 178, 223, 240, 244, 251
Destroyed 21, 24, 45, 91, 101, 108, 134, 140
Destroying 48, 215
Destroys 15, 18, 42, 99, 230
Destruction 22, 25-27, 32, 42, 52, 67, 69, 83, 92, 102, 134, 156, 158, 200, 206, 223, 241

Destructive xii, 14, 19, 21, 23-25, 27, 45, 73, 91-94, 100, 121, 132, 136, 148, 150, 158-159, 161, 164, 170, 178, 201, 203, 210-211, 214-215, 226, 236
Destructive Atoms xii, 19, 21, 23-25, 27, 94, 164
Determination 95, 144, 177-178
Determinative energy xiii, 94, 104, 124, 177-179, 181-183, 191, 204, 211-212, 238
Determine 15, 94, 103, 177-178, 238, 248
Determined 11, 14, 43, 88, 113, 121, 177, 194, 238
Determines xiii, 98, 112, 153, 178, 204-205
Devitalise 48
Devitalised 151
Devitalising 34-35
Diadem 63
Diagnose 157, 164
Die 141, 187
Died 35-36, 195, 206
Dies 143-144, 159
Diet 74, 102
Dietetics 74
Digestive 77, 198
Discarded 68-69, 250
Discarnate 2, 15, 29, 88, 93, 95, 197
Discharge 24, 168
Discharged 42
Discharges 163
Disease 27, 32, 52, 73, 81, 97-98, 101, 108, 129, 163-164, 195, 204, 206, 223, 239
Diseased 24, 26, 34, 49, 89, 108-110, 205, 239
Diseases 97, 103, 110, 157, 164, 205, 231, 239
Disharmony 134, 184
Dishonesty 14, 59
Disintegrate 19, 21, 83-84, 93-94, 154, 238-239
Disintegrated 103, 215, 235, 239
Disintegrates 15
Disintegrating 47, 132, 235

Disintegration xii, 36, 84, 157, 165
Divine Reality 167
Divine Revelation 11
Divinity 185, 189, 235
Divorce 165
Divorced 22, 33, 59, 154, 165
Doctor 37, 45, 108
Doctors 137
Dominate 4, 42, 44-45, 122, 126, 156, 167, 180, 230
Dominated 20, 22, 43, 52, 74, 250
Dominates 122
Domination 25, 30, 88, 134, 155, 233
Dream 45, 60, 187
Dreamer 186
Dreams 21, 62-63, 117, 186
Druid 161
Dryads 65
Dual xi, 83
Dungeon 195
Dweller 20-21, 83, 85, 142
Dwelling 90, 128
Ear 93
Ears 188
Earth 1, 5, 36-37, 39, 45, 47-48, 56, 62-64, 69, 82, 89, 97, 102, 117-118, 128-129, 133, 136-137, 142, 150, 154, 161, 179, 194, 199-200, 211-212, 216, 227, 237, 242, 244-245
Earth-bound 17, 20, 30, 50, 141, 180, 184
Earth-current 216, 224
Earthly 25, 136, 165, 239
Earthquakes 91
East 3, 45, 52, 73-74, 76-77, 79, 81, 108, 117-118, 137, 158, 183, 193, 223, 227, 241
Eastern 20, 76-77, 79, 141, 182, 193, 214, 227, 231, 234
Eastern Yoga 77
Eastern Yogi 182
Eastern Yogis 234
Eat 15, 97, 101, 182
Eaters 102
Eating 23

Eats 102
Ecclesiastical 43
Economic 45
Ecstasies 234
Education 14, 40, 110, 160, 194, 219, 247
Ego 74
Egotism 94
Egotistic 167, 220
Egotistical 45
Egotists 187
Egypt 37, 56, 61, 107, 121, 203-204, 209-215, 217
Egyptian 7, 30, 203, 209-210, 212-215, 226
Egyptian Masonry 213
Egyptians 203, 209, 211-212
Eight 71
Eighteen 145, 206
Einstein 235
Elastic 111, 183
Elasticity 52
Elder 71-72, 104-105, 214, 228
Elder Brothers 71-72
Elderly 110
Elders 23, 142
Electric 65, 245
Electrical 48, 240
Electricity xiii, 17, 81, 138, 173, 225-226
Element 2, 54-55, 81, 130, 140, 165, 191, 193, 204, 223-227, 229, 231, 236, 238-239, 249
Element of fire 54, 223-225, 227, 229, 231, 236
Elemental xii-xiii, 5, 14, 20, 26, 30, 39-49, 51-57, 59, 68-69, 95, 101-102, 112, 122, 128-129, 132, 138, 142-145, 150, 153-161, 179-180, 182, 184-185, 192, 203-205, 209, 211-213, 215, 238-239
Elemental Advocate xii, 112, 153-161, 213
Elemental Nature 26, 39, 41, 43, 45, 47, 49, 51, 53, 55, 57, 59, 145, 154, 157, 179, 192, 204, 211, 213
Elementals 40, 42-44, 47-50, 52-53, 55-56, 59, 83, 102, 143, 159, 161, 227
Elementary 95
Elements xii, 1, 20, 24, 39, 48, 53-54, 56, 78, 83-84, 103, 141, 144, 154, 161, 170, 176, 204, 212, 223-224, 226, 229, 248-249
Elizabethan 124
Elves 60
Emancipation 182
Embryo 79, 197
Emerald 60
Emerson 160, 235
Emotion 241
Emotional 156, 234
Emotions 30, 123, 129, 224
Emperor Charlemagne 154
Enchantment 186-187
Enemies 23, 26, 45, 52, 158, 203
Energies 2, 80, 148, 169, 180, 219, 234, 236, 240
Energise 178, 241
Energised 110, 141, 200, 228
Energises 98-99, 178
Engaged 22, 136
Engender 108, 225, 237
Engendered 41, 172
Engine 180
Engineer 18, 233
Engineering 44
Engineers 13, 45, 251
Engines 45, 206
England 124, 215, 234
English 219
Enlarged 39, 41
Enlighten 244
Enlightened 210
Enlightenment 6, 8, 17, 53, 59, 95, 118, 124, 148, 171, 173, 177, 252
Envy 14, 163
Eons 48
Epochs 88
Equator 77

Equinox 172, 215-216
Era 1, 149
Esoteric 149, 195
Essence 9, 81, 156, 173-174, 180, 214, 241, 244
Essences 56, 75
Eternal 59, 61-63, 65, 132
Eternal lover 59, 61, 63, 65
Eternity xiii, 121
Ether 87, 204
Etheric 47, 150, 154
Europe 1, 26, 114, 117, 121, 205, 211, 251-252
Evening 47, 199, 206
Evenings 186, 188
Evil xii, 9, 14-15, 17, 19-28, 30, 33, 42-44, 63, 69-71, 79-81, 83, 85, 92, 103, 113, 125-135, 137, 139-141, 143, 146, 149, 151, 154, 157, 160-162, 191-192, 204, 211-212, 226-227, 229, 236, 250, 252
Evils 103
Evoke 6, 19, 23, 39, 43, 54, 67, 69, 85, 135, 141, 155, 168, 181, 192, 220, 223, 225, 227, 229, 233-234, 240, 245, 248-249
Evoked xiii, 17, 21, 47, 81, 99, 142, 163, 188, 210, 225, 234
Evokes 11, 24, 173, 227
Evoking 137, 239
Evolution xii, 4, 21-22, 41, 50, 53, 70, 79, 89, 143-144, 169, 233, 236
Evolve 4, 33, 37
Evolved 6, 42, 89, 93, 107, 130-131, 153, 164, 168-169, 199, 210, 236-237
Evolving 24
Exercise 13, 77-78, 110, 183, 197-198
Exercised 73
Exercises 2, 76, 185, 223, 231
Exercising 73, 110, 183
Exhale 110-111
Exhaling 197
Exist 26, 89, 109, 199
Existed xi, 63

Existence 32, 63, 117, 156, 195
Experience 4-5, 9, 29, 50, 55, 63, 88-89, 103-104, 107, 120, 130, 138, 145, 148, 157-158, 160, 167, 181, 194, 211-213, 217, 219, 230, 233, 239, 247, 250
Experienced 113, 173, 194, 201, 223
Experiences xiii, 9, 17, 40, 55, 88-89, 93, 113, 141, 170, 177, 195, 223
Experiment 67
Experimenting 165
Experiments 142, 165, 199-200
Eye xi-xii, 32, 75, 98, 112, 137, 139, 169
Eyeballs 200
Eyes 53, 61-62, 83, 136-137, 185, 187-188, 229, 235
Fail 4, 177, 230
Failed 56, 161, 209
Failing 115
Fails 8, 11
Failure 164, 237, 245
Failures 194
Faith 3, 19-20, 141, 163, 168, 171
Faithful 14, 27, 137, 141, 220
Faithfully 56, 185, 236
Fall 62, 108, 115
Fallen 158, 187
Falling 160
Families 143
Family 122
Famine 206
Fast 102, 191, 241
Fasting 10, 102
Fasts 147
Father 61, 224
Fathered 43
Fatherhood 154
Fathers 155
Faun 186
Fauns 60, 65
Fear 21, 24, 53, 63, 101, 127, 142, 184, 195, 220, 226, 252
Federation 215-216
Feeler 112
Feelers 226

Feeling 10, 141
Feelings 17, 224
Feet 13, 30, 33, 36, 60-62, 71, 78, 82, 112, 118, 121, 151, 185, 189, 200, 227-229
Feminine 20, 224
Femoral 37
Fertile 7, 60
Fertilise 11, 16, 48, 172, 181
Field 76-78, 133, 197, 200, 241
Fields 25, 52, 61, 65, 121, 206, 219
Fifteen 113
Fifth 43, 63
Fifty 1, 7
Finer forces xi, xiii, 1, 21, 87, 89, 91, 93, 95, 213
Finger 59, 72, 198
Fingers 67, 82, 186-187
Finn 119
Fire 16, 39, 53-56, 81, 186, 189, 195, 206, 223-227, 229, 231, 236-237, 239
Fire elementals 53
Fireman 55
Fireplace 122
Fires 55
Fish 32
Fishlike 136
Five 39, 75, 91, 198, 227
Flame 54, 64-65, 84, 186, 223, 225, 228, 233, 235, 237, 239-241, 243, 245
Flaming 81
Flammable 200
Florence 199
Flower 63, 187, 189, 220
Flowers 35, 60, 65, 185
Fluid 29, 34-35, 73, 108, 124, 136, 147-148, 165, 181, 236
Fluidic xii, 26, 47-48, 52, 141
Fluids 26, 109, 197, 206
Flux 49, 247
Foetus 30
Food 24, 74-75, 97, 101-102, 147, 176, 182, 241, 244
Foods 15, 74, 102, 217
Footlights 192

Forearm 209
Forefinger 188
Forefingers 198
Forehead 25, 61-62, 128, 198
Forgive 91
Forgiven 27, 80, 104, 157
Forgiveness 105, 143, 157
Foundation 82, 118, 140
Foundations 120, 130, 209
Fountain 61-62
Fountains 60, 62
Four 10, 29, 79, 89, 172, 199-200
Fourfold 205
Four-sevenths 15, 124
Fourteen 107
Fourth 64, 124
Fragrance 10, 13, 59-60, 64, 70, 185
Fraternities 74
Fraternity xi
Free 30, 80, 101, 103-104, 125, 158, 171, 181, 188, 212
Freed 21, 60, 84, 136, 188, 212, 236
Freedom 10, 84, 88, 96, 103, 123, 139, 148, 159, 188, 210, 251
Fruit 30, 102
Fruitful 187, 216
Fruitless 195
Fruits 48, 187
Futures 139
Gabalis 50, 54, 124, 199, 230
Ganglia xi, xiii, 30
Gangsters 33
Garden 61
Gardener 11
Gardens 63, 142, 189
Gas 110-111, 133
Gaseous 14, 73, 99
Gem 186
Gemini 156
Generates 16, 120, 245
Generation 18, 21, 160, 179, 226, 250-251
Generations 27, 81, 158, 207, 209, 216, 238
Generative 75, 110, 225, 240
Genesis 30
Genius 24, 72, 123, 139, 159, 178

Genius of Perfection 178
Geniuses 92, 140
Germ 249
Germinate 6, 220
Germinating 102, 109, 151, 206, 235
Germlike 14
Germs 24, 97, 109, 206
Giants 44, 237
Gift 24, 73, 75, 95, 98, 226, 234
Gift of Tongues 234
Gilead 130
Gland xi, 98, 200
Glands 164, 198
Glandular 164
Glastonbury 215-216
Glories 5
Glorification 128
Glorified 69
Glorious 90
Glory 64, 69, 107
Gnome 44-45, 47
Gnomes 45, 49
God xiii, 4, 10-11, 43, 54, 64, 85, 87, 91, 167-168, 181, 187, 196, 201, 230, 252
God Hermes 91
Goddess 62, 185, 188
God-enlightened 236
God-like 4, 6, 21-22, 54, 80, 191, 248
Gods 22, 48, 50, 52, 54, 102, 120, 127, 154, 167, 185-187, 189, 209, 211
Gold 60, 65, 206, 220
Golden 107, 117, 130, 150, 185, 189, 203-204, 209
Golden Age 185, 203-204, 209
Goosequill 45
Gordian 153
Govern 9, 21, 41-42, 67, 80, 92, 95, 131, 141, 169, 194, 247
Governed xiii, 2, 34, 112, 133, 160, 166, 186
Governing 18, 156, 192
Government 2, 41-42, 97, 125, 134
Governors 159
Governs 93, 121
Grafting 165

Grain 19, 23
Grateful 105
Gratitude 135, 224
Graveyards 37, 142
Gravitate 143, 223
Gravitates 193
Gravity 30
Great Atlantean 55, 215-216, 234, 242
Great Illuminate Crown of Victory 92-93
Great Initiate xiii, 7, 90, 93, 121, 128, 137, 166, 210, 212, 214-215, 217, 234, 243, 250-251
Great Initiate Jesus 166, 214
Great Initiates 1, 3, 88-89, 92-93, 117-118, 146, 210, 214, 238, 241, 251
Great Intelligence 27, 89, 134
Great Law 52
Great Liberator 226
Great War 25, 114, 251
Greece 7, 54, 61, 122, 209, 215
Greek 21, 54-55, 83, 166
Greeks 17, 37, 211
Green 89
Green-faced Man 55
Grey 29, 45, 143
Greyish-pink 48
Greyly 187
Greyness 187
Grid 110, 145, 197-198
Guardian 59, 69, 150, 154, 161, 209, 212-213
Guardians 52
Guards 48, 236
Guidance xiii, 69, 83, 88, 91-92, 98, 130, 135-136, 245
Guilds 47
Habit 67, 71, 78, 110, 252
Habitation 110
Habits 35, 73-74, 91, 97, 136
Hades 211
Hair 48, 117, 187
Hallucination 50
Hallucinations 161

Hand 60, 62-63, 65, 77, 87, 119, 200, 230-231, 244
Hand-maidens 62
Hands 60, 63-65, 77, 88, 117, 120, 143, 183, 187, 197-198, 215
Happiness 3, 24, 60, 62-64, 79, 168, 186
Happy 24, 45, 59, 67, 125, 177
Harm 159, 165-166, 224, 245
Harmonies 49
Harmonise xiii, 11, 45, 55, 73, 80, 96, 164, 173, 177, 184, 227, 229, 243
Harmonised 163
Harmonises 6, 193, 230
Harmony 4, 47, 53, 67-68, 73, 90, 98, 124, 146, 172, 184, 191, 194, 215-216, 227
Hate 194
Hatha Yoga 72
Hatred 14, 26, 157, 163
Headstone 87
Headstones 73
Heal 13, 55, 135, 144, 157-158
Healed 108
Healer 157, 163
Healers 158, 163
Healing 123, 157, 163-165, 205, 210, 220
Health 4, 27, 35, 51, 71, 73, 75, 77, 79, 81, 94, 137, 158, 163-164, 204-205
Heart xi, 5, 10-11, 13, 16, 19, 33, 52, 62, 64, 77-78, 90, 98, 128, 166, 169, 187, 189, 231
Hearts 62, 113-114, 185
Heat 23, 55, 78
Heaven 3, 19, 61, 64-65, 74, 78, 84, 122, 142, 167
Heavens 132
Hebrew 166
Hebrews 149, 160, 169
Helium 200
Hell 19, 33, 84, 122, 127, 132, 211
Hells 127, 132, 136
Help 4-5, 7, 13, 15, 20, 56, 70, 91, 95, 104, 117-118, 125, 131, 141- 142, 144, 146, 155, 158, 163, 168, 176, 229-230, 237, 250
Helped 23, 164, 174
Helper 161
Helpers 40, 113, 137, 142, 153
Helpful 14
Helping 230
Helpless 13, 143
Helps 5, 17, 91, 109, 157, 164, 210
Hennogenes 128
Heralds 1
Hercules 131
Hereditary 22, 143, 155
Hermes 90-91
Hermes-Mercury 211
Hermetic 18, 124, 236
Hermit 161
Hero 187
Heroic 186, 211
Hierarchal xi, 1, 59, 68, 70, 129, 153, 160, 172, 181, 201, 203, 210, 212, 215-216, 224, 247-248
Hierarchies 185
Highborn 186
Higher Self xii, 2, 10
Highwaymen 230
Historians 7
Historical 52
History 16, 19, 37, 43, 55, 92, 121, 125, 134, 143, 163, 185, 195, 209, 214, 219, 233, 242
Home 96, 227
Honest 14
Hope 8, 25, 45, 63, 80, 132, 139, 141, 186, 195, 252
Hopeless 131
Hopelessness 64
Hoping 131
Horn 45, 117
Horus 209
Hospitals 89, 206
Hour 57
Hours 233
House xiii, 7, 37, 56, 122, 157, 175
Hyperborean 171
Hypnotic 21, 30, 52, 129, 132
Ice 117

Ice cream 118
Idea 8, 75
Ideal 17-18, 25, 43, 118, 141, 156, 235
Idealise 118
Idealised 118
Idealists 71, 118
Ideals 17, 21, 134, 181, 217, 219, 251
Ideas 22, 59, 121, 216
Idols 204
Ignorance 33, 70, 125, 150, 221
Ignorant 10, 41, 45, 53, 67, 80, 140, 146, 154, 175, 201, 205-206, 237
Illuminate 11, 26, 92-93, 144, 169, 199-200, 215
Illuminate Crown of Victory 92-93, 215
Illuminated 200
Illuminates 145
Illuminating 178
Illumination 10-11, 15-16, 44, 73, 88, 92, 95, 107, 110, 123, 150, 221, 229, 252
Illuminations 11, 233
Illuminative 54, 241
Illumined 6-7, 51, 62, 105, 124, 234
Illumines 19
Illusion 3-4, 6, 9, 14, 20, 27, 33-34, 36, 57, 59-60, 89, 142, 149, 159, 161, 163, 165, 167, 171, 176, 179, 181-182, 194, 201, 210, 212, 229-230, 235, 239-241
Illusionary 136
Illusioned 14, 149, 214
Illusions 40, 127, 156, 167, 243
Illusion thought 109
Illusion world 180
Illusory 3, 141
Image xi, 53, 63, 69, 124, 167, 204, 212, 235, 241, 247, 249
Images 34, 48, 51, 53, 133, 188, 204
Imaginary 117
Imagination 13, 17-18, 60, 94, 109, 136, 161, 164, 220
Imaginations 156

Imaginative 144
Imagine 35-36, 230
Imagined 188
Imagining 231
Immoral 80
Immortal 57
Immortality 50
Immune 24, 102, 137, 146, 150, 251
Impersonal 2, 41, 132, 215
Impersonally xii, 141, 158
Impoverish 97
Impoverishes 26
Impregnate 7
Impregnated 26, 55, 107, 182, 203, 231, 252
Impregnating 128
Impregnation 51
Impress 7, 16, 20, 49, 51, 54, 83, 85, 94, 102, 104-105, 113, 115, 129, 133, 140, 143, 158, 164, 183, 191, 204, 225, 227
Impressed 34, 37, 44, 49, 83-84, 114-115, 129, 166, 179, 194, 247
Impresses 34, 119, 122, 182, 224
Impressing 3, 26
Impression 93, 179, 239, 250
Impressions 10, 21, 47, 99, 101, 109, 112, 117, 161, 198
Imprison 1, 19, 23, 84, 168, 210
Imprisoned xii, 3, 14, 33, 55, 84, 87, 103, 128, 141, 147, 150, 165, 203-204, 210, 216, 236
Imprisonment 93
Impure 15, 97, 99, 101, 129, 197
Impurities 76, 99-100, 111, 164, 183, 198
Incarnate 14, 74, 103-104, 169-170, 177, 239
Incarnated 20, 88, 144, 155, 170, 194, 227
Incarnating 14, 74, 92, 104, 193-194
Incarnation 88, 103, 136, 154, 171, 177, 193, 237
Incarnations 5, 9, 30, 59, 81, 133, 149, 154, 173, 195, 233
Incense 37, 72, 108
Independence 170

Indian 182, 193, 214, 219
Indians 193, 214-215, 234
Individual xii-xiv, 7, 9-10, 14, 17, 22,
    45, 79, 90, 92, 130-131, 144,
    159, 167, 170, 179, 183, 191,
    194, 216, 230, 248-251
Individualise 89, 166
Individualised 120, 160, 166, 216
Individuality 11, 22, 41, 48, 55, 67,
    119-120, 160, 166, 170, 184,
    247-249
Individuals 53, 134, 229-230
Infinite 117
Information 7, 9, 17, 26, 34, 39, 43,
    45, 50, 78, 85, 91, 95, 124,
    135, 138, 147, 163, 165, 173,
    177, 204, 214, 230, 233, 235,
    244
Informer Atoms xii
Informers 135
Inhale 8-9, 37, 76-77, 97, 110-111,
    197, 225
Inhaled 9, 164, 197
Inhales 151
Inhaling 8, 76, 107, 197
Inheritance xiii, 5-7, 23, 50, 81, 109,
    148, 155-156, 171, 175, 181-
    182, 211, 215-216, 223, 252
Initiate xiii, 6-7, 30, 68, 77, 90, 92-93,
    121, 123, 128, 132, 134, 137,
    166, 176, 203, 210, 212, 214-
    217, 234, 240, 243, 250-251
Initiate Atoms xiii
Initiate Jesus 166, 214
Initiate Pharaoh 212
Initiated 18, 25, 34, 40, 149, 206,
    213-216, 219, 240
Initiates 1, 3, 19, 23, 37, 39, 49, 54,
    65, 69-70, 78, 88-89, 92-93,
    95-96, 117-118, 121, 125,
    134, 146, 179, 203, 205, 210,
    214-215, 226, 235, 238, 241,
    251
Initiates of Egypt 210
Initiation xi, 34, 209, 243
Initiations 55, 70

Innermost xiii-xiv, 1, 6, 8-11, 13-14,
    16, 18, 20, 22, 24, 33, 41,
    61, 68-69, 75, 81, 83, 87, 90,
    93, 95, 103, 110, 123, 130,
    139, 143, 145, 147, 157-158,
    166-169, 175, 177-178, 181,
    195, 197-198, 221, 226-228,
    230-231, 233-234, 237-238,
    243, 247-249
Insane 132, 161
Insanity 52, 108
Insects 111, 251
Inspiration 59, 87, 122, 185, 187-188
Inspirational 151
Inspire 44, 78, 133, 224
Inspired 94, 179, 185
Inspiring 5
Instinct 24, 156
Instinctive 131, 250
Instinctively 101, 137, 182, 216
Instincts 155
Instruct 9, 55, 81, 94, 149, 161, 176,
    203, 217, 226, 243
Instructed 40, 43, 88-89, 108, 130,
    142, 179
Instructing 221
Instructions 16, 252
Instructive 95, 168, 224
Instructor 57, 87, 103, 107, 141, 156
Instructors 128, 156, 164
Instructs xiii, 55
Instrument xiii, 1, 10-11, 34, 47, 54,
    56, 88, 99, 111, 118, 128,
    134, 147, 165, 173, 180-181,
    191-192, 204-205, 224, 227,
    234, 238-239
Instrumental 215
Instruments 27, 92, 133, 135, 143,
    203
Intellect 129, 201
Intellects 201
Intellectual 136, 160, 200-201
Intelligences 2, 5-6, 11, 15, 17-18, 20,
    26, 30, 39, 44, 50, 68, 79, 81,
    88, 94, 107, 131, 171, 176,
    201, 221, 234, 243
Intelligent 34

Intercourse 30, 120
Interior 4-5, 8-9, 15, 37, 75, 80, 109, 138, 239
Intermediary xii
Intermediate 15, 228-229
Interspaces 44, 87, 199, 236
Intestinal 182
Intestine 73
Intestines 182-183
Intolerance 51, 127
Intuitions 15
Intuitive 164
Invent 133, 203
Invention 67, 205
Inventions 44, 133, 205
Inventor 133
Invisibility 138
Invisible 81, 91, 113-114, 149, 161
Invocation 164, 191-193, 234
Invocations xiii, 203, 227
Invoke 229
Invoking 183
Inwardly 1-3, 14, 17-19, 36, 40, 67, 70, 77-78, 88, 94, 98, 110, 120-121, 131, 134-136, 141, 144, 147, 163-165, 168, 174-175, 177-178, 192, 223, 227, 229, 233, 252
Iron 128, 200
Irrational 71
Istar 61
Japan 195
Japanese 48, 72, 239
Jesus 19, 43, 69, 87, 96, 118, 123, 125, 128, 160, 166, 209, 214, 227, 230
Jewels 60
Jews 47, 183
Joan of Arc 54
John 187-188
Jove-like 54
Joy 5, 7, 37, 40, 78, 92, 236
Joyful 188, 252
Joyfulness 186
Joys 186
Ju-Jitsu 72

Judge 20, 43, 51, 105, 108, 143, 171, 186, 217
Judged 2, 105, 159
Judges 22, 235
Judgment 108, 115
Jupiter 186-187
Juste 23, 40
Justice 4, 6, 34, 52, 61, 70, 81, 89, 104-105, 130, 143, 159, 170, 186, 203, 205, 212, 223, 228, 235, 242, 250-252
Justice Ray 89
Ka 210, 212
Karma 27, 59, 80, 101, 103-105, 157, 215
Karmic 103-104, 144, 166
Keats 24
Keynote 5, 42, 98, 156, 191, 194, 225, 227
Kindness 170
King 47, 55, 154, 159, 211
King Arthur 154
Kingdom 3, 11, 33, 43, 74, 165, 167, 169, 237
Kingdoms 19, 39, 41, 44, 53-54, 180, 237-238
Kingly 41, 57, 155
Kings 48-49, 155
Kipling 75
Klodyke 72
Kneel 189
Kneeling 198
Knees 39
Knew 6, 14, 65, 108, 125, 136, 143, 187, 193, 195, 210
Knight 159
Knights 154
Know Thyself 181
Knower 51
Knowing 63, 143, 193, 195, 203
Knowledge 3, 7-9, 17, 21, 30, 40-41, 47-50, 53, 56, 70-72, 79-83, 85, 89, 91, 104, 114, 118-120, 132, 134, 138, 149-150, 163, 169, 175, 191, 195, 203, 205-206, 215, 219, 221, 227, 239, 242, 244, 252

Knows 51, 67, 81, 84, 101, 123, 141, 161, 182, 213, 223
Kubla Khan 140
Labour 9, 13, 88, 110, 118, 130, 143, 186, 242
Labourer 13, 121
Labours 44, 88
Ladder 124
Lama 231
Lamas 138
Lambent 65, 185
Language 59, 219, 234-235
Larvae 137
Laugh 118
Laughter 45, 60-62
Law 40, 42, 52-53, 71, 84, 103, 115, 123-124, 132, 134, 136, 149-150, 156, 171-172, 182, 191, 197, 214-216, 221, 224, 230, 238, 249, 251
Lawchamber 56
Lawgiver 123, 209, 223
Laziness 35, 140
Lazy 35
Lcmurian 130
Lead 53-54, 73, 95, 113, 136
Lemuria 167
Lemurian 22-23, 203
Leonardo 140
Lesser 18, 87, 99, 211, 244
Lesser Mysteries 18, 87
Levitate 30, 115, 131, 135
Levitation xi, 40, 113, 142
Liberate 14, 33, 157
Liberated xii, 123, 166, 175
Liberates 17
Liberating 192
Liberation 175
Liberator 226
Liberty 230
Lie 37, 88, 173, 240, 244
Lies 8, 10, 13-14, 24, 39, 54, 77, 156, 187, 191, 215, 219, 225
Light Bringers 136
Lightning 65, 157, 226, 245
Lightnings 186, 189
Lightwaves 18

Linen 63
Linga Sharira 160
Liquids 102, 204, 206
Listen 78
Listened 61, 117, 131, 188
Listeners-in 44
Listenin 17, 67, 146, 151, 192, 198
Listening 45, 47, 224
Listening-in 83, 93, 95, 193, 243
Literary 50, 122, 177
Literature 33, 41, 79-80, 83, 103, 117, 124, 151, 154
Livelihood 52
Liver 13, 75
Locomotives 206
Lodge 213
Lodges 47
Loggia 62
Longevity 207
Lord 17, 20, 89
Lord of Mercury 89
Lordly 188
Lords 43, 91, 192-193, 211
Lotus 79, 201, 234
Love 5, 9-10, 13, 37, 43, 45, 48, 60, 64-65, 78, 84, 101, 123-125, 142-143, 147, 153, 167-169, 173, 183, 186, 188, 217, 233
Loved 36-37, 62, 165
Loveliness 44, 48, 63, 128, 186
Lovely 23, 185, 188
Lover 59, 61, 63, 65, 117, 186
Lovers 61
Loving 40, 42
Luciferian 237
Luminosity 44, 132
Lunar xii, 76, 81, 99, 112, 151, 153, 157, 163, 197, 213, 225, 234, 236, 245
Lung 16
Lungs 16, 73, 75, 110-111
Lust 128, 157, 163
Lusts 89, 101, 147
Lute 187
Luxembourg Museum 139
Lying 200
Lyre 186-187

Machine 26, 49, 62, 186-188
Machine-made 26
Machinery 18
Machines 45
Magdalen 125
Magic 21, 23, 40, 47, 52, 61, 84,
    126, 129, 134-135, 143, 156,
    187, 191-193, 203-205, 207,
    211-212
Magical 16, 41, 67, 192
Magician xii, 30, 44, 71, 112, 114,
    135, 143, 179, 181, 191, 209,
    212, 219, 235, 251
Magicians 23, 26-27, 30, 42-43, 71,
    82, 128-129, 135, 143, 235
Magnet 35, 72, 97
Magnetic 76-78, 111, 197, 200, 219,
    241
Magnetise 53, 122
Magnetised 22
Magnetism 130
Mahatmas 120
Mahomet 3
Mammon 42, 150
Manna 149
Mantras xiii, 191-194, 195, 198, 201
Mantric 142, 158, 193
Marble 7, 186-187
Mark 25, 171, 227
Married 44, 237
Mars 34
Martyrs 159
Mary Magdalen 125
Mason 82, 87, 213
Masonic Lodges 47
Masonry 47, 213
Masons 69, 213
Mass 34, 84, 92, 142, 193, 197, 228,
    230-231
Master Atom xiii, 70, 90-93, 99,
    123-125, 145-149, 166, 171,
    175-176, 178, 180, 203, 205,
    211, 213, 239-240
Master Builder 13-15
Master Jesus 118
Master Mason 82
Master Melchizedec 124

Masterpiece 139
Masterpieces 7, 124, 140
Masters 23, 55, 117-119, 121, 123,
    125-126, 131, 134, 191, 229
Mastery 23, 132
Material 24, 41, 45, 48, 79, 87-89, 93,
    118, 120, 127, 139, 171, 179,
    193, 201, 237
Materialise 29, 49, 56, 178
Materials 22, 48, 72, 103, 114, 156,
    172, 251
Matrix 30
Meal 242
Meals 76, 183
Meat 102
Mediaeval Europe 121
Medical 72, 163-164
Medicines 5
Meditate 68, 118, 193
Meditates 6
Meditation 85, 153, 196
Meditations 189
Mediterranean 7
Medium 29, 52, 136-137
Mediums 53, 133, 234
Melancholy 188
Melchizedec 124
Melody 158, 188
Melting pot 170
Membrane 32, 108-109, 147, 192,
    228
Membranes 53, 76, 94, 133, 221
Memories 48, 50, 115, 155, 173, 187
Memorise 114, 164, 198, 251
Memorising 201
Memory 49, 51, 134, 138, 156, 193
Mental xi-xiii, 1, 5-6, 17, 21-22, 26,
    29-30, 33-35, 43-44, 52-53,
    55, 72-76, 84, 89-91, 94, 97-
    98, 103, 107-110, 112-115,
    119-120, 123-124, 128-130,
    132-133, 135, 137-138, 140,
    144-145, 147-149, 151, 157-
    158, 165-166, 169, 171-172,
    175, 180, 193-194, 204,
    210-211, 223, 229-231, 241,
    247, 252

Mental body xii, 1, 5, 21, 26, 34, 91, 112, 175
Mental travelling 113, 115
Mentalities 39, 131
Mentality 26, 36, 134
Mentally 24-25, 72, 97, 105, 120, 146-147, 151, 210
Merciful 65
Mercury 89-90, 187, 193, 226
Mercy 143, 205
Merlin 43
Message 18, 55, 64, 134, 203, 224
Messages 30, 138, 209, 216, 227, 242, 251
Messenger 61, 69, 90-91
Messenger of Light 90
Messengers 61, 68
Metal 177
Metallic 235
Metals 47, 206
Mexico 242
Michael Angelo 140
Michael Juste 23, 40
Microscope 97
Middle-aged 77
Millet 23
Millikan 199-200
Mind xiii-xiv, 3-4, 7-8, 11, 13-15, 17, 19, 22, 24, 26-27, 30, 32, 36-37, 40, 49, 51-54, 56, 60-62, 64, 67, 69, 74, 76-77, 80, 84, 89-94, 96, 98-99, 104, 107-110, 119-120, 122, 124-126, 130, 132-133, 136-138, 141, 143-147, 149, 153, 158, 161, 164-167, 169, 174, 176, 178-180, 182, 188, 191-195, 198, 210-211, 213, 217, 219-221, 229-231, 239, 241, 248, 250-253
Mind-atmosphere 111, 217
Mind-atmospheres 156
Mind-body 6, 34, 44, 72, 84, 92, 120, 145, 147, 197, 223
Mind-matter 40
Minds xi, 1, 3, 7-9, 14, 16, 19, 23-26, 32, 35, 39-43, 45, 49-50, 52-54, 56, 60, 62-63, 68, 71, 79, 84, 89-90, 92, 98, 101, 108-109, 113, 121-122, 126, 129, 132, 134-136, 138-140, 145, 147-148, 156, 160-161, 168, 170, 185-187, 199, 201, 204, 207, 216, 220, 234-235, 250
Mind-stuff 40, 44, 48, 161, 201
Mind-waves 164
Mind-world xiii, 90, 166, 176, 179
Mineral 44-45, 52
Minerals 45, 249
Minerva 185, 187-188
Miracle 53
Miracles 16, 20, 30, 40, 149
Mission 7, 159
Mist 65, 114
Mists 56, 117
Mitscherlich 249
Mme Curie 199-200
Modern 139, 158, 213
Mohammedan Initiates 205
Moist 21, 150, 228
Moisture 35, 98
Monad 215-216
Monadic 215-216
Monet 140
Money 52
Mongolian 211
Moon 47, 51, 55, 60-61, 76, 79, 81, 128, 138, 150-151, 172-173, 176, 209, 214, 227-228, 240
Moral 17, 52-53, 80, 134, 138, 183, 213, 217, 220, 224, 237
Morals 33, 214
Moses 124, 209-210
Mother 40, 61, 63-64, 67, 139, 155, 159, 205, 224
Mother Nature 67, 224
Motherhood 154, 173
Motherly 173
Mothers 155, 173
Mountain 60, 65, 113, 188
Mountains 64, 194, 200
Mummified 212
Muscle 77, 186
Muscles 75, 110-111

Muscular 110
Museum 139
Museums 133, 140
Music 56, 59-61, 65, 158, 173, 186-188, 219
Musical 131
Musician 17, 47
Muslims 121
Mustard 19-20
Mystic 10, 153
Mysticism 233
Mystics 195, 233
Myth 212
Mythological 211
Naiads 185
Name xi, 6, 23, 39, 55, 114, 121, 185, 193, 206
Named 6
Names 6, 128, 171, 213
Napoleon 104
Nasal 8-9, 111, 145, 197-198, 219, 226, 241
Nation 4, 7-8, 25, 53-55, 92, 121, 124-125, 133-134, 143, 150, 169, 171, 252
Nations 15, 17, 54, 91, 128, 133-134, 251
Natural Magic 134, 156, 203-205, 207
Navel 4, 17, 29-30, 191, 226
Nazarene 138
Necromancy 52
Negative 94, 137, 157, 224, 226, 240
Neptune 176, 209
Neptunian 51, 209-211, 241
Neptunian-Amentian 210
Nerve 13, 30, 71, 73, 77, 100, 151, 192, 204, 243
Nerves 10, 15, 73, 200, 240, 249
Nervous xi, 2, 9-10, 17-18, 21-22, 30, 80-81, 87, 114, 147-148, 151, 153, 223, 225, 228, 245
New England 234
Newspapers 75
Nile 7
Nirvana 93, 130, 139
Nocturnal 135

Node xii, 30, 102, 108-110, 112, 147, 151, 176
Node Points xii, 30, 102, 108-110, 147, 151, 176
Nodes 21, 34, 107, 109, 227
Nodic 176
Noguchi 239
Nomadic 150
North 117, 211, 216
Northern 77, 211
Northern Latitudes 211
Northwards 215
Nose 77, 197
Nostril 76-77, 197-198
Nostrils 76, 197
Notation 49, 191
Note 6, 10, 19, 22, 34, 39, 51, 64, 87, 92, 109, 112, 147, 157-158, 164, 173, 184, 186, 191-192, 194, 205, 213, 225, 235, 249
Notes 55, 158, 164, 193-194
Nourish 11, 102, 144, 182
Nourished 5, 26, 64, 217, 224
Nourishes 40
Nourishment 17, 34-35, 71, 74, 89, 101, 147, 164, 172-173, 176, 182, 225, 228, 241
Nous Atom xi-xii, 13-19, 21, 25, 74, 77-78, 81-82, 87-88, 94, 98-99, 101, 111-112, 124, 127, 165-166, 168, 204, 225, 236, 239, 247, 249
Nun 59
Objectively 40, 108, 172
Observances 204
Observant 9, 17, 250
Observation 10, 25, 51, 71, 75, 102, 109, 127, 216, 250
Observations 200, 224
Observe 5, 33, 98, 103, 155, 159, 192, 216, 237
Observed 11, 34, 39, 75, 185, 226, 243, 249
Observer 133, 242
Observers 133
Observing 200

INDEX

Occult xii, 3, 33, 37, 49, 51, 69-70, 72, 74, 117, 121, 124, 163, 185, 197, 212, 216, 219, 229, 231
Occultism 3
Occultist 19, 37, 55, 76, 82, 99, 103, 178, 234, 251
Occultists 52, 55, 114, 124, 181, 195
Ocean 117, 177, 215-216
Ophthamic 200
Oppose 19, 23, 102, 149, 229, 248
Opposes 15, 165, 192, 249
Opposing xii-xiii, 23, 71, 114, 132, 148, 151, 159, 215, 251
Opposite 19, 21, 24, 55, 77, 83, 226
Opposites 148
Oracle 54, 122, 216
Oracles 53-54, 204
Ordeal 53, 128, 195
Oreads 188
Organ xi, 108
Organisation 182
Organisations 49, 51, 129, 143, 209, 230
Organise 209
Organised 182
Organism 13, 173
Organisms 97
Organs xiii, 18, 44, 75, 77, 96, 109-110, 179-180, 192, 204, 219, 223, 225-226, 234, 239-241
Origin 7, 142, 170-171, 173, 199
Orpheus 187
Ossendowski 211
Osteopath 71
Outwardly 14, 17, 19, 110, 164, 192, 252
Overlords 135
Overseer 23, 34
Overseers 13, 99
Oversoul 93, 179
Oxford 138
Oxygen 111, 200
Pagan 59, 188
Pain 4, 15, 20, 30, 62, 69, 77, 101, 103, 125, 159, 195, 228-229
Painful 125

Pains 103
Painters 62
Painting 48, 159, 201
Palestine 121, 128
Palms 197-198
Pamphlet 195
Parables 69
Paradises 57
Parasite 49
Parasites 16, 34-35
Parasitic 102
Parasitical 2
Parent 169, 181, 226, 239
Parental xii, xiv, 121, 170, 227, 248-249, 251
Parental Stem xii, xiv, 121, 170, 227, 248-249, 251
Parents 105, 183
Paris 195, 200
Parrotlike 201
Parsifal 196
Particle 249
Particles 87, 98, 150, 228, 249
Passion 26, 29, 128
Passions xii, 8, 27, 29-30, 34, 42, 49, 83, 134, 141, 237, 251
Passport 211
Past xi-xiii, 1, 4, 6-9, 15-18, 20-22, 24, 27, 29-30, 34, 41, 47-48, 50, 52, 55, 59, 63, 68-69, 79-83, 88-89, 92-93, 102-105, 107-108, 112, 117, 121, 127, 130-131, 134, 139, 143, 145, 148, 150-151, 153, 155, 157-158, 160, 171, 176, 184, 189, 193, 195, 209, 214-215, 217, 223-225, 228, 233-234, 236-237, 244, 249-250
Pasts 139, 157, 167-168
Path xi, 4, 20, 22, 34, 60, 65, 78, 101, 120, 130, 134, 148, 153, 159, 171, 192, 216, 231, 250, 252
Paths 28, 62, 85, 117, 134
Patience 71, 145, 243
Patient 32, 108, 157-158, 163, 165, 228
Pattern 30, 133

Paul of Tarsus 40
Peace 4, 10-11, 25, 36, 48, 59, 91,
    123, 130, 159, 168, 215
Pearl 60, 63-64
Pearls 63
Pendulum 213
Perceive 3, 101-102
Perceived 3, 34, 55
Perceives 137, 179, 200
Perceiving 98
Perception 10, 15, 53, 70, 140, 150
Perceptions 93, 114
Perfected xi, 111, 234
Perfection 104, 168, 175, 178
Perfume 13, 37, 45, 61, 64, 72, 130,
    156, 241
Perfuming 63
Periods xi, xiii, 4, 6-8, 10-11, 14, 17,
    19, 26, 30, 34, 70, 87, 95, 107,
    109, 124, 145, 150-151, 166,
    173, 181, 205, 212, 224, 236,
    244
Personalities 83, 248
Personality 2, 41, 85, 92, 94, 108,
    138, 160, 167, 178, 220, 230
Pharaoh 54, 209, 212
Pharaoh Akhenaten 209
Pharmacopoeia 192
Phidias 7
Philadelphia 122
Philosopher 50
Philosophers 220
Philosophy 50, 195
Phosphorescent 49
Physically 25, 72, 105, 108, 123
Physician 192
Physicians 164
Physicists 199
Pianos 191
Pierce 3, 225, 228
Pierces 81, 233, 238
Pike 200
Pillar 62
Pineal Gland xi, 98, 200
Pink 34
Pipe 186
Pizzaro 242

Plagues 91
Plane 33-34, 59, 72, 89, 95, 109, 115,
    123, 135, 142, 155, 161, 164,
    174, 177-179, 194, 205-206,
    230, 234, 243
Planet 5, 22, 34, 90, 173, 176, 244
Planetary 147, 172
Planets 80, 89, 172-173, 199, 226
Planted 7, 64, 118, 220
Planting 216
Plants 11
Plato 134
Pleasant 55, 195
Pleasing 120
Pleasure 25, 63, 118, 159-160, 248
Pleasures 25
Plexus 228
Poem 140
Poems 24
Poet 41, 94, 183
Poetical 122
Poetry 185-186
Poets 41, 62, 95, 185
Poles 176, 226, 242-244
Police 52
Political 128, 250
Politicians 133
Pollux xii, 156, 248
Positive 24, 76, 93-94, 99, 122, 135,
    141, 157-158, 178, 180, 209,
    224, 226, 230, 239-240
Possesion 214
Possessed 20, 24, 48, 59, 68, 71, 119,
    131, 133, 135, 140, 150, 155,
    175, 203, 214
Possesses xii, 1, 6, 17, 19, 30, 41, 51,
    53, 56, 59, 83-84, 96-97, 110,
    112, 127, 134, 141, 144, 149,
    156, 171, 177, 180-181, 184,
    204, 226-227, 236, 240
Possessing xi, 2, 9, 14, 34, 56, 144-
    145, 153, 155, 163, 169, 183,
    210, 221, 240-241, 248, 251
Possession 6, 24-25, 198
Possessions 2, 10, 16, 42, 53, 88, 91,
    117, 134, 143, 153, 160, 180,
    193, 214, 234, 247

Posture 73-74
Postures 231
Poverty 20, 52, 62
Practical 88
Practice xi-xiii, 1, 5, 9-11, 13, 15-16, 19, 25, 30, 32, 71, 75-78, 85, 97, 103, 105, 111-112, 144-146, 158, 167, 173, 175, 183, 197-198, 213, 219, 224, 229, 236-237, 242-244, 248-249, 252
Practices 4, 15, 24, 33, 71, 73, 80, 85
Practise 1, 90, 129, 145, 179
Practised 29, 133
Practising 9, 77, 99, 198, 250
Praxiteles 7
Pray 125, 131, 143, 229-230, 233, 235
Prayed 53, 64, 130, 168, 185
Prayer 37, 113, 119, 125, 153, 229-231
Prayers 11, 55, 168, 230-231
Praying 10, 230
Prays 105
Preachers 129
Pregnant 7
Preparation 40, 47
Preparatory 10, 237
Prepare 4, 10, 60, 64, 75, 81, 92, 98, 113, 137
Prepared 25, 138, 157, 165, 175, 180
Prepares 182, 230
Prescriptions 164
Presence 2, 10-11, 24, 27, 39, 56, 80-81, 83, 90, 96, 119, 123, 144, 154, 156-157, 220, 242
Priest 216
Priesthood 112
Priests 48, 77, 136, 138, 142, 195, 203, 215
Primrose 64
Princes 186
Principal xii-xiii, 13, 27, 30, 100, 112, 172, 226
Principalities 25, 39
Principle 19, 51, 81, 105, 177-179, 193, 201

Principles 6, 13, 121, 125, 159, 191
Prisms 96
Prison xiii, 157, 175
Prisoner 2, 10, 16, 134, 143, 226, 240, 253
Prisoners 163, 182, 212
Procreate 108
Procreative 78
Professor 199-200, 235
Professor Bruno Rossi 199
Professor Compton 200
Professor Einstein 235
Professor Millikan 200
Project 29, 33, 56, 84, 109, 131, 180
Projecting 122
Projections xii
Prophet 3, 21, 90, 159
Prophets 7, 41, 51, 54, 91, 117, 138, 159, 185, 209
Proserpine 42, 211
Protean 24, 37, 47-48
Protect 25, 42, 56, 72, 93-94, 109, 126-127, 145, 161, 171, 205
Protected 22, 72, 74, 96, 121, 159, 210, 214, 217, 238, 245
Protection 21, 28, 42, 54, 125, 129, 141, 148-149, 158-160, 197, 245, 247
Protective 14-15, 24, 37, 76, 109-110, 128, 146, 148, 156, 181, 186, 201, 209, 252
Protectively 143
Protector 55
Protects xiii, 24, 76, 96, 160, 175, 236
Psychic 77, 194
Psychics 154
Psychoanalysts 32
Psychologists 147
Pure Spirit 169
Purgatory 36, 50, 142
Purification 204
Purified 210
Purify 83, 135, 220
Purifying 102

Purity 8, 24, 29, 32, 43, 77, 82, 85, 98, 148, 153, 157, 161, 169, 173, 209, 213, 229, 251
Pyromaniacs 55
Pythagoras 195
Pythoness 54
Queen 44, 46, 55
Quicksilver 44, 228
Race xiv, 26, 39, 72, 121, 148, 163, 166, 170, 183-184, 206, 219, 227
Races 43, 49, 101, 115, 143, 160, 166, 170-171, 184, 216
Racial xii, 39, 121, 166, 170, 184
Radiance 53, 83, 96, 186, 237, 240
Radiant xii, 5, 32, 91, 112, 132, 240
Radiate 18, 29, 33-34, 49, 108, 125, 158, 220
Radiated 233
Radiates 50, 55, 94, 124, 145, 200, 240, 245
Radiating 10, 35, 107, 122, 204
Radiation 1, 29, 98, 123, 200, 251
Radiations 24, 29, 98, 146
Radium 199
Rain 35, 199
Rainbow 61-62
Rainfall 199
Rainstorm 114
Ray 81, 89, 199-201
Rays 51, 73, 119, 172, 199-201, 216
Realisation 78, 131, 133, 139, 144
Realisations 136, 223
Realised 53, 137, 176
Realises 19, 39, 53, 68, 96, 105, 118, 125, 128, 136, 195, 205
Realising 117, 125
Rebirth 79, 103, 157, 223, 243
Reborn 27, 69, 141, 157, 223
Record xiii, 1, 29, 59, 79, 81, 115, 148, 154, 181, 198, 221
Recorded 51, 143, 154, 214
Records 1, 7, 39, 41, 50, 54-55, 59, 88, 91-92, 121-122, 130, 154, 160, 168, 172, 203, 214, 219, 242, 244, 248
Rectum 35, 73

Red 182, 214, 234
Red Indian 182, 214
Red Indians 214, 234
Redeem 182
Redeemed 34
Redemption 4
Reflect 8, 132, 142, 151, 249
Reflected 79, 243
Reflection 51, 62, 193
Reflects 94, 198
Reincarnate 89
Reincarnation 45, 103, 105, 195
Relationship 33, 87, 93, 98, 118, 141, 144, 157, 163, 216
Religion 80, 101, 121, 151, 170, 173-174, 214, 223
Religions 37, 75, 87, 121, 127, 233
Religious 3, 10, 20, 47, 51, 59, 69, 76, 121, 129, 136, 156, 167, 204, 214, 223, 230, 234
Rembrandt 139-140
Remedied 35, 223
Remedy 6, 18, 104, 172, 182, 221
Remember 21-23, 39-40, 45, 50, 74-77, 82, 84, 88, 102-103, 105, 107-108, 118, 141, 146, 155, 161, 163, 167, 175, 183, 194, 215, 252
Remembered 88, 195
Remembering 195
Remembers 95, 215
Remembrance 16, 48, 57, 60, 63, 89, 115, 143, 195
Renounce 91, 180-181, 191, 228
Respect 14, 27, 52, 71, 76, 79, 148, 212, 214, 243
Respected 37, 172
Respects 249
Responsibility 79
Responsible 36, 82, 94, 120, 230
Rest 8, 73, 75, 88, 95, 130, 143, 198
Retina 169
Retreat 16, 108, 127, 145, 191
Retreats 242
Revelation 11
Revelations 96

Reverence 7, 11, 15, 49-50, 52, 54, 150, 164, 173, 183-184, 243, 247
Rhythm 7, 56, 61, 156, 216
Rhythmic 9, 73, 82, 90
Rites 61, 67, 234
Ritual 23, 155, 213, 227
Rituals 50
Robert A. Millikan 199
Robin Goodfellow 13
Robots 200
Rocky Mountains 200
Roman 166, 193
Roman Church 193
Rome 140, 199, 215
Rose 13, 45, 61, 63-65, 186-187, 189, 241
Rosicrucians 205
Round Table 154
Russia 119
Sac 30, 112, 225
Saclike 29-30, 225
Sacral 228
Sacred 3, 41, 70, 81, 121, 151, 193-194, 203, 214, 237, 243
Sacrifice 13, 33, 102, 170, 250
Sacrificed 22, 102, 127, 171
Sacrifices 166
Sad 63, 117, 185
Saint 76
Saintlike 80
Saintly 144
Saints 41
Salvation 24, 141
Sanitation 204
Sapphire 60
Savage 54
Savages 197
Save 25, 48, 53, 131, 149, 151, 160, 193, 217, 226
Saved 37, 167, 195
Saviour 6, 16, 25, 110
Saviours 87, 117, 131
Scarabaeus 226
Sceptre 56, 212, 241
Scholar xiv, 173, 176, 227
Scholar Atoms xiv, 173, 176

Scholars 50
Scholastic 10
School 7, 79, 89, 108, 121, 141, 211, 220, 228
Schoolboy 160
Schooled 159, 161, 204, 250
Schooling 228
Schools 3, 17, 19-21, 24, 27, 49, 79, 85, 88, 93, 104, 121, 129, 133, 148, 150, 159, 164, 171, 211-212, 219, 235
Science 3, 6, 10, 41, 69-70, 80, 153, 163, 167, 171-172, 176, 191, 200, 203, 206, 212, 229, 240, 252
Sciences 43, 70, 72, 141
Scientific 8, 80-81, 133, 140, 151, 153, 177, 216, 224
Scientifically 140
Scientist 165, 239
Scientists 98, 102-103, 158, 172-173, 179, 199-200, 203-204, 206, 238, 242, 244-245
Scourge 91-92, 212, 252
Scourge of Affliction 252
Screen xii, 14, 17, 49, 107-111, 180, 197-198
Screened 242
Screens 107
Scriptures 47
Scroll 213
Sculptors 7, 139
Sculptures 37, 112
Scythes 25
Sea 60, 113, 117, 215
Sea level 108, 200
Seances 35
Seasons 44, 172
Secluded 10, 138, 220
Seclusion 22, 212
Second 10, 63, 75, 111, 124, 247, 250
Secondary System xi, 10-11, 19-20, 27, 33, 35, 67-68, 70, 79, 93-96, 99, 103, 105, 107-108, 110, 113, 123-124, 148, 155, 160-161, 163, 168-170, 175, 177-179, 181, 193-194, 201,

209, 219, 233, 235, 243-245,
  247-248, 252
Seed 19-20, 85, 118, 235, 249
Seeds 25, 27, 118, 220, 240
Seed-thought 220
Seer xi
Seers 154
Self xii, 2-3, 10, 33, 53, 84, 127, 145,
  149, 175, 230, 247
Self-analysis 4
Self-created 84, 120, 176
Self-determination 179
Self-determined 132
Self-developed xiii, 109, 155, 167
Self-esteem 132
Selfish 72, 125, 205, 236
Selfishness 6
Self-praise 72
Self-protection 23
Self-recording 200
Self-sufficient 167
Self-thought 174
Selves 123, 194
Semen 29, 241
Seminal System xiii, 29, 32, 78, 112,
  145, 172, 225, 234, 236-239,
  241, 243, 248
Sensation 5, 60, 78, 175, 195, 228
Sensations 151, 226
Sense 8-9, 15, 25, 34, 41, 54-55, 70-
  71, 74-75, 80, 88, 93, 97, 103,
  105, 107, 111, 114, 118, 130,
  153, 161, 164, 168, 177, 179,
  188, 192, 194, 197-198, 205
Sensed 22, 83, 119, 123, 197
Senses 15, 59, 65, 91, 154, 179, 194
Sensing 197
Sensitive 7, 24, 29, 35-36, 49, 52-54,
  87, 94-95, 97, 109, 133, 137,
  142-143, 146, 151, 156, 183-
  184, 229
Sensitives 43, 52, 95, 156
Sensitivity 39, 43, 47, 93, 140, 145
Sensory 109, 119
Sensual 221
Sentiment 95
Sentinel 243

Sentinels 56, 242-243
Serene 61, 91
Serenity 11, 54, 59, 130, 186
Serpent 81, 183, 225-228, 236, 240
Serpent Fire 81
Servant 187
Servants 4, 24, 236
Serve xii, 5, 14, 25-26, 56, 62, 102,
  135, 141, 153, 155, 168, 205,
  228
Served 154, 167, 236
Service 62, 94, 96, 101, 113, 136,
  154, 220, 227
Services 114
Seven xiii, 6, 43, 63, 67, 85, 124, 180,
  192, 233
Seventeen 127
Seventy 138, 227
Sex 18, 27, 75, 129, 181, 237
Sex-animalism 32
Sex-inclinations 170
Sex-nature 183
Sexual 129, 165, 239
Sexually 80
Shadow 199, 236
Shadowed 25, 185
Shadows 62, 73, 129, 248
Shaker 234
Sharira 160
Sheath xii, 26, 29-35, 37, 39, 67, 84,
  102, 110, 114, 149, 151, 166,
  175, 199, 225, 233, 241
Sheaths 36, 67-68, 94, 149, 165, 209,
  224
Shekinah 203, 215
Shekinahs 117
Sick 137, 158, 163, 205, 230
Sidereal 237
Sight 45, 187
Sign 61, 90, 128, 144, 156, 171, 237
Signal 49, 55, 68-69, 73, 210
Signalling 56
Signals 169
Signs 68, 131, 172, 237
Silence 61-62, 94, 188, 235
Silent 10, 56, 115, 175, 229, 242
Silently 117, 139

Silicon 200
Silken 84, 91, 109, 112, 147, 175, 221
Silver Cord 33, 160
Silver Shield xiii, 32, 79, 93, 137, 145-151, 175-176, 178, 183, 197, 203, 205, 238-241, 245
Silver Shield of Transformation 112
Silver Shields 135, 139, 148
Silvered 186
Silvery 189
Simple 5, 67, 71, 94, 125, 149, 164, 182, 186, 194, 250
Simple-minded 138
Simplicity 189
Sincere 6, 28, 53, 72, 174, 192-193, 198, 230-231, 252
Sincerely 80, 230
Singing 60, 64-65, 186, 188, 193
Sinners 41
Sins 97, 157
Sion 174
Six 59, 77, 79, 157, 220
Sixteen 117
Sixth 55, 64, 161, 198
Skeleton 30, 103
Skull 73, 87, 147, 240
Sleep 18, 45, 60, 75, 77, 88, 160, 164, 213
Sleeping 17, 49, 56, 87, 90, 183, 225, 227-228, 236, 240
Sleeping Serpent 183, 225, 227-228, 236, 240
Sleeps 24, 95
Sleepy 77
Social 52, 73, 164, 214, 250-251
Societies 69, 118
Society 25, 32-33, 52, 169
Socrates 83, 122
Soil 11, 48, 110, 214-215, 242
Sol 193
Solar Flame 228, 233, 235, 237, 239-241, 243, 245
Solar Force xiii, 16, 19, 77, 80, 87, 99, 107, 111, 175, 221, 223, 225, 229, 233-234, 240, 245
Sole 173, 212

Soles 13, 227-228
Solomon 69, 213
Solon 209
Solstice 216
Song 61-62
Songs 60-61
Sons 40, 48
Soul 20, 33, 60-61, 64, 90, 95, 104, 117-119, 122-123, 126, 142-143, 158, 165-166, 186, 201, 206, 210, 220, 241
Soul-group 89, 160, 165
Souls 25, 33, 62, 72, 92, 118, 125, 128-129, 136, 138, 143, 201, 210, 212
Sound xiii, 6, 23-24, 29, 56, 60-61, 64, 117, 141, 144, 164, 167, 175, 178, 180, 191-194, 227, 234-235, 252
Sounded 23, 164, 235
Sounding 29, 32, 56, 112, 153, 166, 180, 192-193, 224, 239, 245
Sounds 6, 16, 23, 52, 78, 120, 131, 137, 164, 191, 193, 211, 219, 235, 241
Soundwaves 191, 227
South America 242
Southern California 242
Southern Mexico 242
Sow 236
Sowed 25
Sowing 61, 250
Space 4, 35, 63, 200
Spacetime 36, 107
Speak 19, 21, 26-27, 34, 51-54, 71, 80, 83, 93-95, 108, 124, 160, 173, 188, 196, 201, 233-235, 243
Speaking 53, 74, 196, 204, 211
Speaks 185, 233
Speech 56, 105, 129, 234, 241, 252
Sphere 9, 23, 33, 36, 40, 42, 48, 68-69, 115, 131, 158-159, 161, 211, 227-228
Sphinx 47-48, 56, 92, 149-150, 212-213, 215

Spinal xi, xiii, 17, 71, 80, 212, 225, 236, 243
Spine 4, 19, 29, 73, 112, 149, 225-226, 240
Spirit 7, 62, 81, 95, 169-170, 183-185, 187-188
Spirits 26, 33, 44, 50, 93, 95, 169
Spiritual xiii, 8, 13, 19, 53-54, 74-76, 80, 103, 129, 136, 138, 143, 223, 230-231, 235
Spiritualism 50, 95
Spiritually 220
Spray 60, 62, 191, 205
Sprayed 220
Sprays 205
Spring 5, 22, 62, 81-82, 110, 121, 172, 179, 185-188, 212, 215
Spring Equinox 172, 215
St. Augustine 233
Star 61-62, 79, 124, 127, 131, 189
Starry 4, 48
Stars 50, 65, 81, 110, 156, 169, 199-200
Statues 187, 203
Steam 180
Steel 186, 188
Stem xii, xiv, 64, 121, 170, 227, 248-249, 251-252
Stems 170, 249
Stillborn Children 54
Stomach 76, 111, 182-183
Stone 60, 63, 87, 120, 186-187
Stone of Remembrance 63
Stones 44, 47, 60
Students 1, 21-22, 42, 45, 47, 55-56, 70-72, 77, 80, 82, 93, 105, 118, 122-125, 129, 134, 141-142, 146, 159, 195, 205, 211, 217, 220, 229, 244, 250
Studied 164
Studies 48, 50, 72, 129, 165
Study 10, 32, 40, 42, 44, 47, 69, 79-80, 95, 127, 139, 164, 205, 249, 252
Studying 182, 201
Subconscious 3, 21, 32
Subconsciously 234

Submarine 133
Submerged 30, 32, 34, 47, 114, 127, 129-131, 133-135, 137, 139, 141, 143, 145, 157-158, 161-162, 167, 180, 211, 248
Submerged Worlds 30, 127, 129-131, 133-135, 137, 139, 141, 143, 162
Subsoil 7, 216, 250, 252
Subterranean 211
Suffer 3, 20-21, 26, 51, 102, 104, 109, 135, 210
Suffered 17, 59, 125, 134
Suffering 44, 59, 63, 65, 79, 115, 145, 164, 184
Sufferings 14-15, 20, 29, 36, 101, 109, 127, 130, 132, 136, 168, 229
Suffers 105
Sufis 195
Sulphur 35
Summer 172, 186, 199
Sun 7, 14, 17, 22, 42, 51, 55, 60-61, 65, 73, 76, 79, 81, 119, 139, 148-149, 151, 172-173, 193, 199-200, 209, 214-216, 223-228, 239-240, 247
Sun-God 215
Sunlight 22, 35, 99, 132, 169, 178, 186, 199-200, 241
Sunlike 50
Sunrise 64, 188
Suns 239
Surgeon 122, 146
Surgeons 137
Sustenance 241
Sword 81, 153, 158-159, 187, 203, 250
Swords 159, 226
Sylph 43, 50-51, 59
Sylphide 51
Sylphides 50-52
Sylphlike 44
Sylphs 50-53, 65, 132, 185, 188
Symbol 34, 47, 49, 61, 68-70, 119, 139, 146-147, 154, 185, 212, 241, 250

Symbolically 148
Symbolise 212, 224
Symbolised 30, 47, 70, 124, 131, 150, 156, 176, 196, 211-213, 235, 244, 248
Symbolises 151, 171, 215, 233, 241
Symbols 49, 68-70, 131, 146, 171, 185
Symphonies 117
Syria 121
Tarsus 40
Tate Gallery 159
Teach 3, 6, 10, 41, 56, 85, 92, 98, 111, 120, 129-130, 143, 158-159, 221, 229, 235
Teachers 3, 10, 43, 76, 94, 117-123, 125, 138, 146, 204, 209, 220
Teaches 3, 10, 14, 122, 134, 148, 157, 172, 220, 245
Teaching 49, 129, 225
Teachings 3, 17-18, 27, 30, 48-49, 72, 80, 89, 110, 137, 141, 149, 156, 167, 169, 171, 173, 179, 185, 214, 219, 223, 225, 227, 235
Technology 200
Telegraph 242
Telepathy 137
Telephone 56
Television 67
Temple xiii, 2, 6, 48, 56, 69, 91-92, 123, 129, 145, 149, 175-176, 181, 187, 212-213, 215-216
Temples 53, 89, 130, 153, 187
Tempted 128
Ten 51, 87, 200
Teraphim 53, 130, 131, 204, 216
Terrestrial 81
Testament 1, 7, 89, 236
Testament of Learning 1
Thousand Petalled Lotus 79, 234
Theories 71, 140, 199
Theosophic 103
Theosophy 95
Theurgic 194, 216
Think 3, 9, 11, 14, 19, 25-26, 36, 51-52, 55-56, 75, 77, 84, 103, 107, 117, 125, 148, 159-161, 164, 167-169, 192, 199, 211, 230, 235, 245, 249-250
Thinker 112, 239
Thinking 9, 14, 62, 74, 85, 97-98
Thinks 11, 16, 59, 250
Third xi-xii, 52, 63, 75, 98, 112, 124, 137, 156, 226, 240-241, 245
Third Eye xi-xii, 75, 98, 112, 137
Thought activity 146
Thought atmosphere 105
Thought creation 126, 154
Thought creations 84
Thought emotion 78
Thought environment 184
Thought form 20, 83
Thought forms 83
Thought image 239
Thoughts 6, 14, 17, 19, 21-24, 26, 32, 39, 49, 51, 56, 59, 63, 68-69, 75, 78, 84, 91, 94, 98, 109, 115, 117, 126, 131, 163, 175, 178, 180-181, 186, 217, 229-230, 235-236, 238-239, 243, 251-252
Thought vibrations xii
Thought wave 163, 227, 239
Thought waves 17, 109
Thought world 122, 175
Thousand 79, 90
Thousand-petalled 234
Three 19, 27, 33, 36, 68, 74-75, 81, 85, 89, 110, 123-124, 138-139, 142, 149, 161, 194, 201, 206, 229, 231, 233, 240, 244
Threshold 20, 83, 85, 142
Thrice-Born Hermes 90
Thrice-Born Mercury 90
Throat 192
Throats 186
Throne 26, 124, 212
Tibet 138, 216, 227, 231
Tibetan 219
Tide 72, 224
Tigerman 74
Tomb 157
Tombs 210

Tongues 234
Torture 23, 69, 101
Tortured 30, 105
Towers 235
Trance 37, 52, 111, 234, 237
Tranquillity 91, 141
Transform 69
Transformation xiii, 78-80, 88-92,
    99, 112, 124, 130, 145-147,
    149-150, 157, 175, 194, 197,
    239, 241, 245, 247
Transformation Atoms xiii, 79-80,
    88, 90-91, 112, 124, 145-146,
    149, 157, 175, 197, 239, 241,
    247
Transformation breathing 197
Transformed 23
Transforming 63
Transforms 24
Transmit 165, 176, 243
Transmitted xii
Transmitter xiii
Transmitting 239
Transmute 149, 206
Transmuted 79, 172, 228
Transmutes 1, 56
Treasure 81, 193
Treasured 186
Treasures 61, 93, 193, 242
Tree 30, 60, 62, 65, 179
Tree of Love 60, 65
Tree of Youth 62
Tremors 187
Trial 25, 170
Tribal 227
Tribes 131, 160, 193, 215
Trident 49, 147, 241
Trinity 228
Truth 5, 10, 14, 69, 81, 118, 122,
    131, 155, 167, 169, 193, 223
Truths 127, 134
Tune xi, 27, 157, 177, 191, 244
Tuned 239, 245
Twilight 131, 133
Twin 128, 154, 157, 248
Twins 156

Two xii, 7, 13, 15, 19-20, 24, 27, 39,
    65, 72, 78-79, 83, 87, 90, 98,
    109, 121, 128, 131-132, 136,
    148-149, 151, 153, 156, 178,
    191, 197, 199-200, 214, 226,
    239-240, 244, 247-248
Tyana 32, 43, 209
Tyler 212-213
Unconscious 84, 139, 183, 249
Unconsciously 32, 67, 73, 121-122,
    131, 137, 139, 177, 184, 192,
    220, 229, 234, 251
Understand 21, 49, 54, 63, 69, 82,
    95, 115, 118, 124-125, 137,
    149, 156, 165, 171, 219-220,
    227, 233
Understanding xi, 4-5, 8, 16, 22, 42,
    56, 61, 69, 137, 155, 158-160,
    171, 180, 184, 186-187, 194,
    217, 219, 229, 238, 252
Understandingly 70
Understands 3, 105, 158
Understood xiii, 4, 6, 17, 70, 133,
    147, 149, 160, 193, 195, 231
Underworld 133, 151
Union xii, 2-4, 10, 27, 78, 81, 87-88,
    153, 157, 180, 216, 230-231,
    238, 247-248
Unite 1, 4-5, 8, 14, 19, 23, 29, 45, 54,
    84-85, 112, 118, 128, 134,
    149-150, 170-171, 178, 181,
    191, 216, 219, 224-225, 228,
    238, 240, 249, 252
United 6, 49, 74, 99, 113, 117-118,
    137-138, 203, 213, 219, 225-
    226, 228, 236, 239-240, 247
United States 118
Unites 7, 10, 67, 79, 81, 99, 148-149,
    209, 233, 240
Unity 9, 175, 215
Universal 4, 93, 102, 146, 176, 178,
    216, 225
Universe xiii, 2-3, 5, 7, 10, 17, 20, 80,
    84, 89-91, 104, 109, 112, 120,
    155, 167, 172, 176, 189, 223,
    235, 237, 240, 243-244, 251
Universities 79

University 4, 6, 8, 54, 199-200, 233
University of Chicago 200
University of Florence 199
Vampire 26
Vampirise 205
Vanities 51
Vanity 132
Vaporous 241
Vapour 47, 88, 112, 181, 194, 237, 241
Vegetables 102
Vegetarian 74
Vegetarians 102
Vehicle 114, 125, 166
Vehicles xii, 10
Veil 187, 191, 194
Veiled 117
Veils 61, 177
Veins 101, 186
Velazquez 139
Venereal 239
Venous 101
Ventricle xi, 13, 98
Venus 62, 244
Venusian 129
Vertebra 71
Vertical 36
Vestments 51, 136
Vesture 161
Vestures 44
Vibrate 56, 79, 125, 145, 158, 163-164, 191-194, 219, 234
Vibrated 63, 65, 142, 235
Vibrates xi, 18, 93, 194, 229
Vibrating 147, 194
Vibration xi, 7-9, 15, 27, 52, 78, 87, 92, 97-99, 111, 136, 138, 145, 154, 194, 223, 225, 227, 235, 239, 245
Vibrations 11, 16, 22-23, 40, 44, 68, 89, 114, 131, 138, 157, 180, 184, 192-193, 234, 236, 239
Vibratory 54, 82, 111, 119, 147, 154, 158
Vice 49, 132
Vices 16
Victory 15, 92-93, 215

View 50, 89, 114, 148, 176
Viewed 14, 178, 199, 233
Viewing 194
Views 33, 117
Vigorous 40
Vigour 73, 81, 99, 229
Vinegar 35
Virtue 81, 194, 235
Virtues 27, 43
Virtuous 41
Visible 3, 56, 199-200
Vision 40, 50, 63, 84, 150, 161, 237
Visionary 233
Visions 59, 75
Visualise 34, 75, 133, 230
Visualised 69
Visualises xi
Vital 22, 71-73, 99, 111, 121, 205, 238
Vitalised 13
Vitality 1, 7, 22, 29, 33, 35, 71, 75, 78, 97-98, 122, 137, 147-148, 151, 205, 233, 241-242
Vocation 121
Vocations 139
Voice 15, 18, 59-65, 126, 149, 153, 189
Voices 93, 95, 117, 187-188
Void 14, 53, 67, 80-81
Voltage xiii, 35, 109-110, 125, 197, 225, 238, 244-245, 248
Voltages 163, 244-245
Volts 199-200
Voodoo 234
Vow 94
Vowel 6, 16, 23, 52, 120, 137, 164, 219
Vowels 6, 192, 235
Wagner 117, 196
Walk 80, 97, 142, 154, 189, 244
Walked 60-61, 63, 187, 242
Walking 77
Wand 71, 89
War 16, 19, 22-23, 25, 74, 92, 109, 114, 132-133, 170, 251
Warden 212
Wardens 214

Warfare 45, 133
Warlike 34, 91, 133
Warlords 114
Warrior 159
Wars 203
Washington Evening Post 199
Waste 33, 73-74, 80
Wasted 148
Wastes 16, 141
Watch xii, 56, 74, 134, 243
Watched 72, 113, 137, 154
Watches 127, 160
Watching 195, 229
Watchman 192, 225, 236-237
Watchmen 34, 67, 161, 242
Watchtower 60-61
Water 37, 39, 46-49, 51, 73, 75-76, 102, 110, 114-115, 183, 193, 223, 231
Water elementals 47-48
Waters 60-61, 185, 187-188
Wave 112, 178, 194
Wavelength 5, 10, 67, 78, 145, 149, 156, 163, 165-166, 169, 179, 184, 192, 194, 209, 227, 245, 248
Wavelengths 94, 170, 177
Waves 29, 98, 110, 114, 154, 157, 177-178, 245
Wealth 25, 27, 41, 62, 70, 121, 134, 150, 252
Weaverbirds 35
West 70, 76, 80, 117-118, 137-138, 163, 182, 184, 195, 217, 219, 227, 231, 241
Western 1, 7, 10-11, 70, 73, 76-77, 93, 117, 137, 141, 147, 150, 153, 170, 181, 219, 231, 240, 250-252
Western Europe 1
Western Yoga 1, 7, 10-11, 137
Western Yogi 141
Westerners 227
Wheat 121
Wheel 231
Wheels 231
Whistler 139, 159

White xii, 19-20, 23, 25, 40, 47, 71, 123, 129, 143, 179, 211, 250
White Brother 23, 40, 123
White Magician xii, 143, 179
Wind 60
Winds 180, 186, 188-189, 191
Wine 22, 62
Winged 226
Wings 61, 64, 144, 209
Winter 98, 172, 186, 206
Wireless 67, 244
Wisdom 3, 5, 7, 9, 14, 21, 23, 25-26, 32, 37, 39, 41, 45, 47-49, 55, 63, 67, 79-81, 84, 88-89, 101, 107, 117-118, 121, 123, 129, 141, 145, 148-151, 155, 159, 169, 172-173, 175, 180-181, 185-187, 189, 194, 203, 209, 212-213, 221, 227, 229-231, 233, 237, 239, 244, 253
Wise 68, 95, 129, 168, 170, 189, 225, 244-245
Wise Men 68, 244
Wish 3, 9, 24, 42, 47, 56, 67-68, 76, 84, 88, 93, 109, 117-118, 129, 140, 160, 167, 179, 191-192, 214, 219, 225, 251
Wished 167
Wishes 20, 29, 44, 48, 51, 54, 156-157, 186, 191, 193-194, 230, 244
Witchcraft 52
Woman 123, 128, 187
Womb 79, 155
Women 44, 48, 51, 74, 115, 117, 121, 125, 173, 215, 237
Word 2-3, 19, 39, 77, 193, 235, 252
Words 39, 49, 78, 81, 90, 94, 138, 172-173, 186, 214
Work xi, 1, 3-4, 7, 14, 16, 19, 23-25, 27-28, 33-34, 42, 44-45, 52, 54-56, 70, 78, 80, 82, 87-88, 90, 92-93, 95, 101, 117-119, 125, 131, 135-137, 139-141, 144-146, 150, 153, 155, 157, 159-161, 163-165, 167, 176-179, 181, 185, 206, 212, 214,

216, 219, 221, 223, 228-229,
236, 238, 242, 244, 248-253
Worked xi-xii, 42, 88, 114, 121, 140,
149, 172, 185, 209, 229, 235
Worker 97, 101-102, 113, 205
Workers 9, 13-15, 25, 73-74, 78, 137,
210, 236
Working 1, 20, 40, 67, 70-71, 117,
119, 121, 128, 139, 159, 213,
224, 229, 233, 247, 251
Workings 44, 147, 177
Workmen 18, 82
Works xii, 26-27, 43, 47, 50, 81, 91,
95, 104, 124, 139-140, 146,
160, 166, 172, 182, 231
The World of Secrets 205
World Saviour 6, 16
Worldly 143, 146, 220-221
Worship 27, 37, 129, 143, 155, 184,
187, 209, 215
Worshipped 48, 50, 54, 61, 127, 129
Worships 150, 188
Wound 61, 108
Wounded 62
Wounds 35
Year 109-110, 172, 216
Years 1, 7, 22, 43, 72, 87, 90, 122,
159, 165, 187, 195, 204, 206-
207, 227
Yellow 88
Yoga Teachings 167, 169, 171, 173
Yogis 56, 74, 130, 133, 135, 138-139,
149, 170, 179, 215, 231, 233-
234, 241, 251
Young 8, 43, 72, 140, 185, 189, 206
Younger 59, 160, 198, 216, 249, 251
Youthful 24
Yucatan 242
Zeal 104
Zend 195
Zodiac 61, 156, 171, 237, 244
Zodiacal xii, 172, 237
Zuni Indians 193

Glorian Publishing is a non-profit publisher dedicated to spreading the sacred universal doctrine to suffering humanity. All of our works are made possible by the kindness and generosity of sponsors. If you would like to make a tax-deductible donation, you may send it to the address below, or visit our website for other alternatives. If you would like to sponsor the publication of a book, please contact us at 877-726-2359 or help@gnosticteachings.org.

Glorian Publishing
PO Box 110225
Brooklyn, NY 11211 US
Phone: 877-726-2359

VISIT US ONLINE AT:

gnosticteachings.org